THE GREAT LENT

TREASURES OF THE FATHERS OF THE CHURCH SERIES

Our paramount objective in this series is to introduce the believers to the *trialogue* of faith—the harmony among the Holy Scriptures, the Church Fathers, and the rites of the Coptic Orthodox Church. Throughout this symphony of discourse, the believer is not only enlightened by the Holy Scriptures, but is further illumined through the homilies, exegeses, and commentaries of the Church Fathers. This is a brief and simple companion to the Coptic Orthodox lectionary. We hope and pray that through this series, the Holy Scriptures, the Church Fathers, and the Church rites are experienced by the believer as a deep source of blessing, wisdom, and faith.

His Grace Bishop Serapion
*Editor-in-Chief*

Father Ishak Azmy Yacoub
Father John Paul Abdelsayed
*Series Editors*

## VOLUME I
*Sunday Gospels of Tute-Amshir*

## VOLUME II
*Sunday Gospels of the Great Lent*

## VOLUME III
*The Holy Pascha*

## VOLUME IV
*Sunday Gospels of the Holy Fifty Days*

## VOLUME V
*Sunday Gospels of Baramhat-Nasie*

## VOLUME VI
*Daily Readings for the Church Year*

✢

Ⲥⲩⲛ Ⲑⲉⲱ Ⲓⲥⲭⲩⲣⲟⲥ

TREASURES OF THE FATHERS OF THE CHURCH
VOLUME II

# The Great Lent

PATRISTIC MEDITATIONS ON THE SUNDAY GOSPELS

*with an Introduction by His Grace Bishop Serapion*

*and a detailed article on A History of the Great Lent*

*St. Paul Brotherhood Press*
Coptic Orthodox Diocese of Los Angeles, Southern California, and Hawaii

THE GREAT LENT

© 2017 BY SAINT PAUL BROTHERHOOD PRESS

## Saint Paul Brotherhood Press

—⚬—

*Coptic Orthodox Diocese of Los Angeles, Southern California, and Hawaii*
Saint Paul Brotherhood
38740 Avenida La Cresta
Murrieta, California 92562
www.SaintPaulBrotherhood.org

ALL RIGHTS RESERVED.

No part of this publication may be reproduced, stored in a retrieval system, or transmitted in any form or by any means—electronic, mechanical, graphic, photocopy, recording, taping, information storage, or any other—without written permission of the publisher.

ISBN 978-0-9721698-4-4
LCCN 20 10921047

SECOND PRINTING – SEPTEMBER 2017

He who prays and fasts is more disposed for almsgiving. He who fasts is light and winged, he prays with wakefulness, and quenches his wicked lusts; he pleases God and humbles his soul when lifted up.

— *St. John Chrysostom*

A brother came to see Abba Poemen in the second week of Lent. He told him his thoughts and obtained peace through his words. He then said to him, "I hesitated to come here today." The elder asked him why, and the brother said, "I thought that you would not let me in because it is Lent." Abba Poemen then said, "We have not been taught to close the wooden door, but the door of our tongues."

— *Paradise of the Fathers*

A full stomach shrinks from examining spiritual questions...A mind full of the world cannot approach the investigation of divine service. Just as fire cannot burn fresh wood; the love of God cannot be kindled in a heart that loves comfort.

— *St. Isaac the Syrian*

**His Holiness Pope Shenouda III**
117th Pope and Patriarch of the
Great See of the City of Alexandria

**His Grace Bishop Serapion**
Bishop of the Coptic Orthodox Diocese of
Los Angeles, Southern California, and Hawaii

# CONTENTS

| | |
|---|---|
| PREFACE | XV |
| ABBREVIATIONS | XVII |

## I

| | |
|---|---|
| INTRODUCTION TO THE GREAT LENT<br>*His Grace Bishop Serapion* | 1 |

## II

| | |
|---|---|
| A HISTORY OF THE GREAT LENT<br>*Father John Paul Abdelsayed and Archdeacon Moses Samaan* | 9 |

## III

| | |
|---|---|
| THE JOURNEY OF LENT<br>*The Late Hegumen Father Pishoy Kamel* | 31 |

## IV

| | |
|---|---|
| OUR FATHER WHO ART IN HEAVEN<br>*Meditations on the Sunday before the Great Lent* | 39 |
| Gospel Reading for the Sunday Before the Great Lent<br>*(Matthew 6:1-18)* | 39 |
| "Entering the Closet"<br>*St. John Chrysostom* | 40 |
| "Our Father"<br>*St. John Chrysostom* | 44 |
| "The Lord's Prayer"<br>*St. Augustine of Hippo* | 51 |

"On the Lord's Prayer" 61
*St. Cyprian of Carthage*

"When God Prayed" 64
*St. Cyprian of Carthage*

## V

SEEK FIRST THE KINGDOM OF GOD 71
*Meditations on the Sunday of Preparation of the Great Lent*

Gospel Reading for the First Sunday of the Great Lent 71
*(Matthew 6:24-34)*

"Do Not Worry" 72
*St. John Chrysostom*

"The Beatitudes and the Stages of Spirituality" 76
*St. Augustine of Hippo*

"Saving Generosity" 80
*St. Cyril of Alexandria*

## VI

INTO THE WILDERNESS TO BE TEMPTED 83
*Meditations on the Sunday of Temptation of the Great Lent*

Gospel Reading for the Second Sunday of the Great Lent 83
*(Matthew 4:1-10)*

Introductory Note 84
*The Late Hegumen Father Pishoy Kamel*

"His Temptation" 85
*St. Jerome*

"His Will in Fasting" 87
*St. Augustine of Hippo*

| | |
|---|---:|
| "Christ, Adam, and the Fast"<br>*St. Ephrem the Syrian* | 88 |
| "The Medicine of Salvation"<br>*St. John Chrysostom* | 92 |
| "Why Forty Days?"<br>*St. Augustine of Hippo* | 106 |

# VII

| | |
|---|---:|
| AND HE AROSE AND WENT TO HIS FATHER<br>*Meditations on the Sunday of the Prodigal Son of the Great Lent* | 109 |
| Gospel Reading of the Third Sunday of the Great Lent<br>*(Luke 15:11-32)* | 109 |
| "The Grace of God"<br>*St. Athanasius the Apostolic* | 110 |
| "Leaving God"<br>*St. Ambrose of Milan* | 111 |
| "A Model of Repentance"<br>*St. Ambrose of Milan* | 112 |
| "The Patience of the Father"<br>*The Scholar Tertullian* | 114 |
| "Returning to the Father"<br>*St. Cyril of Alexandria* | 114 |
| "The Feast above the Clouds"<br>*St. Clement of Alexandria and Another Writer* | 119 |
| "Do Not Love the World"<br>*St. Augustine of Hippo* | 125 |
| A Prayer of Return to our Heavenly Father | 133 |

# VIII

| | |
|---|---:|
| GIVE ME THIS WATER THAT I MAY NOT THIRST | 135 |
| *Meditations on the Sunday of the Samaritan Woman of the Great Lent* | |
| | |
| Gospel Reading of the Fourth Sunday of the Great Lent | 135 |
| (John 4:1–42) | |
| | |
| Introductory Note | 137 |
| "To Save Us" | 138 |
| *St. John Chrysostom* | |
| | |
| "The Living Water as Daily Renewal" | 139 |
| *The Scholar Origen* | |
| | |
| "Encountering the Beloved" | 139 |
| *St. Augustine of Hippo* | |
| | |
| "Worshiping the Father" | 159 |
| *St. Ambrose of Milan* | |
| | |
| "He Restored Our Nature" | 161 |
| *St. Gregory of Nyssa* | |
| | |
| "The Husband of Souls" | 161 |
| *The Scholar Origen* | |
| | |
| "The Spring of Your Love Waters the Depth of My Spirit" | 165 |
| *A Prayer by Hegumen Father Tadros Malaty* | |

# IX

| | |
|---|---:|
| RISE, TAKE UP YOUR BED AND WALK | 169 |
| *Meditations on the Sunday of the Paralytic Man of the Great Lent* | |
| | |
| Gospel Reading of the Fifth Sunday of the Great Lent | 169 |
| (John 5:1–18) | |
| | |
| Introductory Note | 170 |

| | |
|---|---:|
| "Christ, Our Rescue from Despair"<br>*The Late Hegumen Father Pishoy Kamel* | 172 |
| "Do You want to be Made Well?"<br>*St. Cyril of Alexandria* | 173 |
| "The Baptismal Font"<br>*The Scholar Tertullian* | 180 |
| "Water of Renewal"<br>*St. John Chrysostom* | 183 |
| "Heal Me O Lord!"<br>*St. John Chrysostom* | 184 |
| "Spiritual Paralytics"<br>*The Scholar Origen* | 191 |
| "The Great Physician"<br>*St. Cyril of Jerusalem* | 193 |
| "I Have No Man"<br>*A Prayer by Hegumen Father Tadros Malaty* | 193 |

# X

| | |
|---|---:|
| GO, WASH IN THE POOL OF SILOAM<br>*Meditations on the Sunday of the Man Born Blind of the Great Lent* | 195 |
| Gospel Reading of the Sixth Sunday of the Great Lent<br>*(John 9:1-41)* | 195 |
| "Making Clay"<br>*St. Irenaeus of Lyons* | 197 |
| "The Light of the World"<br>*St. Gregory Nazianzen* | 199 |
| "Does God Listen to Sinners?"<br>*St. Augustine of Hippo* | 200 |

"The True Light and His Disciples"     206
*The Scholar Origen*

"The Light of the World"     210
*St. John Chrysostom*

"The Blind World"     217
*St. Augustine of Hippo*

"Commentary on the Sunday of the Man Born Blind"     223
*St. Cyril of Alexandria*

APPENDIX OF SOURCES AND CHURCH FATHERS     281

# PREFACE

As a mother feeds her child—with the proper food, at the proper time, and with the proper utensils—the Church feeds us the Word of God in manageable portions, at different times of the liturgical year, and using the golden spoon of the Church Fathers. In all wisdom, tender care and love, our Mother Church yearns to feed her children the Holy Scriptures and nourish them with the Bread of Life.

With great joy and enthusiasm, we present to you *The Great Lent*, part of the TREASURES OF THE FATHERS OF THE CHURCH series. This book contains excerpts from patristic writings on the readings and themes of the weeks of the Great Lent according to the Coptic Orthodox tradition. In addition, the book features several commentaries and notes on the rites of the Great Lent to enhance the believer's understanding and appreciation of depth of the rites of the Church.

Our paramount objective in this series is to introduce the believers to the *trialogue* of faith—the harmony among the Holy Scriptures, the Church Fathers, and the rites of the Coptic Orthodox Church. Throughout this symphony of discourse, the believer is not only enlightened by the Holy Scriptures, but is further illumined through the homilies, exegeses, and commentaries of the Church Fathers. This is a brief and simple companion to the Coptic Orthodox lectionary. We hope and pray that through this series, the Holy Scriptures, the Church Fathers, and the Church rites are experienced by the believer as a deep source of blessing, wisdom, and faith.

This is Volume II of the TREASURES OF THE FATHERS OF THE CHURCH series, which offers readers a rich treasure of patristic writings from St. Athanasius, St. Cyril of Alexandria, St. John Chrysostom, St. Gregory Nazianzen, the Scholar Origen, and many others. Also included in this volume is a series of three articles containing an introduction to the spirituality of the Great Lent, a liturgical history of its customs and rites, and a general overview of its Sunday gospel readings.

God willing, we hope to also publish the remaining volumes within this series. The projected and published volumes of this series are:

| | |
|---|---|
| Volume I | Sunday Gospels of Tute-Amshir |
| Volume II | Sunday Gospels of Great Lent |
| Volume III | The Holy Pascha |
| Volume IV | Sunday Gospels of the Holy Fifty Days |
| Volume V | Sunday Gospels of Baramhat-Nasie |
| Volume VI | Daily Readings for the Church Year |

May our Lord Jesus Christ, the King of the ages, Who fasted on our behalf forty days and forty nights, receive our fasting unto Himself, forgive our trespasses, remit our transgressions, grant us our Christian perfection that would be pleasing unto Him, and keep us in purity and righteousness all the days of our life.

Through the never-ending intercessions of the Holy Theotokos St. Mary and the prayers of all His angels, apostles, martyrs, and saints who pleased Him from the beginning, we pray that this work will be a source of blessing for the glory of His Name and the spread of His Kingdom, and that you all may receive the blessing of the Fast of the Forty Days of Salvation that belongs to our good Savior.

*Glory be to the Holy Trinity, our God, unto the Ages of all ages, Amen.*

Bishop Serapion
Feast of the Holy Theophany
2010 11 Tubah, 1722 A.M.

# ABBREVIATIONS

| | |
|---|---|
| ANF | Ante-Nicene Fathers Series |
| ACW | Ancient Christian Writers Series |
| FCS | Fathers of the Church Series |
| NPNF | Nicene and Post-Nicene Fathers |
| PG | *Patrologia Graeca* |
| PL | *Patrologia Latina* |
| PLS | *Patrologia Latina, Supplementum* |
| SC | *Sources Chretiennes* |
| SSGF | Sunday Sermons of the Great Fathers |

# I

## Introduction to the Great Lent

*His Grace Bishop Serapion*

The Great Lent is considered the holiest fast because our Lord Jesus Christ fasted it Himself. Therefore, during the Great Lent we follow the example set by our Lord Jesus Christ, Who fasted on our behalf forty days and forty nights (Mt. 4:2). Also, during the Holy Pascha, which comes after the forty days, we live the Passion of Christ day by day and hour by hour.

Because of the significance and holiness of Great Lent, the Church designated a week of preparation to precede the forty days. The Church teaches us to prepare for the Great Lent in a spiritual manner. We fast to prepare ourselves for the forty holy days. In fact, the preparatory week is not the only fast which the Church designated to prepare us for the Great Lent and Holy Week. Two weeks before the Great Lent, we fast Jonah's Fast, which is also known as the Fast of Nineveh. It is a relatively short fast, only three days in length, but nonetheless a fast of sincere repentance. During this fast, we experience with Jonah his fasting and repentance in the great fish's belly. We also live with the Ninevites their fasting and repentance. Just as the fasting accompanied by repentance saved Jonah and the Ninevites from perdition, so also will our fasting accompanied by repentance save us from eternal destruction and death due to sin.

**The Great Lent is an Apostolic Fast**

In *Apostolic Constitutions*, a fourth century compilation of treatises on Early Christian doctrine, spirituality, and worship, we find the following description of the forty-day fast:

After that [i.e. the Feast of the Theophany], you are to observe the fast of the forty days, 'in which you are to remember the Lord's way of life and his commandments.' This fast is to be observed before the fast of Easter, beginning on Monday and ending on Friday. After these days, end this fast, and begin the holy week of the passover, all of you fasting with fear and trembling, and praying during it for the departed.[1]

In Canon 69 from the *Canons of our Fathers the Apostles*, the following is mentioned: "Any bishop, priest, deacon, reader, or chanter who does not fast Great Lent or Wednesdays and Fridays shall be excommunicated, unless he has a physical ailment. As for a lay person, he shall be excluded."

### The Great Lent is an Ascetic Fast[2]

The Church teaches us to fast until sunset. Fish is not allowed during this period. Also married couples should refrain from physical relations to give themselves time for fasting and prayer (1 Cor. 7:5).

The 12th century historian of Coptic canon law, Ibn Al-Assal, refers to several restrictions during the Great Lent. He wrote that there should be no celebrations of the martyrs during the weekdays of the Great Lent.[3] In addition, there were to be no weddings, celebrations, drinking parties, social gatherings, and marital relations during the entire period.[4] Believers were to fast until the eleventh hour (or 5:00 p.m.) Women were not allowed to wear jewelry or makeup during the fast.[5]

Coincidentally, we would like to emphasize the importance of the period of strict abstinence during fasting. It is refraining from eating and drinking for a time, followed by eating vegetarian food. Some people

---

[1] *Apostolic Constitutions* V.13:3-4.
[2] The very word "ascetic" comes from the Greek ascesis, which means "struggle." The fathers and mothers of the desert in the wilderness of Shiheet (or *Scetis* or *Skete* in Greek) struggled in spiritual warfare and prayer. For this reason, the general term "ascetic" was later applied to anyone who bore these characteristics.
[3] *Magmou Al-Safawy Ibn Al-Assal*, translated by Dr. William A. Hanna, based on translation of the Arabic text published by Hegumen Father Philothaos Awad in 1886 A.D., ch. 15, §§25, 78. If the priest broke this fast because of such a feast, he was to be excommunicated, §29.
[4] Ibid., ch. 15, §§26, 35.
[5] Ibid., ch. 15, §§28, 32; ch. 25, §109.

practice fasting by abstaining from meat and they eat vegetarian food, disregarding the period of strict abstention. These people should be regarded as vegetarians and not as fasting. A vegetarian eats only vegetarian food, but is not considered a fasting person. True fasting must be accompanied by abstention from food and drink until sunset as designated by the Church. However, due to variations in people's physical and spiritual abilities, the Church gave the father of confession the authority to designate to his children the length of their strict abstinence. He determines what is suitable for their spiritual benefit according to the nature of their work, as well as their physical ability to endure fasting.

**The Great Lent is a Period of Prayer**

The period of Great Lent is distinctive for its many celebrations of the Divine Liturgy. They become the spiritual treasure for the fasting person to help him throughout the rest of the year. Along with the Divine Liturgy on Sundays, which have specific readings, hymns, and tunes, the Church also arranged special readings for the daily Liturgies during the Great Lent. Also, during the weekdays, there are special hymns that capture the holiness and piety of the period.

The Church celebrates the Divine Liturgy almost daily during Great Lent. It is preferred that these Liturgies start late in the day to offer those fasting the opportunity to practice strict abstinence. It is not permitted to have the Divine Liturgy on weekdays early in the morning, since the Church teaches the believers to pray all the hours until the Compline Prayer.[6] How can believers pray the psalms of the Compline Prayer at 5:00 a.m.? Also, having an early morning Liturgy means there will not be abstention from food, since we cannot abstain from food following the Divine Liturgy. The proper time to end the Divine Liturgy during the weekdays of Great Lent is at sunset. Due to the inability of the elderly and the sick, it is permitted to end the Divine Liturgies earlier, but not before noon. That way, everyone may receive the blessing of Holy Communion while benefiting from abstinence. We hope that the fathers of confession

---

[6] The Compline Prayer in the Book of Hours (Agpeya) of the Coptic Orthodox Church corresponds to the Twelfth Hour of the day, which is at 6:00 p.m., following the ancient practice of designating 6:00 a.m. as the First Hour, 9:00 a.m. as the Third Hour, and so on.

will take great care in guiding their children as to the importance of strict abstinence and how to struggle to keep it for as long as they can.

**The Great Lent is a Period of Repentance**

Fasting without repentance and changing one's life is useless. Unless the fasting person changes his life during fasting, he will only be hungry and exhausted without gaining anything else. Therefore, the Church constantly reminds us of the importance of repentance during fasting. Before the Great Lent, we fast Jonah's Fast and we live the story of Jonah and the Ninevites' repentance.

During the third Sunday of Lent, the Holy Church offers us the gospel reading of the Prodigal Son as a model of repentance, which requires an awakening, confession of sins, leaving the place of sin, and returning to the Heavenly Father with confidence in His mercies and acceptance. This parable reveals to us the depth of God's love for sinners and how He accepts them no matter how horrendous their sin is.

Our Lord Jesus Christ said, "The one who comes to Me I will by no means cast out" (Jn. 6:37). Christ "has come to save that which was lost" (Mt. 18:11). God desires that all men be saved and come to the knowledge of truth (1 Tim. 2:4). Christ is the True Physician Who is needed by those who are ill by sin. He did not come to call the righteous, but sinners to repentance (Mk. 2:17). Repentance is a result of divine action. It is the Spirit of God Who moves the hearts of sinners to repent. It is written in the Holy Scriptures, "For it is God Who works in you both to will and do for His good pleasure" (Phil. 2:13).

God's pleasure is in the return of a sinner so that he will not die in his sin. When God sees his sinful child returning to Him, He has compassion and goes to him, kissing him, and welcomes his return by saying, "It is right that we should make merry and be glad" (Lk. 15:32). The return of a sinner and his repentance results in joy to God, as well as to all the heavenly hosts, because "there will be more joy in heaven over one sinner who repents than over ninety-nine just persons who need no repentance" (Lk. 15:7).

During the Great Lent, we praise God for His many mercies. The Doxology of Great Lent presents to us a magnificent hymn in praising

God and humbly asking for His mercies. The first Doxology of the Sundays of the Great Lent starts with the following: "I will praise you, O Lord, for Your mercies are forever. From generation to generation, my mouth shall declare Your truth."

In this beautiful doxology, we praise God for His mercies. The chanter then remembers his many sins and transgressions by saying, "My sins are heavy over my head." As his sins are revealed in front of him, he then remembers the stories of those who repented and were accepted by God, so that he may not lose hope. Therefore, he remembers the publican, the adulteress, and the thief and asks God to make him like any one of them. Again, he recalls God's attributes by saying, "I know You are good, kind and merciful. Remember me in Your mercy forever." God does not wish the death of a sinner, but that he should return and live. Then the chanter remembers his sins again and says:

I have sinned, O Jesus, my Lord,

I have sinned, O Jesus, my God,

O my King, do not count the sins I have committed.

He asks for God's mercies so that he may not be punished like Sodom and Gomorrah, but rather, that God may have mercy on him like the Ninevites. The chanter ends his praise by saying:

But absolve and forgive my many transgressions

As good and lover of mankind

Have mercy on us according to Your great mercy.

This doxology is beautiful poetry, through which the human soul expresses her feelings resulting from the heaviness of her sins. At the same time, she shows her great hope in our kind and merciful Lord, Who is happy with the return and repentance of the sinner. Yet, He punishes the unrepentant sinners. Therefore, repentance is the means by which we enjoy God's great mercies.

### The Great Lent is a Period for Doing Mercy

The Church reminds us of the importance of doing merciful acts during fasting. Therefore, during Great Lent we chant together praising those who have mercy on the poor. The Holy Bible teaches us that the fasting which is accepted by God is the one in which we do acts of mercy to others. "Is this not the fast that I have chosen: to loose the bonds of wickedness, to undo the heavy burdens, to let the oppressed go free, and that you break every yoke? Is it not to share your bread with the hungry, and that you bring to your house the poor who are cast out; when you see the naked, that you cover him and not hide yourself from your own flesh?" (Is. 58:6, 7).

The Great Lent is a beautiful period of fasting to perform good deeds by helping the poor, feeding the hungry, visiting the sick, and taking care of the needs of others. The person who fasts by not yielding to the needs of the flesh will feel the needs of others and his heart will be moved to serve them. Also, the asceticism of fasting teaches us to care for the heavenly and not be concerned with the earthly. Thus it becomes easy to forsake our material possessions and offer them to the needy.

**The Great Lent is a Period of Reconciliation with Others**

Fasting is an act of worship presented to God, and God does not accept the offering and worship of a person who quarrels with others. Instead, He asks him to go and make peace with his brother before coming to worship and present offerings in front of God's altar. Fasting is an appropriate time to evaluate our relationship with others. As we ask God to forgive us our sins, we must also forgive those who have sinned against us.

**The Great Lent is a Spiritual Journey**

The Great Lent is an important step in the yearly liturgical cycle of the Church, which was instituted to remind us of our renewed state, our journey from this world to Heavenly Jerusalem. The Church organizes its yearly cycle around one single event—our Lord's glorious Resurrection—so that we may organize our lives around our own resurrection in Him. The Great Lent is the spiritual journey that leads us to our resurrection, the end of the old and the beginning of the new. Therefore, let us journey from the lands of Egypt to the Promised Land, from Jerusalem to Golgotha, from this world to the Heavenly Jerusalem, and from the fiery furnace to the Bosom of the Father.

May God grant us a blessed fast by which we can grow in a life of prayer, asceticism, and repentance. May we always increase in doing acts of mercy and living in peace with one another.

# II

# A HISTORY OF THE GREAT LENT[1]

*Father John Paul Abdelsayed and Archdeacon Moses Samaan*

> When a man leaves on a journey, he must know where he is going. Thus with Lent. Above all, Lent is a spiritual journey and its destination is Easter, the "Feast of Feasts."[2]

The Great Lent has oftentimes been likened by the Church Fathers as a spiritual journey of the soul with her Bridegroom through the wilderness of the world to her final resting place in the heavens. Much like the Exodus of the Israelites, tracing this spiritual journey is quite complex and unsettled. As much as biblical scholars have debated the locations of the individual cities and precise plan which the Israelites took, liturgical scholars have debated the precise development of the Great Lent in Christian history.

Perhaps Gregory Dix's work[3] was first in the line of several generations of scholars[4] who assumed that the Great Lent grew from a short one- or

---

[1] We graciously thank Professor Maxwell E. Johnson for his direction and review of this article. Especially helpful was his forthcoming chapter on "Lent and Holy Week," in Paul F. Bradshaw and Maxwell E. Johnson, *The Origins of Fasts, Feasts and Seasons in Early Christianity* (London: SPCK, forthcoming). We also thank Dr. Nicholas Russo for his review and comments. His illuminating doctoral dissertation, *The Origins of Lent* (Ph.D. Dissertation, University of Notre Dame, 2009) has done much to further scholarship in this field thus far. To their scholarship, generosity and friendship we are most grateful.

[2] Alexander Schmemann, *Great Lent: Journey to Pascha* (Crestwood: St. Vladimir's Seminary Press, 2001), 11.

[3] D. Gregory Dix, The Shape of the Liturgy (London: Dacre Press, 1945), 347-360.

two-day fast held before the celebration of the Pascha, to a Holy Week, to a three week fast before baptism (in the West), and ultimately a six-week fast for catechumens that would be baptized on the Feast of the Resurrection.

Recent scholarship—and especially the work of Thomas Talley,[5] Nicholas Russo,[6] and Maxwell Johnson[7]—has cast new light on the development of the Great Lent. It is now believed that the theory of a single origin of the Great Lent cannot be sustained. It is more likely that the emergence of the pre-Paschal Lent is due to the fusion and confusion of several pre-Nicene patterns of fasting, penitence, and pre-baptismal preparation.

This article will explore current trends in scholarship concerning the development of the Great Lent.

**The Development of the Pre-Paschal Fast**

The one- or two-day fast before Pascha mentioned in several early Church sources gradually developed into a longer fast. St. Irenaeus (as chronicled by Eusebius) mentions the variety of pre-paschal fasting in his day (ca. 130-200). Some fasted in anticipation of Pascha for one or two

---

[4] See Adolf Adam, The Liturgical Year: Its History and Meaning after the Reform of the Liturgy (New York: Pueblo, 1981), 91ff.; Pierre Jounel, "The Year," in The Church at Prayer, vol. IV, ed. A.G. Martimort (Collegeville: Liturgical Press, 1986), 65-72.

[5] Thomas Talley, The Origins of the Liturgical Year, 2nd ed. (Collegeville: Liturgical Press, Pueblo, 1986), (hereinafter, "Origins"); idem., "The Origin of Lent at Alexandria," in Worship: Reforming Tradition, ed. Thomas Talley (Washington, D.C.: Pastoral Press 1990), 87-112; reprinted in, Studia Patristica 17:2, ed. Elizabeth A. Livingstone (New York: Pergamon Press, 1982), 97-108, and in Between Memory and Hope: Readings on the Liturgical Year. ed. Maxwell E. Johnson (Collegeville: Liturgical Press, Pueblo, 2000), 183-206.

[6] Nicholas Russo, The Origins of Lent (Ph.D. Dissertation, University of Notre Dame, 2009).

[7] Maxwell E. Johnson, "Lent and Holy Week;" idem., "From Three Weeks to Forty Days: Baptismal Preparation and Origins of Lent," in Living Water, Sealing Spirit: Readings on Christian Initiation, ed. Maxwell E. Johnson (Collegeville: Pueblo, 1995), 118-136; idem., "Lent," in, The New Westminster Dictionary of Liturgy and Worship, ed. Paul Bradshaw (Louisville: Westminster John Knox, 2002), 278-9; idem., "Preparation for Pascha? Lent in Christian Antiquity," in Passover and Easter: The Symbolic Restructuring of Sacred Seasons, Two Liturgical Traditions, volume 6, eds. Paul F. Bradshaw and Lawrence A. Hoffman (Notre Dame: University of Notre Dame Press, 1999), 36-54.

days, as we find in Tertullian or in *Apostolic Tradition!*[8] The early practice in Alexandria seems to be one week around the time of St. Dionysius (ca. 240s) and St. Athanasius in 329.[9] Some have argued that the original two-day pre-Paschal fast eventually developed in Alexandria and Syria into this six-day pre-Paschal fast.[10] Rather than serving as the single origin of the Great Lent, however, the extension of this short fast should be viewed as part of the development of the Holy Pascha week.

In support of his theory that the one- or two-day pre-Paschal fast was the origin of the Holy Week, commemorating the last days and hours of our Lord Jesus Christ, Talley highlighted how the celebration of Lazarus Saturday and Palm Sunday divides the Great Lent from Holy Week.[11] This division is even clear in the modern Coptic rite. The Coptic Orthodox Church calls the Friday immediately before Lazarus Saturday the "Conclusion of the Lent" or the "Seal of the Fast."[12] On this Friday, the hymns of the Church transition from the lenten tune to the annual tune. Because of this separation between the Great Lent and the Holy Pascha week, Talley and others see the development of the original one- or

---

[8] Tertullian, *De ieiunio adadversuspsychicos*, ch. 13-14; *Apostolic Tradition: A Commentary*, eds. Paul F. Bradshaw, Maxwell E. Johnson and L. Edward Phillips (Minneapolis: Fortress, 2002), 172.

[9] St. Dionysiusus (of Alexandria), *The Letters and Other Remains of Dionysius of Alexandria, Letter to Basilides*, trans. Charles Let Feltoe (Cambridge: Cambridge University Press, 1904), 94-5. In his Festal Letter of 329, §10, St. Athanasius describes one week fast as 'the holy fast" in preparation of Pascha. NPNF, s. 2, v. 4, 509-10.

[10] Paul F. Bradshaw, "The Origins of Easter," in *Two Liturgical Traditions, vol. 5: Passover and Easter*, eds. Paul F. Bradshaw and Lawrence Hoffman (Notre Dame: University of Notre Dame Press, 1999), 81-97; reprinted in *Between Memory and Hope: Readings on the Liturgical Year*, ed. Maxwell E. Johnson (Collegeville; Liturgical Press, Pueblo, 2000), 111-124.

[11] Talley, *Origins*, 176-214; *idem.*, "The Origin of Lent at Alexandria," *Studia Patristica* 17:2, ed. Elizabeth A. Livingstone (New York: Pergamon Press, 1982), 97-108.

[12] Russo points out that, historically, different days were treated as the culmination of the fortyday fast in the Coptic Orthodox Church. Abu 'l-Barakat (14th c.) labels Palm Sunday as "The seventh Sunday of the fast...The end of the sacred quarantine [i.e., the forty days]...The pascha [i.e., culmination] of the fast." See Villecourt, Le Museon 38, 314. Macarius of Memphis (10th c.), on the other hand, refers to the sixth day of the sixth week of the fast as: "the day of baptism...Consummation of the sacred quarantine...The day on which the Lord Christ baptized his disciples." See ibid. 36. One way to reconcile the differing accounts is to consider Macarius as speaking of the post-Epiphany forty-day fast while Abu 'l-Barakat as speaking of the Great Lent, as Talley argues.

two-day short fast into a six-day fast as more of a preparation for the Feast of the Resurrection than the development of a Great Lent practice. Primary evidence for this view is found throughout Chapter 21 of the *Didascalia Apostolorum*,[13] which relates this pre-Paschal fast chronologically to events in the last week of our Lord Jesus Christ's life.

### The Three-Week Lenten Fast[14]

While the short pre-Paschal fast is most likely not the single origin of the Great Lent, there are other historical periods of fasting that offer insight into the development of the Great Lent in the Early Church. Rome, for example, knew a three-week Lenten fasting period that was recorded by the Byzantine historian Socrates in the fifth century:

> The fasts before Easter will be found to be differently observed among different people. Those at Rome fast three successive weeks before Easter, excepting Saturdays and Sundays.[15]

Rome, like the other major Christian centers in the world, had an established forty-day fast by the end of the fourth century. What Socrates records here, however, most likely represents an earlier three-week Lenten fast, not fifth century practice. Antoine Chavasse analyzed the readings from the Roman lectionary for the last three weeks of the Great Lent and found the framework of an independent lectionary therein that supported the presence of an original three-week Lenten fast, including the Holy Pascha.[16] Talley concurs in this conclusion, though he does not positively date the three-week Lenten fast in Roman practice.[17]

---

[13] The Didascalia, or the Teaching of the Twelve Apostles and Holy Disciples of Our Saviour, is an early Christian treatise composed in the first part of the third century for a community of Christian converts from paganism in the northern part of Syria. The work is modeled on the Didache and forms the main source of the first six books of the Apostolic Constitutions. See Johannes Quasten, Patrology, vol. 2, 147-148.

[14] Maxwell E. Johnson, "From Three Weeks to Forty Days: Baptismal Preparation and the Origins of Lent," 118-136; *idem*., "Lent and Holy Week," forthcoming.

[15] *Historia Ecclesiastica* 5.22.

[16] Antoine Chavasse, "La structure du Carême et les lectures des messes quadragesimales dans la liturgie romaine," *La Maison-Dieu* 31 (1952):76-120; *idem*., "La preparation de la Pâque, à Rome, avant le Ve siècle. Jeûne et organisation liturgique," in *Memorial J. Chaine* (Lyon: Facultés catholiques, 1950), 61-80; *idem*., "Temps de préparation à la Pâque, d'après quelques livres liturgiques romains," *Recherches de science religieuse* 37 (1950): 125-45. For a

This three-week Lenten period was not confined to Rome only. Some scholars argue that the fourth century Jerusalem rite contained a three-week fast similar to the Roman practice above. The possibility of a three-week fast in fourth century Jerusalem practice was discovered through an analysis of the lectionary of the Armenian Church, which is generally accepted as a fair reflection of fourth century Jerusalem practice. The three-week fast in Jerusalem would have been for the preparation of catechumens for baptism on the Feast of the Resurrection. By examining the rites of baptism in the Armenian Church, which require catechumens to prepare for baptism *three weeks or more* before the baptism, scholars such as Mario F. Lages argued that this period of preparation constituted a three-week fast before baptism on the Feast of the Resurrection.

In several other liturgical traditions, including North Africa, and Constantinople among others, there is ample evidence of a similar three-week (or longer) period of preparation for baptism. The ninth- and tenth-century Byzantine liturgies in Constantinople, for example, prohibit anyone from become a catechumen any later than three weeks before Lazarus Saturday. This preservation of at least three weeks before Lazarus Saturday is indicative of a defined preparation period for baptism that oftentimes—but not always—preceded the Feast of the Resurrection.

A *prima facie* examination of this three-week preparatory fast may lead one to the conclusion that it is the origin of the Great Lent, especially in the early Christian centers that observed it. Unfortunately, this conclusion ultimately cannot be sustained. In the aforementioned liturgical traditions, the three-week fast was directly related to preparation for baptism as opposed to a general preparation by the faithful for the Feast of the Resurrection. Although this was commonly practiced prior to the Feast of the Resurrection, it was done so only because there was a preference that catechumens be baptized on the Feast of the Resurrection in early Christian centers such as Rome, Constantinople and North Africa. The same rite would presumably have been followed for baptism on any other day. In the early Armenian and Syrian traditions, for example,

---

more detailed summary and is cussion of Chavasse's work see Maxwell E. Johnson, "From Three Weeks to Forty Days: Baptismal Preparation and the Origins of Lent."
[17] Talley, *Origins*, 167.

catechumens were oftentimes baptized on the Feast of Epiphany, reflecting a *mimesis* or commemoration of our Lord Jesus Christ's baptism. The same three-week preparation was prescribed for catechumens receiving the grace of baptism on the Feast of the Epiphany just as it was for those on the Feast of the Resurrection. For these reasons, it is not possible to conclusively state that the three-week preparatory fast is the single origin of the Great Lent.

**Alexandria: The Key to Understanding the Origin of the Great Lent**

In recent times, scholars have directed their attention to the great early Christian center of Alexandria to discover the origins of the Great Lent. The earliest documented liturgical tradition in Alexandria did not have baptism on the Feast of the Resurrection. Although the Alexandrian tradition did have a one-week pre-Paschal fast, there is no evidence of a longer pre-Paschal fast, such as the three-week fast discussed above. Alexandrian tradition did, however, include a forty-day fast (the *Quadragesima* or *Tessaracosti*) that was separate and distinct from the one-week pre-Paschal fast. As to why the fast was forty days in length, the number forty has Biblical significance, such as the forty years the Israelites spent in the wilderness before reaching the promised land (Ex. 16:35), Moses' fast on Mt. Sinai (Ex. 34:28), Elijah's fast on his journey to Mt. Horeb (1 Kg. 19:8), and most importantly our Lord's fast in the wilderness (Mt. 4:1).

Talley, Johnson and Russo all point to an Alexandrian root for the forty-day practice, which seems to have originally followed Epiphany. Their work acknowledges three pivotal Egyptian sources: *Origen's Homilies on Leviticus 10.2*, St. Peter of Alexandria's *Canonical Epistle* (ca. 305), and the *Canons of Hippolytus* 12 and 20 (ca. 336-340).

Origen may be referring to this fast in his *Homilies on Leviticus* 10, 2:

> They fast, therefore, who have lost the bridegroom; we having him with us cannot fast. Nor do we say that we relax the restraints of Christian

abstinence; *for we have the forty days consecrated to fasting,* we have the fourth and sixth days of the week, on which we fast solemnly.[18]

Some like Charles Renoux have argued for a link between Origen's commentaries and a forty-day fast;[19] such arguments bear serious difficulties. Origen's words should be read with caution, because there is a chance that his words were enhanced or otherwise modified by Rufinus, who translated his homilies from the original Greek into Latin. Unfortunately, there is no extant Greek version of many homilies and the Latin versions are not conclusive, because of Rufinus' own admission that he built upon the foundations Origen laid when he translated these homilies. Also problematic is the fact that Origen delivered this homily *ex tempore* in Caesarea, to which he fled after teaching in Egypt for many years. For this reason, it is not clear who the "we" are in his statement "for we have the forty days consecrated to fasting." It could refer to Egypt, but it could also refer to Caesarea. As a result of these issues, Origen's words are helpful, but not conclusive, in establishing the presence of an ancient forty-day fast in Alexandria. There are, thankfully, other sources that help in establishing the presence of this ancient fast.

In Canon 1 of St. Peter of Alexandria, the "Seal of Martyrs," this forty-day fast is documented in the context of a rule to readmit penitents who left the Church in the face of persecution:

> [F]or they did not come to this of their own will, but were betrayed by the frailty of the flesh; for they show in their bodies the marks of Jesus, and some are now, for the third year, bewailing their fault: it is sufficient, I say, that from the time of their submissive approach, *other forty days* should be enjoined upon them, to keep them in remembrance of these things; *those forty days* during which, though our Lord and Savior Jesus Christ had fasted, He was yet, after He had been baptized, tempted by the devil. And when they shall have, during these days, exercised themselves much, and constantly fasted, then let them watch in

---

[18] English translation from Talley, *Origins,* 192 [emphasis supplied].
[19] Charles Renoux, "Origen and the Georgian Jerusalem Lectionary," in *First scholarly Conference Devoted to Svetitskovloba, 1995* (Tbilissi: n.p., 1998), 337-340; *idem.,* "Origène dans la liturgie de Jérusalem,"*Adamantius* 5 (1999): 37-52.

prayer, meditating upon what was spoken by the Lord to him who tempted Him to fall down and worship him: 'Get behind me, Satan, for it is written, "Thou shalt worship the Lord thy God, and Him only shalt thou serve."[20]

St. Peter here refers to an *additional* forty-day period of fasting specifically for the apostates who abandoned the Church during persecution. Notably, he refers to this additional period as "other forty days," possibly demonstrating the presence of another forty day fast in Alexandrian tradition.

The forty day fast in Alexandrian tradition may be further documented in the *Canons of Hippolytus* (ca. 336-340), part of the *Apostolic Tradition* that prescribes various church orders and rules in the Early Church. These canons survive only in an Arabic version, which, in turn, is based on a Coptic version. Canon 12 states, "during forty days [the catechumens] are to hear the word and if they are worthy they are to be baptized." [21]Canon 20 offers perhaps the clearest evidence:

> The fast days which have been fixed are Wednesday, Friday, *and the Forty*. He who adds to this list will receive a reward, and whoever diverges from it, except for illness, constraint, or necessity, transgresses the rule and disobeys God [W]ho fasted on our behalf.[22]

The reference to "the Forty" is a clear reference to this ancient forty-day fast, but perhaps more importantly, the last words of the warning reflect the purpose of this fast: it was an icon of our Lord's own forty-day fast in the wilderness.

In response to these references, and after a thorough examination of extant Egyptian liturgical sources, Talley concluded that the Alexandrian tradition included an ancient practice of a forty-day fast that was completely separate from the Holy Week and the Feast of the Resurrection. This fast was instead connected to the Feast of Epiphany, which commemorates the baptism of our Lord Jesus Christ. The fast

---

[20] ANF, v. 6, 269 [emphasis supplied].
[21] Documents of the Baptismal Liturgy, ed., E.C. Whitaker, Rev. and expanded ed., 3rd ed. Maxwell E. Johnson (Collegeville: Liturgical Press, 2003), 129.
[22] Bradshaw, *The Canons of Hippolytus*, 25 [emphasis supplied].

started on the day after this Feast in strict imitation of our Lord Jesus Christ, Who fasted immediately after His Baptism (Mt. 3:16, 4:2; Lk. 4:1, 2).

Nicholas Russo argues for the authenticity of this ancient fast by pointing to the work of F.C. Conybeare, who speculated that this forty-day fast originated in the first century among early Jewish-Christian Quartodecimians.[23] Among the evidence proffered by Conybeare was the testimony of a certain 12th century hierarch, Catholicos Isaac, who said, "Christ, after He was baptized, fasted forty days, and only (that); and for 120 years such was the tradition, which prevailed (in the Church)."[24] Russo sees this testimony as concrete evidence of the ancient Alexandrian practice of a forty-day fast after the Feast of the Epiphany. In addition, he found that this fast is ubiquitous in the Alexandrian tradition from the various circumstances in which it has been used. The forty-day fast has been connected, for example, with catechesis, pre-baptismal preparation, penance, and more.

Once it is accepted that Alexandrian tradition included an ancient forty-day fast that commenced on the day after the Feast of the Epiphany and was related to a strict imitation of our Lord Jesus Christ Who fasted immediately after His baptism, the question becomes how this fast contributed to the universal practice of the Great Lent. The answer is likely found in the Council of Nicaea. Rene-Georges Coquin believed that the Great Lent became a universal forty-day fast before the Feast of the Resurrection because of the Council's decision to use a calculation to determine the date of the Feast throughout the Church.[25] Moreover, the practice of baptism on the Feast-which, as Maxwell Johnson notes, had theretofore been a mere "preference" limited to a few Christian centers, such as Rome and North Africa-became universal throughout the Church after Nicaea. The sole exception was Alexandria, which persisted in the

---

[23] *The Key of Truth: A Manual of the Paulician Church of Armenia: The Armenian Text Edited and Translated with Illustrative Documents and Introduction by Fred. C. Conybeare* (Oxford: Clarendon Press, 1898), lxxviii. Quartodecimians were early Christians who celebrated the Feast of the Resurrection from the eve of the 14th day of the Jewish month of Nisan, which was the day of the Lord's Passover in the Holy Scriptures.

[24] Ibid.

[25] René-Georges Coquin, "Une Réforme liturgique du concile de Nicée (325)?" *Année* 111:2 (1967): 178-92.

absence of baptism on the Feast. Nonetheless, the forty-day fast in Alexandria shifted to a position immediately before the Feast of the Resurrection to conform with the rest of the Church. The combination of a universal calculation of the date of the Feast of the Resurrection and the almost universal practice of baptism on the Feast led to a standardization of preparation for baptism in the form of the Great Lent.

After the Great Lent developed into a universal practice accepted by the catholic (i.e., universal) Church at the Council of Nicaea (325), the Alexandrian patriarch was appointed to announce the date of the Feast of the Resurrection as well as the days of fasting by way of paschal letters. These letters were written on the Feast of Epiphany to designate both the Great Lent and the Feast of the Resurrection. The first to write such letters was Pope Dionysius of Alexandria. Since this reorganization, the days have not been altered or changed in the Coptic Orthodox Church.

Thus, at least from the time of Nicaea and perhaps at the time of Origen, Alexandria had a forty-day, pre-paschal Lent, which after Nicaea was shifted from a post-Epiphany position to pre-Pascha.[26] Despite the various critiques and shortfalls of Talley's theory,[27] the Great Fast, which ends up as eight weeks by the time of Egeria,[28] owes much to the development in Alexandria from the simple fast of two days, or one week, to forty days following Epiphany, which was later moved and extended to a pre-Paschal fast.

---

[26] Johnson, "Lent," 278.
[27] Paul F. Bradshaw, "Diem baptismo sollemniorem" (1993), in ΕΥΛΟΓΗΜΑ: *Studies in Honor of Robert Taft, S.J.*, eds. E. Carr et al., (Rome, 1993), 41-51; repr. in *Living Water, Sealing Spirit: Readings in Christian Initiation*, ed. Maxwell E. Johnson (Collegeville: Liturgical Press, 1995), 137-147; *idem.*, "Tertullian's 'Diem Baptismo sollemniorem' Revisited: A Tentative Hypothesis on Baptism at Pentecost," in *Studia LiturgicalDiversa: Essays in Honor of Paul F. Bradshaw*, eds. M.E. Johnson and L.E. Phillips (Portland: The Pastoral Press, 2004), 31-44.
[28] Talley notes that Egeria's repeated insistence on eight weeks demonstrates a more general practice, 173-4.

## The Catholic Church in the Fourth Century

By the fourth century, many Church Fathers, such as St. Hippolytus, St. Athanasius, and St. Basil, refer to a fast of forty days.[29] Even when the local churches throughout the world agreed about the number of forty days, there were significant differences as to how they understood and calculated these days. This depended on whether they included the Holy Pascha, Saturdays and Sundays, and the preparation weeks as part of these forty days.[30] For example, in Jerusalem, Cyprus, and Antioch, the forty days were understood as the days of strict abstinence. Thus, it included the Holy Pascha, but not Saturdays and Sundays, which resulted in eight weeks with five days of fasting in each.[31] On the other hand, Constantinople understood the forty days as days of preparation. Thus it included Saturdays and Sundays, but not the Holy Pascha, Lazarus Saturday, or Palm Sunday.[32]

In eleven of his festal letters, St. Athanasius the Apostolic explains the forty days' fast. The most important of these is perhaps the sixth letter written for the Feast of the Resurrection in 334 A.D. in which the blessed Father wrote:

> We begin the fast of forty days on the first day of Baramhat (February 25); and having prolonged it till the fifth of Baramouda (March 31), suspending it upon the Sundays and the Saturdays preceding them. We then begin again on the holy days of Pascha—on the sixth of Baramouda (April 1) and cease on the eleventh of the same month (April 6) late in the evening of Saturday, whence dawns on us the holy Sunday, on the twelfth of Baramouda (April 7), which extends its beams with unobscured grace to all the seven weeks of the holy Pentecost.[33]

---

[29] Socrates-PG 67:833; Leo-PL 44:633; St. Jerome-PL 22:475; Eusebius-FCS, 336, n. 17; St. Athanasius, "Letter 6" NPNF, s. 2, v. 4, 1248-1249.

[30] Schmemann, 136; Chavasse, "La structure."

[31] Ibid.; *Peregrinatio Etheriae* 27:1. From the writings of Epiphanius and St. John Chrysostom (387), we know that Cyprus and Antioch followed the example of the calculation begun in Jerusalem

[32] Schmemann, 136.

[33] St. Athanasius, "Letter 1: Of Fasting, Trumpets and Feasts," NPNF, s. 2, v. 4, 1215, 1219.

Moreover, many ancient church canons indicate this forty day period of fasting.[34] Some of these include:

> Great Lent should be honored before Holy Week. It starts on the Monday following the Saturday and is completed on the Friday preceding Holy Week. After it, you must pay great attention to Holy Week and fast it with fear and piety;[35]

> The fast of Lent is to be observed by you as containing a memorial of our Lord's mode of life and legislation. But let this solemnity be observed before the fast of Passover...after which begin the holy week of the Passover fasting in the same all of you with fear and trembling;[36]

and

> If any bishop, or presbyter, or deacon, or reader, or singer does not fast the forty days of the Holy Lent, or the forth day of the week and the day of Preparation, let him be deprived, except he be hindered by weakness of body. But if he is one of the laity, let him be excommunicated.[37]

Also during this time, the Spanish pilgrim nun, Egeria, explains that the differences of the forty days fast were calculated on whether Saturday was included as a fast day (as in the West) or not (as in the East):

> In our part of the world, we observe forty days before Easter, but here [in Jerusalem] they keep eight weeks. It makes eight weeks because there is no fasting on the Sundays or the Saturdays (except one of them, which is a fast because it is Easter vigil). So the eight weeks, less eight Sundays and seven Saturdays...make forty-one fast days. The local name for Lent is Heortae."[38]

---

[34] *Apostoloic Canons*, 69; Canons of Laodicia, 50.
[35] *Didascalia Apolostorum*, ch. 18.
[36] *The Constitutions of the Holy Fathers*, 5.18, 443.
[37] *Constitutions*, Canon 69, 504; *Apostolic Canons*, 69, 598; Denver Cummings, *The Rudder (Pedalion) of the Metaphorical Ship of the One Holy Catholic and Apostolic Church of Orthodox Christians* (Chicago: Orthodox Christian Educational Society, 1957), 122.
[38] Marcel Metzger, *History of Liturgy: the Major Stages* (Collegeville: Liturgical Press, 1997), 93.

Generally speaking, there were three primary reasons for the forty days' fasting: (1) to share in the sufferings of the Lord; (2) to fast on behalf of the Jews during their period of feasting; and (3) to prepare oneself to receive the Communion at the Paschal Feast. As St. Augustine noted, the forty-day fast is related to the forty days from Resurrection to Ascension:

> He fasted for forty days when He was tempted in the desert before the death of His body, as is written in the Gospel (Mt. 4:1-3); and again He spent forty days with the disciples, as Peter says in the Acts of the Apostles (Acts 1:3-5),[39] coming in and going out, eating and drinking after the Resurrection of His body.
>
> In the use of the number forty to designate this period of time, a reference seems to be made of those who are called to grace through Him Who came not to destroy the Law but to fulfill it. For there are ten precepts of the law. Now, the grace of Christ has been diffused throughout the world and the world is divided into four parts. Furthermore, when ten is multiplied by four, since those "that have been redeemed [by the Lord, He has] gathered out of the lands, from the east and from the west, and from the north and from the south" (Ps. 107:2-4), the result is forty.
>
> Hence, He fasted for forty days before the death of His Body as if to say, "Abstain from the desires of this world." But He ate and drank during the forty days after the Resurrection of His Body, as if to say, "Behold I am with you...even to the end of the age" (Mt. 28:20).
>
> Fasting is, indeed, proper in the trial of the contest, since he who strives in a contest abstains from all things (1 Cor. 9:25); but food is proper in the hope of peace which will not be achieved until our body, whose redemption we hope for, will have put on immortality. However, we now feast by anticipation upon that in which we do not yet take glory by actual possession. St. Paul predicted our doing both these things at the same time when he said, "Rejoicing in hope, patient in tribulation" (Rom. 12:12), as if the former were contingent on food, the latter on

---

[39] This reference to St. Peter as the author of Acts instead of St. Luke leads one to question whether St. Augustine was referring to one of the apocryphal Acts of the Apostles. See O. Bardenhewer, *Patrologie* (trans. Shahan), 97-110.

fasting. In fact, when we enter upon the way of the Lord, let us fast from the vanity of this present life and refresh ourselves with the hope of the future life, not focusing our heart on things here, but feasting it on things above.[40]

### Alexandrian Influence on the Manner of Fasting

Additionally, hitherto unexplored evidence suggests Egypt was a source not only for the time of fasting but for the way which one fasted. The *apotactitae* mentioned by Egeria[41] who fast entire week at a time seem to be related to the rigorous weekly fasting in the Egyptian desert of the Pachomian monks and nuns. As it is mentioned

> "There were some monks who went in to partake of food at the third hour of the day, and others at the sixth hour, and others at the ninth hour, and others in the evening, and others who ate once a day only; and there were some who ate only once a week; and according as each one of them knew the letter which had been assigned to him, so was his work."[42]

Moreover, the custom of their eating of water and gruel, but no oil or bread, also seems rooted in the tradition on the mountain of St. Antony.[43] One could further surmise that such a close connection of ascetic practices between the monks in Egypt and Palestine later developed into similarity of periods of fasting.

### A Period of Baptism, Repentance and Reflection

Originally, the Great Lent in Alexandria was not known as a preparation for the Feast of Resurrection, but was instead connected with

---

[40] St. Augustine, Sermon 263, FCS, v. 38, 391-396.
[41] Egeria, 28.3; John Wilkinson, *Egeria's Travels*, 3rd edn. (Warminster: Aris & Phillips, 1999), 149, 72-74.
[42] *The Paradise or Garden of the Holy Fathers* trans. by Sir Ernest Alfred Wallis Budge (London: Chatto & Windus, 1907), vol. 1, ch. 33, 146. The same is written about Abba Hor, 335; Elijah the Hermit, ch. 8, 340. See also "Introduction," liv.
[43] The *Apothegmata* mentions story of Bishop of Nilopolis who was fed water and gruel by Abba Sisoes on the mountain of St. Antony and his hospitality," *Sisoes* 15; Graham Gould, *The Desert Fathers on the Monastic Community* (New York: Oxford University Press, 2002), 146-147.

the Feast of Epiphany. Most scholars have concluded that this fast was specifically for catechumens, who would fast following the example of the Lord's forty day fast following His baptism during the Feast of Epiphany. Thus, forty days later, the fast would be concluded with the baptism of the neophytes on the Friday of the sixth week.[44] Weeks later, the Church held a separate fast for the Feast of Resurrection (some say two days up to six days).[45] Afterwards, the Holy Chrism (Myroun) would be prepared on Holy Thursday and the newly baptized would be Chrismated. Rene-Georges Conquin traced this rite throughout several Coptic manuscripts, such as *The Lamp of Darkness,* the 14th century Coptic Church encyclopedia by the scholar Abu al-Barakat, the 13th century Coptic Synexarium, and the Annals of the 10th century Melkite patriarch Eutychius.

Similarly, in the Early Church, the main purpose of Lent was to prepare the catechumen for baptism, which was usually performed during the Divine Liturgy on the Feast of the Resurrection.[46] In fact, those who desired to be baptized by Easter had to begin their instruction before the second week of the Great Lent, since they had to fast from its beginning.[47] This discipline of catechumens was first instituted in the second century, and became widespread during the fourth century.[48]

Concerning the instruction of the catechumen, St. Augustine tells us the names of those recommended for baptism were handed in at the beginning of Lent.[49] When they finished their studies, they were brought to the bishop on Apocalypse Saturday to be baptized. The Mystery of Baptism was performed on this day because this vigil was in remembrance of the death, burial, and resurrection of our Lord Jesus Christ.[50] Similarly,

---

[44] Talley, "The Origin of Lent."
[45] By the time of St. Dionysius (247-264 A.D.), we see clearly a six-day fast preceding the Feast of Resurrection.
[46] Schmemann, 14; J. Danielou, *The Bible and the Liturgy* (Notre Dame: University of Notre Dame Press, 1956).
[47] Canon 45, Council of Ancyra, NPNF, s. 2, v. 14, 415.
[48] A Monk of the Eastern Church (Fr. Lev Gillet), *The Year of Grace of the Lord* (Crestwood, NY: St. Vladimir's Seminary Press, 1980), 128 (hereinafter, "Year of Grace").
[49] Sermon 13, *Ad. Neophitos.*
[50] Archimandrite (Bishop) Kallistos Ware, "The Meaning of the Great Fast," in *The Lenten Triodion* (London: Faber and Faber, 1938): 13-68, 31

Baptism is an initiation into the crucifixion and resurrection with Christ (Rom. 6:3, 4).

Those already baptized into the faith, reminded of the day of their own baptism, would spend this period in repentance. Those who were convicted of notorious sin were put to open penance. Initially, such repentance was required for sins like idolatry, murder, and adultery. This would last until the end of the Great Lent, when the bishop would "reconcile" these penitents.[51] They were punished in this world so that their souls might be saved in the day of the Lord.[52] Later, this punishment was promoted by St. Basil and St. Gregory of Nyssa,[53] until it prevailed Rome and the rest of the Early Church, except for the Church of Alexandria.[54]

To meet these needs of catechism and repentance, many of the Fathers extended the number of homilies during this period. St. John Chrysostom, for example, would preach between two to five days each week during the Great Lent as opposed to only Sundays.[55] Many of these sermons led to the conversion of hundreds of nonbelievers.[56] Moreover, many of the monks would leave their monasteries for the inner wilderness, seeking solitude and fellowship with the Lord. At the end of Lent, they would return to their monasteries, as explained in the story of St. Mary of Egypt.

### The Fast Today in the Coptic Orthodox Church

The Great Lent in the Coptic Orthodox Church today consists of fifty-five days. Forty of these commemorate the days on which our Lord fasted. Though these include Saturdays and Sundays, believers do not practice strict abstinence during these days, although they are still to refrain from meat and dairy food products and marital relations. The

---

[51] *Year of Grace*, 128.
[52] *Excursus on the Public Discipline or Exomologesis of the Early Church*, NPNF s. 2, v. 14, 106.
[53] Ibid.
[54] *Year of Grace*, 128.
[55] Philip Schaff, "Prologoumena: The Life and Works of St. John Chrysostom," NPNF, s. 1, v. 9:1-24, 20.
[56] Ibid., 21. During the Lent of 387 A.D., for example, St. John delivered a series of 21 sermons called "Homilies on the Statutes," which led to the conversion of many. For more detail, see NPNF s. 1, v. 9, 619-825.

rational for treating Saturdays and Sundays of the Great Lent differently is that Saturday is the day of the Lord's Sabbath and Sunday is the day of the Lord's Resurrection.

Along with these forty days, the Church added the final period for the Holy Pascha and a preparation week. However, more than one interpretation exists for the meaning of these extra weeks of fasting. Some reason[57] that the addition was made up for the exclusion of Saturdays and Sundays from the Great Lent. Again, there is no abstinence (between the 1st and 11th hour) on these two days in the Church during any time of the year, except on the last Saturday before Passion Week, or the Great Saturday. Al-Safi Ibn Al-'Assal, a famous Coptic historian, stated that "all men and women should observe the Great Lent for eight weeks extending from the end of winter until the beginning of summer."[58]

Others say the extra weeks are linked to the Fast of Heraclius, a seven-day fast attributed to the Emperor Heraclius (575-642 A.D.) who rescued the Holy Cross from the Persians in 629 and restored it to Golgotha. Ibn al-Assal called this preparation week "Heraclius week."[59] However, this connection is likely erroneous.[60] The addition of a week to expiate Heraclius' sin of massacring Jews at Jerusalem and its environs, at the requests of the Miaphysites,[61] was an assertion began in 17th century. Moreover it does not account for the fact that according to the *History of the Patriarchs of Alexandria,* Pope Benjamin I remained in hiding in the monastery during the reign of Heraclius, who persecuted many of the

---

[57] These include Ibn al' Makin (1205-1273), Jurjis ibn al-Amid, Abu-Shakir ibn al-Rahib ibn- Butrus ibn al-Muhadhab (thirteenth century).
[58] ch. 15, 142.
[59] ch. 15, §4.
[60] "Fasting," *Coptic Encyclopedia,* 1095.
[61] This allegedly includes the Miaphysites in Egypt, Ethiopia, and Syria, but not the Melkites. Abu Salih, al Arrmani, et al., *The Churches and Monasteries of Egypt and Some Neighbouring Countries* p. 39, n 1 Jo. Mich. Vansleb, *Histoire de l'église d'Alexandrie* (Paris, 1677), 74-76; Danhauer, *Ecclesia Aethiopica* (Strasburg, 1672), cap. vi. Alfred Joshua Butler, *The Arab conquest of Egypt and the Last Thirty Years of the Roman Dominion,* (London: Clarendon Press, 1902), 134. By Even Bulter is uncertain whether Copts directly participated and does not discuss the legend of the fast in detail.

Miaphysite faithful and clergy and "appointed bishops throughout the land of Egypt and Antinoe."[62]

Additionally, if this fast were requested by the Miaphysites alone, little comparison and contrast has been properly made with the Byzantine addition of Cheesefare week,[63] or the connection between Maximus the Confessor, who is believed to have been the first secretary of the court of Emperor Heraclius, the head of the Imperial Chancellory before he became a monk.[64] More modern scholars such as Kaegi, recognizing these inconsistent records, have acknowledged that the link between the lenten fast and the massacre under Heraclius as both controversial and unclear.[65]

Sa'id ibn Bartiq (887-940 A.D.), the Melkite patriarch in Egypt commonly known as Eutychius, explains that this was made for some type of preparation. Many attribute these weeks to the final preparation week of fasting, prayer and teaching for catechumens ready to be baptized into the Christian faith on the Feast of the Resurrection.[66]

Moreover, as noted above, the practice of the forty days and the celebration of Great Lent in the Church of Alexandria was clearly defined from a very early time by the great St. Athanasius the Apostolic. In his seventh letter during the celebration of the Feast of the Resurrection in 335 A.D., St. Athanasius notes that the fast starts one week early:

> We begin the fast of forty days on the twenty-third of Meshir (February 17) and the holy fast of the blessed feast on the twenty-

---

[62] Severus of Al'Ashmunein (Hermopolis), *History of the Patriarchs of the Coptic Church of Alexandria, v. 2: Peter I to Benjamin I (661)*, ed. and trans. B. Evetts, *Patrologia Orientalis* 1 (1904): 489-492.

[63] Elena Velkova Velkovska, "Liturgical Year in the East," in *Handbook for Liturgical Studies: Liturgical Time and Space*, vol. 5, ed. Anscar J. Chupungco (Collegeville: Liturgical Press, 2001), 157-176, 159; A. Rahlfs, "Die alttestamentlichen Lektionen der griechischen Kirche," *Mitteilungen des Septuaginta-Unternechmens der K. Gesellschaft der Wisesenschaften zu Göttingen* (Berlin, 1909-1915) 1:202-205; cf. J. Herburt, *Die ieiunio et abstinentia in ecclesia byzantine ab initiis usque ad saec. XI, Corona Lateranensis* 12 (Rome, 1968), 57-58; Talley, *Origins*, 181.

[64] Andrew Louth, *Maximus the Confessor* (New York: Routledge, 1996), 4.

[65] Walter Emil Kaegi, *Heraclius: Emperor of Byzantium* (New York: Cambridge University Press, 2003), 205.

[66] High Wybrew, *Orthodox Lent, Holy Week and Easter: Liturgical Texts with Commentary* (Crestwood, NY: St. Vladimir's Seminary Press, 1997), 5.

> eighth of Phamenoth (March 24); and having joined to these six days after them, in fastings and watchings, as each one is able, let us rest on the third of the month Pharmuthi (March 29) on the evening of the seventh day.
>
> Also, that day which is holy and blessed in everything, which possesses the name of Christ, namely the Lord's day, having risen upon us on the fourth of Pharmuthi (March 30), let us afterwards keep the holy feast of Pentecost.[67]

Thus, by the time of St. Athanasius, the Church of Alexandria celebrated the forty day fast for the Great Lent, which included a week for the Holy Pascha. Because the dates for Easter and the Great Lent changed each year, St. Athanasius was accustomed to send out a festal letter which explained the dates for these fasting days as well as the fifty days of Pentecost that would follow.[68] With great urgency, St. Athanasius told the leaders of the church to read this message to the people

> before the fast of forty days, so that they may not make this an excuse for neglect or fasting. Also, when it is read, they may be able to learn about the fast. But O, my beloved, whether in this way or any other, persuade and teach them to fast the forty days.[69]

In the same letter, he explains how the whole world participates in such a fast, and if any in Egypt would break from such a fast, it would be a disgrace.[70]

Also, there was no abstinence on Saturdays and Sundays since the Divine Liturgy was celebrated on those days. The same is practiced in the church today.

---

[67] St. Athanasius, "Letter 7," NPNF, s. 2, v. 4, 1257
[68] "According to custom, I give you notice respecting Easter, my beloved, that you also may notify the same to the districts of those who are at a distance, as is usual." St. Athanasius, "Letter 17," NPNF, s. 2, v. 4, 1232.
[69] St. Athanasius, "Letter 12 to Serapion," NPNF, s. 2, v. 4, 1232.
[70] Ibid.

### The Byzantine Tradition

At Constantinople, Saturdays were not considered days of fasting in the calculation except for Holy Saturday immediately before the Feast of the Resurrection. Therefore, the forty days began on Monday in Lent and ended six weeks later on Friday. This was followed by Lazarus Saturday, Palm Sunday, and the Holy Pascha (which is treated separately than the Great Lent).[71]

Beginning in the sixth or seventh century, Constantinople added an eighth or preliminary week of fasting, also called the "Week before Lent," "Cheesefare Week," or the "Week without Meat." During these days, meat is forbidden but cheese and other dairy products are permitted. It also contains some Lenten liturgical features. It seems to have originated as a compromise with Palestinian monks, which attached this period to their eight-week Great Lent. Final unification of the Byzantine Lenten tradition was achieved after the Arab conquest of Egypt and Syria and their independence from Constantinople.[72] St. John of Damascus, writing in the first half of the eighth century, indicates that this additional week was not universal in the Christian east.[73]

In time, two more pre-Lenten weeks were added to Cheesefare Week: the week of the Prodigal Son developed from Meat-Fare Sunday, mentioned in the ninth century by Theodore the Studite.[74] The week of the Publican and the Pharisee developed from anti-Armenian polemics and is first mentioned in the eighth century. It is virtually unanimous among scholars that this pre-Lenten period probably did not occur before the sixth or seventh century.[75]

### Western Practices

Contrary to our practices in the East, the Church in Rome came to keep a fast of a total of forty days before Easter. Because it did not allow any fasting on Sunday, the day of the Lord's Resurrection, it fasted for six

---

[71] Ware, 32-33.
[72] Schmemman, 137.
[73] John of Damascus, *On the Holy Fasts*, PG 95:64-77.
[74] Sermon 50, PG 99:577.
[75] Ware, 29.

days a week, for six weeks, thus totaling thirty-six days.[76] Centuries later, four additional days were added to reach forty days.[77] Thus, Lent began in Rome on a Wednesday, commonly known today as "Ash Wednesday," a rite that remains today.[78] The main difference between this western rite and the East is that in the latter tradition, the forty days did not include Holy Week nor did it include Saturday as a fast day.

Until the fourteenth century, most Western Christians abstained from meat and animal products, as we Copts do today along with our sister Oriental and Eastern Orthodox Churches. But over the past five hundred years, the Western Church has steadily reduced the physical requirements of fasting. As Bishop Kallistos Ware noted:

> One reason for this decline in fasting is surely a heretical attitude towards human nature, a false 'spiritualism' which rejects or ignores the body, viewing man solely in terms of his reasoning brain. As a result, many contemporary Christians have lost a true vision of man as an integral unity of the visible and the invisible; they neglect the positive role played by the body in the spiritual life, forgetting St. Paul's affirmation: "Your body is the temple of the Holy Spirit...glorify God with your body" (1 Cor. 6:19, 20).[79]

**The Fast of the Soul**

In a world where people are afraid to fast because it may seem too difficult, inconvenient, and burdensome, the Church reminds us of the meaning of fasting—to hunger and tire to the point of physical exhaustion for the sake of uniting with our heavenly Bridegroom. Fasting is to toil to obtain the blessing of the fullness of the Spirit, as promised by our Lord, "Blessed are those who hunger and thirst for righteousness, for they shall be filled" (Mt.5:6). Ibn Al-Assal said, "Fasting is not the abstaining from

---

[76] Ibid, 32. Regarding the Latin custom of fasting on Saturday, see Pope Innocent I, Letter to Decentius, 4 (PL 56:516A); Augustine, Letter 36 to Casulanus, §2 (PL 33:136); John Cassian, *Institutes*, 3, 9-10.

[77] Although the earliest testimony to adding these four days dates to the eighth century in the Gelasian Sacramentary, hints of this addition go back to the fifth century. A. Allan McArtur, *Evolution of the Christian Year* (London: SCM Press, 1953), 137.

[78] Wybrew, 10-11.

[79] Ware, 15.

food and water, but a fast acceptable to God is a pure heart. If the body goes hungry, but the soul is occupied with evil desire and the heart is defiled with high living, fasting benefits you nothing."[80]

For this reason, the Church not only sets this period of austere fasting, but also provides much spiritual food to feed the soul. One custom in many churches is the daily celebration of Divine Liturgy, usually celebrated between the 9th and 11th canonical hours (3:00-5:00 pm). However, on Saturdays and Sundays, it is celebrated at its usual time in the morning. It is also customary, although not obligatory,[81] to pray either the entire Liturgy according to St. Cyril or simply just the Cyrillian Anaphora prayer.[82] It has also become a time for many churches to increase the number of spiritual meetings, Bible Studies, and retreats in its yearly program.

---

[80] Ibn Al-Assal, ch. 15, §§34, 67.
[81] The Byzantine Rite fixes certain liturgies to be celebrated on specific dates of the year. For example in the Antiochian Orthodox Church, the liturgy of St. Basil is required to be prayed for the Feast of the Nativity.
[82] *Coptic Encyclopedia*, 1095.

# III

## THE JOURNEY OF LENT[1]

*The Late Hegumen Father Pishoy Kamel*

*The forty days of fasting is a gift from our Lord Who fasted for us, and a gift from the Church to her children that they may struggle and become liberated from bitter slavery—the slavery of hatred and grudges; the slavery of worldly desires, idleness in prayer and obedience of the commandments. The Great Lent is a time of rejoicing for the children of the Church, to pass over the weakness of the soul, particularly very difficult matters which we cannot solve. Our Lord, Who is fasting with us, will pass over with the Cross to His children and show them the glory and the power of His Resurrection.*

— Fr. Pishoy Kamel[2]

The Church has a strong program during Great Lent instituted by the Fathers through the inspiration of the Holy Spirit, which became to the soul a source of survival and spiritual filling, and to the Church a source of communal repentance and deep fellowship with the Lord Jesus Christ in His fast. For Christ fasted for us and with us, and certainly He is a partner with each fasting soul.

The monks used to take this opportunity of the holy fast to leave their monasteries to the wilderness in solitude and in the fullness of the company of the Lord Jesus and the fellowship of the Holy Spirit. At the

---

[1] Originally printed in *Coptic Church Review*, 3:1 (1982), 9-13, trans. Lily H. Soliman. Fr. Pishoy Kamel, *The Passover by the Blood: The Holy Pascha*, 17.
[2] Fr. Pishoy Kamel, *The Passover by the Blood: The Holy Pascha*, 17.

end of Lent they returned to their monasteries, as was recorded for us in the tale of St. Mary the Egyptian and her meeting with St. Zosima the priest.

In addition, the Church considered the Great Lent a dedication program for the teaching of catechumens who were admitted to the faith, and were baptized in the name of the Holy Trinity at the Feast of Resurrection; that is, they were buried and resurrected with Christ. The procession which the Church conducts during these days for the newly baptized baby was in the past the procession of Resurrection which the catechumens experienced at their baptism and resurrection with the Lord during the Feast of Resurrection.

These days of fasting, the Church as a Body practices absolute abstention, daily liturgies, the life of repentance and contrition before God. We can find through meditation on the Sunday readings a strong spiritual program for every soul, which may be titled, "The Journey to the Bosom of the Father." The journey starts in a frank and clear invitation in the gospel reading of Preparation Sunday for entry into the closet for a dialogue with the Father.

### 1. Preparation Sunday (Mt. 6:1-8)

"When you pray enter into your closet...shut your door, pray to your Father Who is in secret..." Also if you give alms or fast that also should be to the Father in secret.

*The Point of Departure of the Journey*

The Church declares to us that the closet is the point of departure of the journey of Lent. If it does not start at the closet then the journey of our fast has deviated from its true course. The fact that the Church starts the fast by directing us to the closet means that the fast is not only related to the flesh but it is related more to the spirit and to Kingdom of God. The week of preparation is the week of the closet.

*Close Your Door*

The journey starts after closing the door, the door that looks at the world. Then there opens before us another door that faces heaven, "Our Father Who Art in heaven," "I looked, and, behold a door was opened in heaven" (Rev 4:1). Fasting is not a fetter or a prison to the senses but a soaring without hindrance towards contemplation of God.

*Pray to Your Father*

The Church has set a standard to the level of faith of the catechumens before they are allowed to receive the Mystery[3] of Baptism. The standard is the church continues teaching the catechumens about the Lord's prayer, starts with "Our Father" and at the moment they perceive and comprehend the paternity of God to them, they are entitled to receive the Mystery of Baptism.

*Your Father Who Sees in Secret*

This is the secret of the prayer of the closet which the Church perceived so allotted to it the deepest of prayers like the prayer of the five wise virgins awaiting the coming of the Bridegroom, and the prayer of the one who is at the feet of the Lord Jesus. When we are in the closet, we discover our sins. And we hold the feet of the Lord to free our feet the prodigal road, and we taste the love of God, and learn contrition, and thus the goal of the journey of our fast becomes the withdrawal of the soul into itself (in secret) where the Lord purifies it with His Blood and dedicates her a temple for Him and adorns her with His talents so that she may participate with the wise virgins in the meeting of the Bridegroom.

Since the journey is with the soul, it should be done in secret. The relationship between the human soul and Christ, is an invisible relationship that begins in the chamber. So fasting is accompanied by a

---

[3] The word "mystery" is used here instead of "sacrament" reflecting a more accurate translation of the word in both Coptic (ⲙⲩⲥⲧⲏⲣⲓⲟⲛ) and Arabic ("al-Seir"), which are both used as liturgical languages in the Coptic Orthodox Church. Using the word "mystery" instead of "sacrament" reflects the Orthodox understanding of these events as divine grace "mysteriously' working with human action in a manner that cannot be explained.

reduction in talking and visits and by concentrating on spiritual readings and attending the Divine Liturgy.

Brother, our heavenly Father is calling you to a holy participation with Him in secret, through which you may start your fast, your prayers, and your alms-givings. So beware of negligence.

Practice: The practice in the week of preparation is the prayer of the chamber and the worship in secret which will continue with us all through after the period of fasting.

**2. Surrender of Life to the Heavenly Father (Mt. 6:24-34)**

The gospel of the first Sunday of Lent calls for the surrender of life to the Father. "Take no thought for your life, what you shall eat...nor yet for the body, what you shall wear...do not worry about tomorrow." The reason for not worrying is that, "your heavenly Father knows that you have of all these things" (Mt. 6:32).

The practice of this week is a call to a secure life in the care of the Father and the carrying out of what comes in the verse, "Do not worry about tomorrow," physically, mentally and spiritually.

The Christian commandment is full of risks but its assurance is the care of the Father. The woman who gave the two mites was risking her meal. During the fast, Satan wages his war by convincing us that we are risking the necessities of the body and causes us to worry about our health. Likewise, in charity, there is a risk of wealth.

In this week, we experience the complete surrender to the care of the Father and to His commandment.

**3. Why does God Forget Us if He is Our Father? (Mt. 4: 1-10)**

The gospel of the Second Sunday deals with the temptation of doubting God's paternity toward us, "If you are the son of God, why does He leave you hungry? Why does God allow the presence of disease, failure and the death of His beloved?"

Practice: It is our duty this week to examine our faith in the love of the Father Who gave His Son for us. Our faith should surpass all temptations and emotions. Faith in the Father should be a faith that fortifies us against the temptation of the adversary, the hardships of this world and the sufferings and desires of the body.

### 4. Repentance in the Father's Bosom (Lk. 15:11-32)

Repentance in Christianity is different from any other repentance. It is the return of the son to his Father and the Father falling on the neck of His son to embrace him and kiss him (Lk. 15:20). This is the gospel of the third Sunday of the Great Lent.

The Father's paternity to us is not because of our righteousness, but because of His paternity to His children, especially the sinners. The Father's paternity for us challenges all our sins, our failures, our betrayal of His love and our mistreatment of His Name.

Practice of this week, brother, is simple. Do not permit this week to go by without a true repentance and resorting to the Father's embrace. Examine this in your chamber and taste the Father's embrace and His kisses which are reserved only for those who repent. This is the week of repentance in the Father's bosom, the repentance of the whole Church— the communal repentance.

### 5. Worship of the Father in Spirit and in Truth (Jn. 4:1-42)

The next step after repentance is worship of the Father Who accepted and loved me and cleansed me from my sins and put me in His bosom. Contrition of the spirit and submission to the Father and the love of frequent prostrations in worship are the expressions of our love for Him Who opened His arms for us sinners and kissed us. This is the end of the road of repentance in the Father's bosom, and this is the sweetest fruit of the chamber and which the Father gives us in secret.

The Church, inspired by the Spirit, stresses in the period of Lent the use of prostrations during private prayers and in the Divine Liturgy, during the Offering of Incense, after the readings of the prophets.

The practice of this week is to worship the Father in spirit and truth "for such the Father seeks to worship Him" (Jn. 4:23)

### 6. Bethsaida and Baptism (Jn. 5:1-18)

The gospel of the fifth Sunday talks about Bethsaida which symbolizes Baptism. We, the crowds of Christians, were beside it sick, lame, blind and paralyzed, suffering every spiritual sickness. The Angel that moves the water symbolizes the Holy Spirit Who comes down on the water of baptism.

This is our share in Christ: those who are baptized have ever in the Father even if they have been sick for 38 years.

The practice of this week is to hope and never to despair. Baptism has given us the grace of sonship and children are never disappointed in their hopes in the love of the Father.

### 7. Sonship is a Spiritual Enlightenment (Jn. 9:1-41)

The last Sunday in Lent is the Sunday of Baptism, during which we read the gospel of the man born blind.

*"I was blind and now I see."*

This is our everlasting experience as children of the Heavenly Father. We were blind and He opened our sight so we beheld miracles of His laws and we saw what the prophets longed to see, and He gave us understanding of the Scriptures.

*"Go wash in the pool of Siloam."*

Baptism means washing in the pool of Siloam, so we become pure. Repentance is a continuous washing, so we may see clearly. Repentance is a continuation of Baptism and it is the means through which we can see Christ clearly all our life. Lasting repentance cleans our heart, renews the intellect, protects the contrite soul in the obedience of the Father, and through repentance, we can discover all the graces and secrets of the Heavenly Father.

**8. The Kingdom of the Beloved Son (Mt. 21:1-17; Mk. 11:1-11; Lk. 19:29-48; Jn. 12:12-19)**

This week begins with the entrance of Christ to rule Jerusalem, riding on a donkey and ends by Him ruling from the Cross on Calvary where He draws all to Him—all the children to rule with Him in the Kingdom of His Father.

## Table of Readings and Topics in the Great Lent

| Weeks | Title | Passage | Topics |
|---|---|---|---|
| Preparation | *Sermon on the Mount* | Mt. 6:1-18 | Prayer, Fasting, Alms Giving |
| First Sunday | *Kingdom of Heaven* | Mt. 6:24-34 | Surrender to the Heavenly Father |
| Second Sunday | *Temptation* | Mt. 4:1-10 | Faith and Doubt |
| Third Sunday | *Prodigal Son* | Lk. 15:11-32 | Repentance and Renewal in Baptism |
| Fourth Sunday | *Samaritan Woman* | Jn. 4:1-42 | Living Water and Baptism |
| Fifth Sunday | *Paralyzed Man* | Jn. 5:1-18 | Baptism & Hope |
| Sixth Sunday | *Man Born Blind* | Jn. 9:1-41 | Baptism and Enlightenment |
| Seventh Sunday | *Palm Sunday* | Mt. 21:1-17<br>Mk. 11:1-11<br>Lk. 19:29-48<br>Jn. 12:12-19 | Kingdom and Reign |

# IV

## Our Father Who Art in Heaven

*Meditations on the Sunday before the Great Lent*

### Gospel Reading for the Sunday Before the Great Lent

#### (Matthew 6:1-18)

*Take heed that you do not do your charitable deeds before men, to be seen by them. Otherwise you have no reward from your Father in heaven. Therefore, when you do a charitable deed, do not sound a trumpet before you as the hypocrites do in the synagogues and in the streets, that they may have glory from men. Assuredly, I say to you, they have their reward. But when you do a charitable deed, do not let your left hand know what your right hand is doing, that your charitable deed may be in secret; and your Father who sees in secret will Himself reward you openly.*

*And when you pray, you shall not be like the hypocrites. For they love to pray standing in the synagogues and on the corners of the streets, that they may be seen by men. Assuredly, I say to you, they have their reward. But you, when you pray, go into your room, and when you have shut your door, pray to your Father who is in the secret place; and your Father who sees in secret will reward you openly. And when you pray, do not use vain repetitions as the heathen do. For they think that they will be heard for their many words.*

*Therefore do not be like them. For your Father knows the things you have need of before you ask Him. In this manner, therefore, pray: Our Father in heaven, Hallowed be Thy name. Thy kingdom come. Thy will be done, on earth as it is in heaven. Give us this day our daily bread. And forgive us our debts, As we forgive our debtors. And do not lead us into temptation, But deliver us from the evil one. For Thine is the kingdom and the power and the glory forever. Amen.*

*For if you forgive men their trespasses, your heavenly Father will also forgive you. But if you do not forgive men their trespasses, neither will your Father forgive your trespasses.*

*Moreover, when you fast, do not be like the hypocrites, with a sad countenance. For they disfigure their faces that they may appear to men to be fasting. Assuredly, I say to you, they have their reward. But you, when you fast, anoint your head and wash your face, so that you do not appear to men to be fasting, but to your Father who is in the secret place; and your Father who sees in secret will reward you openly.*

## "Entering the Closet"

### *St. John Chrysostom*[1]

"And when you pray, you shall not be like the hypocrites. For they love to pray standing in the synagogues and on the corners of the streets, that they may be seen by men. Assuredly, I say to you, they have their reward. But you, when you pray, go into your room, and when you have shut your door, pray to your Father Who is in the secret place; and your Father Who sees in secret will reward you openly."

These, too, He calls "hypocrites," and very fitly, for while they are pretending to pray to God, they are looking round after men, wearing the garb, not of suppliants, but of ridiculous persons. For he, who is to do a suppliant's office, letting go all other, looks to Him alone Who has power to grant his request. But if you leave Him and go about wandering and casting around your eyes everywhere, your will depart with

---

[1] St. John Chrysostom, *Homily 19 on the Gospel of St. Matthew*, NPNF, s. 1, v. 10, 293-296.

empty hands. For this was your own will. Therefore He did not say, "Such shall not receive a reward," but, "they have received" that is, they shall indeed receive one, but from those of whom they themselves desire to have it. For God does not will this; He rather, for His part, was willing to bestow on men the recompense that comes from Himself. But they, seeking that which is from men, can be no longer justly entitled to receive from Him, for whom they have done nothing.

But I ask you to consider the loving kindness of God, in that He promises to bestow on us a reward, even for those good things which we ask of Him. Having then discredited them, who order not this duty as they should, both from the place and from their disposition of mind, and having shown that they are very ridiculous: He introduces the best manner of prayer, and again gives the reward, saying, "Enter into your closet."

Some may say, "Then, should we not pray in church?" Indeed we should by all means, but in this spirit. Because everywhere God seeks the intention of all that is done. For, even if your enter into your closet and shut the door, if you do it for display, the doors will do you no good.

It is worth observing in this case also, how exact the definition, which He made when He said, "That they may be seen by men." So that He desires you duly to shut your doors—and more importantly, even to shut the doors of the mind. For as in everything it is good to be freed from vainglory, so most especially in prayer. For if even without this, we wander and are distracted, when shall we attend unto the things which we are saying, should we enter in having this disease also? And if we who pray and beseech do not attend, how do we expect God to attend?

But there are some, who after such and so earnest charges, behave themselves so unseemly in prayer, that even when their person is concealed, they make themselves manifest to all by their voice, crying out disorderly, and rendering themselves objects of ridicule both by gesture and voice. Don't you realize that even in a market place, if any acts like this, and begging clamorously, the person he is asking will ward him off. But if he quietly, and with the proper gesture, requests, he instead wins over the one that can grant the favor.

Then, let us not make our prayer by the gesture of our body, nor by the loudness of our voice, but by the earnestness of our mind—without noise or clamor and for display, so as even to disturb those that are near us, but with all modesty, and with contrition in the mind, and with inward tears.

But are you troubled in mind, and cannot not help but cry out loud? Then, surely it is the part of one exceedingly troubled to pray and entreat even as I have said. Moses was also troubled, and prayed in this way and was heard. Because of this, God also said to him, "Why do you cry out to Me?" (Ex. 14:15). Also Hannah, again her voice not being heard, accomplished all she wished, forasmuch as her heart cried out. But Abel did not only pray in silence, but even when he was dying, his blood cried out louder than a trumpet.

Then I do not think that you are groaning as that holy man. But as the Prophet commanded, "Rend your heart, and not your garments" (Joel 2:13) Call upon God out of the deep, as it is said, "Out of the depths I cry to You, O Lord" (Ps. 129:1). From beneath, out of the heart, draw forth a voice, make your prayer a mystery. Don't you see that even in the houses of kings all uproar is put away, and silence is great on all sides? When you enter a palace —not one on the earth, but one far greater than that, which is in heaven— don't you show a great deal of respect? Yes, for you are joined to the choirs of angels; you are in communion with archangels; you are singing with the Seraphim. And all these tribes display great, proper order—singing that mystical melody, and their sacred hymns to God, the King of all, with great awe. Then, when you are praying mingle yourself with these and emulate their mystical order. For you are not praying to men, but to God—Who is present everywhere, Who even hears the voice before [it sounds], Who knows the secrets of the mind.

If you pray this way, you will receive a great reward. For He says, "Your Father Who sees you in secret, will reward you openly." He did not say, "[He] will freely give you," but, "[He] will reward you." Yes, for He has made Himself a debtor to you, and even from this has honored you with great honor. For because He Himself is invisible, He would like your prayer to be the same.

Then He says even the words of the prayer, "When you pray, do not use vain repetitions as the heathen do" (Mt. 6:7). You see that when He was speaking of almsgiving, He removed only that mischief which comes of vainglory, and added nothing more. Neither did He say when one should give alms, as from honest labor, not from evil nor covetousness, this being abundantly acknowledged among all. And before that, He had thoroughly cleared up this point when He blessed those "who hunger and thirst for righteousness" (Mt. 5:6).

But touching prayer, He adds somewhat over and above "not to use vain repetitions." And as there He derides the hypocrites, so here the heathen, shaming the hearer everywhere most of all by the vileness of the persons. For since this, in most cases, is especially biting and stinging, I mean our appearing to be likened to outcast persons. By this topic, He dissuades them, calling frivolousness, here, by the name of "vain repetition," as when we ask of God things unsuitable, kingdoms, and glory, and to get the better of enemies, and abundance of wealth, and in general the things that do not at all concern us.

When saying, "For your Father knows what you need before you ask Him," He seems to me to command here that we also should not make our prayers long—I mean long, not in time, but in the number and length of the things mentioned. For perseverance indeed in the same requests is our duty, His word being "continuing steadfastly in prayer" (Rom. 12:12).

And by that example of the widow who prevailed with the pitiless and cruel ruler, and by the continuance of her intercession and by that of the friend, who came late at nighttime, and roused the sleeper from his bed, not for his friendship's, but for his importunity's sake. What did He Himself do other than to lay down a law that all should continually make supplication unto Him?

He did not, however, forbid us to compose a prayer of ten thousand clauses, and so come to Him and merely repeat it. For this He obscurely signified when He said, "For they think that they will be heard for their many words...For your Father knows the things you have need of before you ask Him" (Mt. 6:7, 8). One may say, "If He knows the things you have need of, why do we have to pray?" Not to instruct Him, but to prevail with Him; to be made intimate with Him, by continuance in supplication; to be humbled; to be reminded of your sins.

## "Our Father"

### St. John Chrysostom[2]

Our Father in heaven, Hallowed be Thy Name. Thy Kingdom come. Thy will be done; on earth as it is in heaven. Give us this day our daily bread. And forgive us our trespasses, as we forgive those who trespass against us. And lead us not into temptation, but deliver us from the evil one...For Thine is the Kingdom and the power and the glory forever. Amen.

See how He immediately stirs up the hearer, and reminded him of all God's bounty in the beginning? He who calls God Father will receive in this single title remission of sins, elimination of punishment, righteousness, sanctification, redemption, adoption, inheritance, brotherhood with the Only-Begotten, and the supply of the Spirit. For one cannot call God Father, without attaining all those blessings. Therefore, He awakens their spirit, both by the dignity of Him Who is called on, and by the greatness of the benefits which they have enjoyed.

But when He says, "in Heaven," He does not speak this as shutting up God there, but as withdrawing him who is praying from earth, and fixing him in the high places, and in the dwellings above.

He teaches, moreover, to make our prayer common, on behalf of our brethren also. For He does not say, "My Father, Who art in Heaven," but, "Our Father," offering up His supplications for the body in common, and nowhere looking to his own, but everywhere to his neighbor's good. By this, He immediately takes away hatred, quells pride, casts out envy, brings in the mother of all good things—even charity, exterminates the inequality of human things, and shows how far the equality reaches between the king and the poor man—if at least in those things which are greatest and most indispensable, we are all of us fellows.

For what harm comes of our family below, when we are all knit together on high? No one should have more than another, neither the rich

---

[2] St. John Chrysostom, *Homily 19 on the Gospel of St. Matthew*, NPNF, s. 1, v. 10, 289-303.

more than the poor, nor the master than the servant, neither the ruler than the subject, nor the king than the common soldier, nor the philosopher than the barbarian, nor the skillful than the unlearned. For He has given all one nobility, having desired to be called the Father of all alike.

Therefore, when He has reminded us of this nobility, of the gift from above, of our equality with our brethren, of charity. And when He has removed us from earth and fixed us in heaven, let us see what He commands us to ask after this. Not but, in the first place, even that saying alone is sufficient to implant instruction in all virtue. For he who has called God Father, and a common Father, would be justly bound to show forth such a conversation, as not to appear unworthy of this nobility, and to exhibit a diligence proportionate to the gift. Yet is He not satisfied with this, but adds, also another clause, thus saying,

**"Hallowed be Thy Name."**

Worthy of him who calls God Father, is the prayer to ask nothing before the glory of His Father, but to account all things secondary to the work of praising Him. For "hallowed" is glorified. He has completed His own glory, and ever continuing the same, but He commands him who prays to seek that He may be glorified also by our life. Which very thing He had said before likewise, "Let your light so shine before men, that they may see your good works, and glorify your Father in heaven" (Mt. 5:16). Yea, and the Seraphim, giving glory, also said in this manner, "Holy, Holy, Holy" (Is. 6:3). So that "hallowed" means "glorified." By this, he says "Grant that we may live so purely, that through us all may glorify You." Which thing again appertains unto perfect self-control, to present to all a life so reprehensible, that every one of the beholders may offer to the Lord the praise due to Him for this.

**"Thy Kingdom come."**

And this again is the language of a right-minded child, not to be riveted to things that are seen, neither to account to things present some great matter, but to hasten unto our Father and to long for the things to come. And this springs out of a good conscience, and a soul set free from things that are on earth. This, for instance, Paul himself was longing after every day: why he also said, that "we also who have the first-fruits of the

Spirit, even we ourselves groan within ourselves, eagerly waiting for the adoption, the redemption of our body" (Rom. 8:23). For he who has this fondness can neither be puffed up by the good things of this life nor abashed by its sorrows, but as though dwelling in the very heavens, is freed from each sort of irregularity.

**"Thy will be done, on earth, as it is in heaven."**

Behold a most excellent train of thought! He called us indeed long for the things to come and hasten towards that sojourn, and, till that may be, even while we abide here, to be earnest in showing forth the same conversation as those above. For you must long, He says, for heaven, and the things in heaven. However, even before heaven, He has asked us to make the earth a heaven and do and say all things, even while we are continuing in it, as having our conversation there. So much that these too should be objects of our prayer to the Lord. For there is nothing to hinder our reaching the perfection of the powers above, because we inhabit the earth, but it is possible even while abiding here, to do all, as though already placed on high. What He says therefore is this: "As there all things are done without hindrance, and the angels are not partly obedient and partly disobedient, but in all things yield and obey, for He says, 'Mighty in strength, performing His word' (Ps. 102:20). So grant that we men may not partially do Your will, but perform all things as You will."

He has also taught us to be modest, by making it clear that virtue is not only our endeavor, but also of the grace from above? And again, He has enjoined each one of us, who pray, to take upon himself the care of the whole world. For He did not at all say, "Thy will be done" in me, or in us, but everywhere on the earth so that error may be destroyed, truth implanted, all wickedness cast out, virtue return, and no difference in this respect be henceforth between heaven and earth. "For if this comes to pass," He says, "there will be no difference between things below and above, separated as they are in nature, the earth exhibiting to us another set of angels."

**"Give us this day our daily bread."**

What is "daily bread?" It refers to bread for one day. For because He had said thus, "Thy will be done in earth as it is in heaven," but was discoursing to men encompassed with flesh, subject to the necessities of nature and incapable of the same impassibility with the angels. While He enjoins the commands to be practiced by us also, even as they perform them, He condescends likewise, in what follows, to the infirmity of our nature. Thus, "perfection of conduct," He says, "I require as great, not however freedom from passions. No, for the tyranny of nature does not permit this, for it requires necessary food." But mark, I pray you, how even in things that are bodily, that which is spiritual abounds. For He has commanded us to make our prayer neither for riches, nor for delicate living, nor for costly raiment, nor for any other such thing, but for bread only. [We are to pray for] "daily bread," so as not to "worry about tomorrow" (Mt. 6:34). Because of this He added, "daily bread," that is, bread for one day.

He then adds another expression afterwards, saying, "Give us this day" so that we may not, beyond this, wear ourselves out with the care of the following day. For why do you submit to the cares of that day, the interval before which you do not know whether you will see?

As He proceeded, He also more fully commanded, saying, "Therefore do not worry about tomorrow" (Mt. 6:34). He would have us be on every hand unencumbered and winged for flight, yielding just so much to nature as the compulsion of necessity requires of us. Then forasmuch as it comes to pass that we sin even after the washing of regeneration, He, showing His love to man to be great even in this case, commands us for the remission of our sins to come unto God Who loves man, and thus to say,

**"Forgive us our trespasses, as we also forgive those who trespass against us."**

See your surpassing mercy? After taking away so great evils, and after the unspeakable greatness of His gift, if men sin again, He counts them such as may be forgiven. For that this prayer belongs to believers, is taught to us both by the laws of the Church, and by the beginning of the prayer. For the uninitiated could not call God, "Father." If then the prayer belongs to believers, and they pray, entreating that sins may be forgiven them, it is clear that not even after the laver is the profit of repentance taken away. Since, had He not meant to signify this, He would not have made a law that we should so pray.

Now He Who both brings sins to remembrance, bids us to ask for forgiveness, and teaches how we may obtain remission, and so makes the way easy. It is perfectly clear that He introduced this rule of supplication, as knowing and signifying that it is possible even after the baptismal font to wash ourselves from our offenses. By reminding us of our sins and persuading us to be modest; by the command to forgive others, setting us free from all revengeful passion; and by promising in return for this to pardon us also, He extends good hopes and instructs us to have high views concerning the unspeakable mercy of God toward man.

But what we should observe most is this, that whereas in each of the clauses He had made mention of the whole of virtue, and in this way had included also the forgetfulness of injuries—for so, that "Hallowed be His Name," is the exactness of a perfect conversation; and that "His will be done," declares the same thing again; and to be able to call God "Father," is the profession of a blameless life; in all which things had been comprehended also the duty of remitting our anger against them that have transgressed—still He was not satisfied with these, but meaning to signify how earnest He is in the matter, He sets it down also in particular, and after the prayer, He makes mention of no other commandment than this, saying, "For if you forgive men their trespasses, your heavenly Father also will forgive you" (Mt. 6:14), so that the beginning is of us and we ourselves have control over the judgment that is to be passed upon us.

For in order that no one, even of the senseless, might have any complaint to make, either great or small, when brought to judgment, He causes the sentence to depend on you, who are to give account: "and with the measure you use," He says, "it will be measured back to you" (Mt. 7:2). And if you forgive your fellow servant, you will obtain the same favor from Me, though indeed the one be not equal to the Other. For you forgive in your need, but God, is in no such need. You forgive your fellow slave, God forgives His own slave. You are liable for numerous charges, God is without sin. Even after all this, He shows forth His loving-kindness toward man.

Although He could indeed, even without this, forgive you all your offenses, He wills that you by this also to receive a benefit, affording you on all sides innumerable occasions of gentleness and love to man, casting out what is brutish in you, and quenching wrath, and in all ways cementing you to him who is your own member.

For what do you have to say? That your have wrongfully endured some ill on your neighbor? (For these only are trespasses and an act done with justice is not a trespass.) But, you also are drawing near to receive forgiveness for such things, and for much greater. Even before the forgiveness, you have received no small gift, in being taught to have a human soul, and in being trained to all gentleness. By this a great reward shall also be laid up for you elsewhere, even to be called to account for none of your offenses.

What sort of punishment then do we not deserve, when after having received the privilege, we betray our salvation? And how shall we claim to be heard in the rest of our matters, if we will not, in those which depend on us, spare our own selves?

**"And lead us not into temptation, but deliver us from the evil one: for Thine is the Kingdom, and the power, and the glory, forever. Amen."**

Here, He teaches us plainly our own vileness, and silences our pride, instructing us to deplore all conflicts, instead of rushing upon them. For so both our victory will be more glorious, and the devil's overthrow will be more ridiculed. I mean, that as when we are dragged forth, we must stand nobly, so when we are not summoned, we should be quiet, and wait for the time of conflict, that we may show both freedom from vainglory, and nobleness of spirit. And He here calls the devil "the evil one," commanding us to wage against him a war that knows no truce, and implies that he is not such by nature.

For wickedness is not of those things that are from nature, but of them that are added by our own choice. And he is so called preeminently, by reason of the excess of his wickedness, and because he, in no respect injured by us, wages against us implacable war. Why did He neither say, "deliver us from the evil ones," but, "from the evil one?" So to instruct us in no case to entertain displeasure against our neighbors, for whatever wrongs we may suffer at their hands, but to transfer our enmity from these to him, as being himself the cause of all our wrongs.

Having then made us anxious as before conflict, by putting us in mind of the enemy, and having cut away from us all our remissness, He again encourages and raises our spirits, by bringing to our remembrance the King under whom we are arrayed, and signifying Him to be more powerful than all.

*"For Thine is the Kingdom..."*

So it follows that if His be the Kingdom, we should fear no one, since there can be none to withstand, and divide the empire with Him. For when He says, "Thine is the Kingdom," He sets before us even him, who is warring against us, brought into subjection, though he seems to oppose God for a while. For in truth, he also is among God's servants, though of the degraded class, and those guilty of offense. He would not dare set upon any of his fellow servants, had he not first received license from above. And why do I say, "his fellow servants?" Not even against swine did he venture any outrage, until He Himself allowed him, nor against flocks, nor herds, until he had received permission from above.

*"And the power..."*

Therefore, manifold as your weakness may be, your way of right be confident, having such a one to reign over you, who is able fully to accomplish all, and that with ease, even by you.

*"And the glory, forever. Amen."*

Thus He not only frees you from the dangers that are approaching you, but can make you also glorious and illustrious. For as His power is great, so also is His glory unspeakable, and they are all boundless, and no end of them. Do you see how He has by every means anointed His champion, and has framed him to be full of confidence?

Then, as I said before, meaning to signify, that of all things He most loathes and hates bearing malice, and most of all accepts the virtue which is opposite to that vice. He has after the prayer also again put us in mind of this same point of goodness, both by the punishment set and by the reward appointed, urging the hearer to obey this command.

Therefore, considering these things, let us cast up that venom, let us put an end to our enmities, and let us make the prayers that become such as we are. Instead of the brutality of devils, let us take upon us the mildness of angels, and in whatever things we may have been injured, let us, considering our own case, and the reward appointed us for this commandment soften our anger. Let us relieve the waves, that we may both pass through the present life calmly, and when we have departed from there, may find our Lord such as we have been towards our fellow-servants.

And if this is a heavy and fearful thing, let us make it light and desirable, and let us open the glorious gates of confidence toward Him. And what we had not strength to effect by abstaining from sin, let us accomplish it by becoming gentle to them who have sinned against us (for this surely is neither grievous nor burdensome) and let us by doing kindnesses to our enemies lay up beforehand much mercy for ourselves.

For so both during this present life all will love us, and above all others, God will both befriend and crown us and will count us worthy of all the good things to come, unto which may we all attain, by the grace and love towards mankind of our Lord Jesus Christ, to Whom be glory and might forever and ever. Amen.

## "The Lord's Prayer"

### St. Augustine of Hippo [3]

### 1.

The order established for your edification requires that you learn first what to believe, and afterwards what to ask. For so the Apostle says, "Whoever shall call upon the Name of the Lord, shall be saved" (Joel 2:32; Rom. 10:13). The blessed Paul cited this testimony from the Prophet, for by the Prophet were those times foretold, when all men should call upon God: "How then shall they call on Him in Whom they have not believed? And how shall they believe in Him of Whom they have not heard? And

---

[3] St. Augustine, Sermon 7, *Sermons on Selected Lessons of the New Testament*, NPNF, s. 1, v. 6.

how shall they hear without a preacher? And how shall they preach unless they are sent?" (Rom. 10:14, 15).

Therefore, preachers were sent. They preached Christ. As they preached, the people heard, by hearing they believed, and by believing called upon Him. Because then it was most rightly and most truly said, "How shall they call on Him in Whom they have not believed?" Thus, you have first learned what to believe: and today have learned to call on Him in Whom you have believed.

2.

The Son of God, our Lord Jesus Christ, has taught us a prayer, and although He is the Lord Himself, as you have heard and repeated in the Creed, the Only Son of God, yet He would not be alone. He is the Only Son, and yet would not be alone, He has granted to have brethren. For to whom does He say, "Say, 'Our Father in heaven'" (Mt. 6:9)? Whom did He wish us to call our Father, except His own Father? Did He permit us this?

Parents sometimes when they have gotten one, two, or three children, fear to give birth to any more, lest they reduce the rest to poverty. But because the inheritance which He promises us is such as many may possess, and no one be straitened. Therefore He has called into His brotherhood the numerous brethren who say, "Our Father, Who Art in heaven." So said they who have been before us, and so shall say those who will come after us. See how many brethren the Only Son has in His grace, sharing His inheritance with those for whom He suffered death. We had a father and mother on earth, that we might be born to labors and to death. But we have found other parents—God our Father, and the Church our Mother, by whom we are born unto life eternal. Let us then consider, beloved, whose children we have begun to be and let us live so as becomes those who have such a Father. Realize, then how our Creator has condescended to be our Father!

3.

We have heard Whom we should call upon, and with what hope of an eternal inheritance we have begun to have a Father in heaven. Let us now hear what we must ask of Him. Of such a Father what shall we ask? Do we not ask rain of Him, today, and yesterday, and the day before? This is no great thing to have asked of such a Father, and yet you see with what sighing's, and with what great desire we ask for rain, when death is feared, when that is feared which none can escape. For eventually every man must die, and we groan, and pray, and travail in pain, and cry to God, that we may die a little later. How much more should we cry out to Him, that we may come to that place where we shall never die!

### 4.

Therefore is it said, "Hallowed be Thy Name." This we also ask of Him that His Name may be hallowed in us, for Holy is it always. And how is His Name hallowed in us, except while it makes us holy. For once we were not holy and we are made holy by His Name, but He is always Holy, and His Name always Holy. It is for ourselves, not for God, that we pray. For we do not wish well to God, to Whom no ill can ever happen. But we wish what is good for ourselves, that His Holy Name may be hallowed, that that which is always Holy, may be hallowed in us.

### 5.

"Thy Kingdom come" (Mt. 6:10). Surely, it will come, whether we ask or not. Indeed, God has an eternal Kingdom. For when did He not reign? When did He begin to reign? For His Kingdom has no beginning, neither shall it have any end. But that we may know that in this prayer also we pray for ourselves, and not for God (for we do not say, "Thy Kingdom come," as though we were asking that God may reign). We shall be ourselves His Kingdom, if believing in Him we make progress in this faith. All the faithful, redeemed by the Blood of His Only Son, will be His Kingdom. And this, His Kingdom, will come when the resurrection of the dead has taken place, for then He will come Himself. And when the dead are risen, He will separate them, as He Himself said, "and He will set the sheep on His right hand, but the goats on the left" (Mt. 25:33). To those who shall be on the right hand He will say, "Come to Me, O blessed of My Father, inherit the Kingdom" (Mt. 25:34).

This is what we wish and pray for when we say, "Thy Kingdom come," that it may come to us. For if we shall be reprobates, that Kingdom will come to others, but not to us. But if we shall be of that number who belong to the members of His Only-Begotten Son, His Kingdom will come to us, and will not delay. For are there as many ages yet remaining, as have already passed away? The Apostle John has said, "Little children, it is the last hour" (1 Jn. 2:18). But it is a long hour proportioned to this long day and see how many years this last hour lasts. Nevertheless, be as those who watch, and so sleep, and rise again, and reign. Let us watch now, let us sleep in death; at the end we shall rise again, and shall reign without end.

6.

"Thy will be done on earth, as it is in heaven" (Mt. 6:10). The third thing we pray for is, that His will may be done as in heaven so in earth. And in this also we wish well for ourselves. For the will of God must necessarily be done. It is the will of God that the good should reign, and the wicked be damned. Is it possible that this will should not be done? But what good do we wish for ourselves, when we say, "Thy will be done on earth as it is in heaven?" Listen. For this petition may be understood in many ways, and many things are to be in our thoughts in this petition, when we pray God, "Thy will be done on earth, as it is in heaven." As Your angels do not offend You, so may we also not offend You.

Again, how should we understand "Thy will be done on earth, as it is in heaven?" All the holy patriarchs, all the prophets, all the apostles, all the spiritual are God's heaven, and we in comparison to them are earth. "Thy will be done on earth, as it is in heaven" — as in them, so in us also.

Again, "Thy will be done on earth, as it is in heaven." The Church of God is heaven, His enemies are earth. So we wish well for our enemies, that they also may believe and become Christians, and so the will of God be done, as in heaven, so also in earth.

Again, "Thy will be done on earth, as it is in heaven." Our spirit is heaven, and the flesh, earth. As our spirit is renewed by believing, so may our flesh be renewed by rising again and "Thy will be done on earth, as it is in heaven."

Again, our mind through which we see truth, and delight in this truth, is heaven, as, "For I delight in the law of God according to the inward man" (Rom. 7:22). What is the earth? "I see another law in my members, warring against the law of my mind, and bringing me into captivity to the law of sin which is in my members" (Rom. 7:22, 23).

When this strife has passed away, and a full concord brought about of the flesh and spirit, the will of God will be done as in heaven, so also in earth. When we repeat this petition, let us think of all these things, and ask them all from the Father. Now all these things which we have mentioned, these three petitions, beloved, have respect to the life eternal. For if the Name of our God is sanctified in us, it will be for eternity. If His Kingdom come, where we shall live forever, it will be for eternity. If His will be done as in heaven, so in earth, in all the ways which I have explained, it will be for eternity.

### 7.

There remain now the petitions for this life of our pilgrimage. Therefore, it follows, "Give us this day our daily bread" (Mt. 6:11). Give us eternal things, give us things temporal. You have promised a Kingdom, do not deny us the means of subsistence. You will give everlasting glory with Yourself hereafter, give us in this earth temporal support. Therefore is it "day by day," and "today," that is, in this present time. For when this life shall have passed away, shall we ask for daily bread then? For then it will not be called, "day by day," but "today." Now it is called, "day by day," when one day passes away, and another day succeeds. Will it be called "day by day," when there will be one eternal day?

This petition for daily bread is doubtless to be understood in two ways, both for the necessary supply of our bodily food, and for the necessities of our spiritual support. There is a necessary supply of bodily food, for the preservation of our daily life, without which we cannot live. This is food and clothing, but the whole is understood in a part. When we ask for bread, we by this understand all things.

There is a spiritual food also which the faithful know, which you too will know, when you shall receive it at the altar of God. This also is "daily Bread," necessary only for this life. For shall we receive the Eucharist when we shall have come to Christ Himself, and begun to reign with Him forever? So then the Eucharist is our daily bread, but let us in such wise receive it, that we be not refreshed in our bodies only, but in our souls. For the virtue which is apprehended there, is unity, that gathered together into His Body and made His members, we may be what we receive. Then will it be, indeed, our daily bread. Again, what I am handling before you now is "daily bread," and the daily lessons which you hear in church, are daily bread, and the hymns you hear and repeat are daily bread. For all these are necessary in our state of pilgrimage.

But when we shall have got to heaven, shall we hear the word, we who shall see the Word Himself, and hear the Word Himself, and eat and drink Him as the angels do now? Do the angels need books, and interpreters, and readers? Surely not. They read in seeing, for the Truth Itself they see, and are abundantly satisfied from that fountain, from which we obtain some few drops. Therefore has it been said touching our daily bread, that this petition is necessary for us in this life.

8.

"Forgive us our debts, as we forgive our debtors" (Mt. 6:12). Is this necessary except in this life? For in the other we shall have no debts. For what are debts, but sins? Realize that you are on the point of being baptized, then all your sins will be blotted out, none whatever will remain. Whatever evil you have ever done—in deed, word, desire, or thought—all will be blotted out.

Yet, if in the life which is after baptism there were security from sin, we should not learn such a prayer as this, "Forgive us our debts." Only let us certainly do what comes next, "As we forgive our debtors." Do you then who are about to enter in to receive a universal and entire remission of your debts, do you, above all things, see that you have nothing in your hearts against any other, so as to come forth from baptism secure, as it were, free and discharged of all debts, and then begin to purpose to avenge yourselves on your enemies, who in time past have done you wrong. Forgive, as you are forgiven. God can do no one wrong, and yet He forgives those who owe nothing. How then should he not forgive, who is himself forgiven, when [God] forgives all but owes nothing [to anyone and needs] no one to forgive Him?

## 9.

"Lead us not into temptation, but deliver us from the evil one" (Mt. 6:13). Will this again be necessary in the life to come? "Lead us not into temptation," will not be said, except where there can be temptation. We read in the book of holy Job, "Is not the life of man upon earth a temptation?" (Job 7:1). What then do we pray for? Listen. The Apostle James says, "Let no one say when he is tempted, 'I am tempted by God'" (Jas. 1:13). He spoke of those evil temptations by which men are deceived and brought under the yoke of the devil. This is the kind of temptation he spoke of. But, there is another sort of temptation which is called a "testing." Concerning this kind of temptation it is written, "The Lord your God is testing you to know whether you love the Lord your God with all your heart and with all your soul" (Deut. 13:3).

What means "to know?" It means "to make you know," for He knows already. With that kind of temptation, whereby we are deceived and seduced, God tempts no man. But undoubtedly in His deep and hidden judgment He abandons some. And when He has abandoned them, the tempter finds his opportunity. For he finds in him no resistance against his power, but immediately presents himself to him as his possessor, if God abandoned him.

Therefore, so that He may not abandon us, we say, "Lead us not into temptation." "For every one is tempted," says the same Apostle James, "when he is drawn away by his own desires and enticed. Then, when desire has conceived, it gives birth to sin; and sin, when it is full-grown, brings forth death" (Jas. 1:14, 15). What then has he taught us by this? To fight against our lusts. For you are about to put away your sins in Holy Baptism, but lusts will still remain. Against these lusts you will still remain fighting against after your regeneration, for a conflict within yourselves still remains.

Let no enemy from without be feared. Conquer your own self, and the whole world is conquered. What can any tempter from without, whether the devil or the devil's minister, do against you? Whoever sets the hope of gain before you to seduce you, let him only find no covetousness in you; and what can he who would tempt you by gain effect?

Whereas if covetousness is found in you, you take fire at the sight of gain and are taken by the bait of this corrupt food. But if he finds no covetousness in you, the trap remains spread in vain. Or, should the tempter set before you some woman of surpassing beauty. If chastity is within, external iniquity is overcome. Therefore that he may not take you with the bait of a strange woman's beauty, fight with your own lust within.

You have no sensible perception of your enemy, but of your own lust you have a sensible perception. You do not see the devil, but you see the object that engages you. So, gain mastery over that which you are sensible within. Fight valiantly, for He Who has regenerated you is your Judge. He has arranged the lists; He is preparing the crown.

Since you will surely be conquered if you do not have Him to help you if He abandons you, therefore you say in this prayer, "Lead us not into temptation." The Judge's wrath has given over some to their own lusts as the Apostle says, "Therefore God also gave them up to uncleanness, in the lusts of their hearts" (Rom. 1:24). How did He give them up? Not by forcing, but by forsaking them.

### 10.

"Deliver us from evil," may belong to the same sentence. Therefore, that you may understand it to be all one sentence, it runs thus, "Lead us not into temptation, but deliver us from evil." Therefore he added "but," to show that all this belongs to one sentence, "Lead us not into temptation, but deliver us from evil." How is this? I will propose them singly. By delivering us from evil, He leads us not into temptation; by not leading us into temptation, He delivers us from evil.

### 11.

And truly it is a great temptation, dearly beloved, it is a great temptation in this life, when that in us is the subject of temptation, whereby we attain pardon, if in any of our temptations we have fallen. It is a frightful temptation, when that is taken from us, whereby we may be healed from the wounds of other temptations.

I know that you have not yet understood me. Give me your attention, that you may understand. Suppose greed tempts a man, and he is conquered in any single temptation (for sometimes even a good wrestler and fighter may get roughly handled). So, greed has got the better of a man, even though he is a good wrestler, and he has done some avaricious act.

Or there has been a passing lust; it has not brought the man to fornication, nor reached unto adultery, for when this does take place, the man must at all events be kept back from the criminal act. But, "whoever looks at a woman to lust for her has already committed adultery with her in his heart" (Mt. 5:28). He has let his thoughts dwell on her with more pleasure than was right; he has admitted the attack. Although he may be an excellent combatant, he has been wounded, but he has not consented to it. He has beaten back the motion of his lust. He has chastised it with the bitterness of grief. He has beaten it back and has prevailed.

Still in the very fact that he had slipped, has he ground for saying, "Forgive us our debts." And so of all other temptations, it is a hard matter that in them all there should not be occasion for saying, "Forgive us our debts." What then is that frightful temptation which I have mentioned, that grievous, that tremendous temptation, which must be avoided with all our strength, with all our resolution? What is it? When we go about to avenge ourselves. Anger is kindled and the man burns to be avenged. O frightful temptation! You are losing that with which you had to attain pardon for other faults. If you had committed any sin as to other senses, and other lusts. Hence, you might have had your cure, in that you might say, "Forgive us our debts, as we forgive our debtors." But whoever instigates you to take vengeance, will lose for you the power you had to say, "as we forgive our debtors." When that power is lost, all sins will be retained; nothing at all is remitted.

## 12.

Our Lord, Master, and Savior, knowing this dangerous temptation in this life, when He taught us six or seven petitions in this prayer, took none of them for Himself to treat of, and to commend to us with greater earnestness, than this one. Have we not said, "Our Father, Who Art in heaven" and the rest which follows? Why after the conclusion of the prayer, did He not enlarge upon it to us, either as to what He had laid down in the beginning, or concluded with at the end, or placed in the middle? Why didn't He, if the Name of God is not hallowed in you, or if you have no part in the Kingdom of God, or if the will of God is not done in you, as in heaven, or if God does not guard you so that you do not enter into temptation? Why none of all these? But what does He say? "For if you forgive men their trespasses, your heavenly Father will also forgive you" (Mt. 6:14), in reference to that petition, "Forgive us our debts, as we also forgive our debtors." Having passed over all the other petitions which He taught us, this He taught us with a remarkable force. There was no need of insisting so much upon those sins in which if a man offend, he may know the means whereby he may be cured: need of it there was, with regard to that sin in which if you sin, there is no means whereby the rest can be cured.

Because of this, you should always be saying, "Forgive us our debts." What debts? There is no lack of them, for we are but men. I have talked somewhat more than I should; I have said something I should not, have laughed more than I should, have eaten more than I should, have listened with pleasure to what I should not, have drunk more than I should, have seen with pleasure what I should not, have thought with pleasure on what I should not. "Forgive us our debts, as we also forgive our debtors." If you have lost, you are yourself lost.

### 13.

Take heed, my brethren, my sons, sons of God, take heed, I beseech you, in that I am saying to you. Fight to the uttermost of your powers with your own hearts. And if you shall see your anger making a stand against you, pray to God against it, that God may make you conqueror of yourself, that God may make you conqueror, I say, not of your enemy without, but of your own soul within. For He will give you His present help, and will do it.

But He prefers that we ask this of Him, more than rain. For you see, beloved, how many petitions the Lord Christ has taught us and there is scarce found among them one which speaks of daily bread, that all our thoughts may be molded after the life to come. For what can we fear that He will not give us, Who has promised and said, "Seek first the Kingdom of God and His righteousness, and all these things shall be added unto you." "For your heavenly Father knows that you need all these things. But seek first the Kingdom of God and His righteousness, and all these things shall be added to you" (Mt. 6:33, 34).

For many have been tried even with hunger, and have been found [as] gold, and have not been forsaken by God. They would have perished with hunger, if the daily inward bread were to leave their heart. After this, let us chiefly hunger. For, "blessed are those who hunger and thirst for righteousness, for they shall be filled" (Mt. 5:6).

But He can in mercy look upon our infirmity, and see us, as it is said, "He remembers that we are dust" (Ps. 102:14). He Who from the dust made and gave life to man, for that His work of clay's sake, gave His Only Son to death. Who can explain, who can worthily so much as conceive, how much He loves us?

## "On the Lord's Prayer"
### *St. Cyprian of Carthage*[4]

**"Our Father Who Art in heaven."**

Anyone who is renewed, reborn, and restored to his God by grace, first of all says 'Father,' because he is now become a son. "He came," He says, "to His own, and His own did not receive Him. But as many as received Him, to them gave He right to become the children of God, to those who believe in His Name" (Jn. 1:11, 12). Whoever therefore believes in His Name is made a son of God, and hence should begin to give thanks and show himself a child of God as he names his Father at his rebirth, that he renounces his earthly father and fleshly father and acknowledges that he has begun to have the Father in heaven as his only Father...

---

[4] St. Cyprian, *Treatise 4:On the Lord's Prayer*, §§9-18, ANF, v. 5., 449-452.
St. Cyprian devoted the entirety of his fourth treatise on the subject of the Lord's Prayer, comprised of three sections. First, he explains how the Lord's Prayer is the most excellent of all prayers— profoundly spiritual and most effectual for obtaining our petitions. In the second part, he explains the prayer; and then explains its seven chief clauses. Finally, he considers the conditions of prayer, and tells us what prayer should be.

So great is the mercy of the Lord, so abundant His condescension and His prosperity of goodness toward us, seeing that He has wished us to pray in the sight of God in such a way as to call God "Father," and to call ourselves "sons" of God, even as Christ is the Son of God—a name which none of us would dare to venture on in prayer, unless He Himself had allowed us thus to pray! We should then, beloved brethren, remember and know that when we call God "Father," we should act as children of God.

**"Hallowed be Thy Name."**

We say this, not wishing that God should be made holy by our prayers, but asking the Lord that His Name should be hallowed in us. Indeed, how could God, Who is Himself the One Who hallows, be hallowed? The Apostle states the nature of the hallowing which is conveyed to us from the grace of

God when he says: "Do you not know that the unrighteous will not inherit the Kingdom of God? Do not be deceived. Neither fornicators, nor idolaters, nor adulterers, nor homosexuals, nor sodomites, nor thieves, nor covetous, nor drunkards, nor revilers, nor extortioners will inherit the Kingdom of God. And such were some of you. But you were washed, but you were sanctified, but you were justified in the name of the Lord Jesus and by the Spirit of our God" (1 Cor. 6:9-11). He says that we have been sanctified in the Name of the Lord Jesus Christ and in the Spirit of our God and we in turn, because our Master and Judge warns the one who has been healed and revived by him to sin no more lest something worse should befall him (Jn. 5:14), pray that this sanctification should remain within us.

**"Thy Kingdom come."**

We ask that the Kingdom of God be made known to us. For when does God not reign or when does that which always was, and shall never cease to be, begin? We ask that our Kingdom, promised us by God, may come, won by Christ's Blood and passion, so that we who have served him in the world should afterward come to reign with Christ as Lord...It is indeed possible, beloved brothers, that Christ Himself is that Kingdom Whose coming we daily desire, Whose coming we desire soon to see. Also we do well to ask for the Kingdom of God, that is the heavenly Kingdom, because there is an earthly Kingdom, but whoever renounces the world is greater than its honors and its Kingdom alike.

**"Thy will be done, on earth as it is in heaven."**

We say this not so that God might do what He wishes, but that we should be able to do what God wishes. For who can stand in the way of God to prevent Him from performing His will? But since we are opposed by the Devil, and our thought and deeds are so prevented from complete submission to God, we pray requesting that the will of God might be done in us. For this to be done in us there is need of God's will, that is His aid and His protection, since nobody is strong in his own strength, but is kept safe in God's kindness and mercy.

Now, if the Son was obedient in the performance of His Father's will, how much more should the servant be obedient in doing the will of his Master? We ask that the will of God be done in heaven and on earth. Each pertains to the completion of our safety and salvation. Since we are in possession of a body from the earth and a spirit from heaven, we are ourselves both earthly and heavenly, and we pray therefore that the will of God be done in both, that is both in our body and in our spirit.

For there is strife between the flesh and the spirit, a daily contest as they clash with one another so that we do not the things we desire. While the spirit seeks the things which are heavenly and godly, the flesh lusts after the things which are earthly and worldly. Therefore, we ask that the reconciliation be brought about between the two through the help and assistance of God. Thus, while the will of God is undertaken both in the spirit and in the flesh, the soul which is reborn through Him may be saved.

**"Give us this day our daily bread."**

This may be understood both spiritually and literally, since both understandings lead to salvation through the divine plan. For Christ is the Bread of Life, and thus He is not the bread of anybody but ourselves...

Moreover we ask that this bread should be given to us daily lest we who are in Christ, and receive His Eucharist daily as the food of salvation, should be prevented by the interposition of some terrible sin and so be separated from the Body of Christ, inhibited from and not receiving the heavenly bread. It is also possible to understand the request as thus: that we who have renounced the world and its wealth and its pomp, abandoning them through faith in his spiritual grace, are asking for as much food and sustenance as is needful. He [God] promises to provide everything for those who seek the Kingdom and the righteousness of God for, since all things are God's, the one who has God will lack nothing if he is not lacking in God.

## "When God Prayed"
### *St. Cyprian of Carthage*[5]

What wonder is it, beloved brethren, if such is the prayer which God taught, seeing that He condensed in His teaching all our prayer in one saving sentence? This had already been before foretold by Isaiah the Prophet, when, being filled with the Holy Spirit, he spoke of the majesty and loving-kindness of God, "consummating and shortening His word," He says, "He will finish the work, and cut it short in righteousness: because the Lord will make a short work in all the world" (Is. 10:23). For when the Word of God, our Lord Jesus Christ, came unto all, and gathering alike the learned and unlearned, published to every gender and every age the precepts of salvation He made a large treasury of His precepts, that the memory of the scholars might not be burdened in the celestial learning, but might quickly learn what was necessary to a simple faith. Thus, when He taught what is life eternal, He embraced the mystery of life in a large and divine brevity, saying, "And this is eternal life, that they may know You, the only true God, and Jesus Christ Whom You have sent" (Jn. 17:3).

Also, when He would gather from the Law and the Prophets the first and greatest commandments, He said, "Hear, O Israel; the Lord your God is one Lord: and you shall love the Lord your God with all your heart, with all your soul, and with all your mind.' This is the first and great commandment. And the second is like it: 'You shall love your neighbor as yourself.' On these two commandments hang all the Law and the

---

[5] St. Cyprian, *Treatise 4: The Lord's Prayer*, §§28-36, ANF, v. 5, 978-983.

Prophets" (Deut. 6:5, Mt. 22:37-40). And again: "Whatever you want men to do to you, do also to them, for this is the Law and the Prophets" (Mt. 7:12).

Nor was it only in words, but in deeds also, that the Lord taught us to pray, Himself praying frequently and beseeching, and thus showing us, by the testimony of His example, what it behooved us to do, as it is written, "So He Himself often withdrew into the wilderness and prayed" (Lk. 5:16). And again, "He went out into a mountain to pray, and continued all night in prayer to God" (Lk. 6:12). But if He prayed Who was without sin, how much more should sinners pray? And if He prayed continually, watching through the whole night in uninterrupted petitions, how much more should we watch nightly in constantly repeated prayer?!

But, the Lord prayed and besought not for Himself—for why should He Who was guiltless pray on His own behalf? Rather, He prayed for our sins, as He Himself declared, when He said to Peter, "Indeed, Satan has asked for you, that he may sift you as wheat. But I have prayed for you that your own faith should not fail; and when you have returned to Me, strengthen your brethren" (Lk. 22:31, 32).

And subsequently He beseeches the Father for all, saying, "I do not pray for these alone, but also for those who will believe in Me through their word; that they all may be one, as You, Father, are in Me, and I in You; that they also may be one in Us" (Jn. 17:20, 21). The Lord's loving-kindness, no less than His mercy, is great in respect of our salvation, in that, not content to redeem us with His Blood, He in addition also prayed for us. Behold now what was the desire of His petition, that like as the Father and Son are one, so also we should abide in absolute unity. From this it may be understood how greatly he sins who divides unity and peace, since for this same thing even the Lord besought, surely desirous that His people should thus be saved and live in peace, since He knew that discord cannot come into the Kingdom of God.

Moreover, when we stand praying, beloved brethren, we should be watchful and earnest with our whole heart, intent on our prayers. Let all carnal and worldly thoughts pass away, nor let the soul at that time think on anything but the object only of its prayer. For this reason also the priest, by way of preface before his prayer, prepares the minds of the brethren by saying, "Lift up your hearts," that so upon the people's response, "We lift them up unto the Lord,"[6] he may be reminded that he himself should think of nothing but the Lord. Let the breast be closed against the adversary and be open to God alone nor let it suffer God's enemy to approach to it at the time of prayer. For frequently he sneaks upon us, penetrates within, and by crafty deceit snatches away our prayers from God, that we may have one thing in our heart and another in our voice, when not the sound of the voice, but the soul and mind, should be praying to the Lord with a simple intention.

But what carelessness it is, to be distracted and carried away by foolish and profane thoughts when you are praying to the Lord, as if there were anything which you should rather be thinking of than that you are speaking with God! How can you ask to be heard by God, when you yourself do not hear yourself? Do you wish that God should remember you when you ask, if you yourself do not remember? This is absolutely to take no precaution against the enemy; this is, when you pray to God, to offend the majesty of God by the carelessness of your prayer; this is to be watchful with your eyes, and to be asleep with your heart, while the Christian, even though he is asleep with his eyes, should be awake with his heart, as it is written in the person of the Church speaking in the Song of Songs, "I slept, but my heart was awake" (Song 5:2). Therefore the Apostle anxiously and carefully warns us, saying, "Continue earnestly in prayer, being vigilant in it with thanksgiving" (Col. 4:2), teaching, that is, and showing that those are able to obtain from God what they ask, whom God sees to be watchful in their prayer.

Moreover, those who pray should not come to God with fruitless or naked prayers. Petition is ineffectual when it is a barren entreaty that beseeches God. For as every tree that does not bring forth fruit is cut down and cast into the fire; assuredly also, words that do not bear fruit cannot deserve anything of God, because they are fruitful in no result. And thus Holy Scripture instructs us, saying, "Prayer is good with fasting and almsgiving" (Tob. 12:8). For He Who will give us in the day of judgment a

---

[6] This liturgical greeting is perhaps one of the oldest in the liturgical tradition, the earliest manuscripts of which contain minor variations. The congregational response cited by St. Augustine here, is also found in St. Cyril of Jerusalem's *Catechetical Lecture* 23.4.

reward for our labors and alms, is even in this life a merciful hearer of one who comes to Him in prayer associated with good works.

For instance, when Cornelius the centurion prayed, he had a claim to be heard. He was in the habit of doing many alms-deeds towards the people, and of ever praying to God. To this man, when he prayed about the ninth hour, appeared an angel bearing testimony to his labors, and saying, "Cornelius, your prayers and your alms have come up for a memorial before God" (Acts 10:4).

Those prayers quickly ascend to God which the merits of our labors urge upon God. Thus also Raphael the angel was a witness to the constant prayer and the constant good works of Tobias, saying, "It is honorable to reveal and confess the works of God. Now, therefore, when you prayed, and Sarah, your daughter-in law, I did bring the remembrance of your prayers before the Holy One. And when you buried the dead, I was with you likewise. And when you did not delay to rise up and to leave your dinner, to go out and cover the dead, your good deed was not hidden from me. And now God has sent me to heal you, and Sarah, your daughter-in-law. I am Raphael, one of the seven holy angels who present the prayers of the saints, and who go in and out before the glory of the Holy One" (Tob. 12:12-15).

By Isaiah also the Lord reminds us, and teaches similar things, saying, "I have not chosen such a fast...but do you loose every burden of iniquity, do you untie the bonds of hard bargains, set the bruised free, and cancel every unjust account. Break your bread to the hungry, and lead the unsheltered poor to your house: if you see one naked, clothe him, and you shall not disregard the relations of your own seed. Then shall your light break forth as the morning, and your health shall speedily spring forth: and your righteousness shall go before you, and the glory of God shall surround you. Then you will cry, and God shall hearken to you; while you are yet speaking He will say, 'Here I am!'" (Is. 58:6-9).

He promises that He will be at hand, and says that He will hear and protect those who, loosening the knots of unrighteousness from their heart, and giving alms among the members of God's household according to His commands, even in hearing what God commands to be done, do themselves also deserve to be heard by God. The blessed Apostle Paul, when aided in the necessity of affliction by his brethren, said that good works which are performed are sacrifices to God. "I am full," he says, "having received from Epaphroditus the things sent from you, a sweet-smelling aroma, an acceptable sacrifice, well pleasing to God" (Phil. 4:18). For when one has pity on the poor, he lends to God and he who gives to the least gives to God; he sacrifices spiritually to God a sweet-smelling aroma.

And in discharging the duties of prayer, we find that the Three Youth with Daniel, being strong in faith and victorious in captivity, observed the third, sixth, and ninth hour, as it were, for a mystery of the Trinity, which in the last times had to be manifested. For both the first hour in its progress to the third shows forth the consummated number of the Trinity, and also the fourth proceeding to the sixth declares another Trinity; and when from the seventh the ninth is completed, the perfect Trinity is numbered every three hours, which spaces of hours the worshippers of God in time past having spiritually decided on, made use of for determined and lawful times for prayer.

Subsequently the thing was manifested, that these things were of old Mysteries, in that anciently righteous men prayed in this manner. For upon the disciples at the third hour the Holy Spirit descended, Who fulfilled the grace of the Lord's promise. Moreover, at the sixth hour, Peter, going up unto the housetop, was instructed as well by the sign as by the word of God admonishing him to receive all to the grace of salvation, whereas he was previously doubtful of the receiving of the Gentiles to baptism (Acts 10:9-16). And from the sixth hour to the ninth, the Lord, being crucified, washed away our sins by His Blood. He then accomplished His victory by His passion that He might redeem and raise us.

But for us, beloved brethren, besides the hours of prayer observed of old, both the times and the mysteries have now increased in number. For we must also pray in the morning, that the Lord's resurrection may be celebrated by morning prayer. And this formerly the Holy Spirit pointed out in the Psalms, saying, "Listen to the sound of my cry, my King and my God, for to You I pray. O Lord, in the morning You will hear my voice; in the morning I plead my case to You, and watch" (Ps. 5:2, 3). And again, the Lord speaks by the mouth of the Prophet: "In their affliction they will seek Me early, saying, 'Let us go and return to the Lord our God'" (Hos. 6:1).

Also at sunset and at the decline of day, of necessity we must pray again. For since Christ is the true sun and the true day, as the worldly sun and worldly day depart, when we pray and ask that light may return to us again, we pray for the Advent of Christ, which shall give us the grace of everlasting light. Moreover, the Holy Spirit in the Psalms manifests that Christ is called the day: "The stone," he says, "which the builders rejected has become the chief cornerstone. This is the Lord's doing; it is marvelous in our eyes. This is the day which the Lord has made; let us rejoice and be glad in it" (Ps. 118:22-24). Also the Prophet Malachi testifies that He is called the Sun, when he says, "But to you who fear My Name the Sun of Righteousness shall rise, and healing shall be in His wings" (Mal. 4:2).

But if in the Holy Scriptures the true Sun and the true Day is Christ, there is no hour excepted for Christians wherein God should not frequently and always to be worshipped, so that we who are in Christ—that is, in the true Sun and the true Day—should be instant throughout the entire day in petitions, and should pray. And when, by the law of the world, the revolving night, recurring in its alternate changes, there can be no harm arising from the darkness of night to those who pray, because the children of light have the day even in the night. For when is he without light who has light in his heart, or when has not he the sun and the day, whose Sun and Day is Christ?

Let not us, then, who are in Christ-that is, always in the lights cease from praying even during night. Thus the widow Anna, without intermission praying and watching, persevered in deserving well of God, as it is written in the Gospel that she "did not depart from the temple but served God with fastings and prayers night and day" (Lk. 2:37).

Let the Gentiles look to this, who are not yet enlightened, or the Jews who have remained in darkness by having forsaken the light. Let us, beloved brethren, who are always in the light of the Lord, who remember and hold fast what by grace received we have begun to be, reckon night for day; let us believe that we always walk in the light, and let us not be hindered by the darkness which we have escaped. Let there be no failure of prayers in the hours of night-no idle and reckless waste of the occasions of prayer. New created and newborn of the Spirit by the mercy of God, let us imitate what we shall one day be. Since in the Kingdom we shall possess day alone, without intervention of night, let us so watch in the night as if in the daylight. Since we are to pray and give thanks to God forever, let us not cease in this life also to pray and give thanks.

# V

## SEEK FIRST THE KINGDOM OF GOD

*Meditations on the Sunday of Preparation of the Great Lent*

### GOSPEL READING FOR THE FIRST SUNDAY OF THE GREAT LENT

#### (Matthew 6:24-34)

*No one can serve two masters; for either he will hate the one and love the other, or else he will be loyal to the one and despise the other. You cannot serve God and mammon.*

*Therefore I say to you, do not worry about your life, what you will eat or what you will drink; nor about your body, what you will put on. Is not life more than food and the body more than clothing? Look at the birds of the air, for they neither sow nor reap nor gather into barns; yet your heavenly Father feeds them. Are you not of more value than they? Which of you by worrying can add one cubit to his stature?*

*So why do you worry about clothing? Consider the lilies of the field, how they grow: they neither toil nor spin; and yet I say to you that even Solomon in all his glory was not arrayed like one of these. Now if God so clothes the grass of the field, which today is, and tomorrow is thrown into the oven, will He not much more clothe you, O you of little faith?*

*Therefore do not worry, saying, "What shall we eat?' or "What shall we drink?' or 'What shall we wear?' For after all these things the Gentiles seek. For your heavenly Father knows that you need all these things. But seek first the kingdom of God and His righteousness, and all these things shall be added to you. Therefore do not worry about tomorrow, for tomorrow will worry about its own things. Sufficient for the day is its own trouble.*

## "Do Not Worry"
### *St. John Chrysostom*[1]

After He has shown the hurt to be unspeakable, then and not before He makes the commandment stricter in that He not only bids us to cast away what we have, but forbids us to take thought even for our necessary food, saying, "Take no thought for your soul, what you shall eat" (Mt. 6:25).

[He told us not to worry about food], not because the soul does not need food, for it is incorporeal, but He spoke according to the common custom. For though it needs not food, yet can it not endure to remain in the body, except that it be fed. In saying this, He puts it not simply so, but here also He brings up arguments, some from those things which we have already, and some from other examples.

From what we have already, thus saying: "Is not the soul more than food and the body more than clothing?" (Mt. 6:25). He, therefore, has given the greater, how shall He not give the less? He Who has fashioned the flesh that is fed, how shall He not bestow the food? Why neither did He simply say, "Take no thought what you shall eat," or "what you will wear;" but, "for the body" and "for the soul." Because from them He was to make His demonstrations, carrying on His discourse in the way of comparison. Now the soul He has given once for all, and it abides such as it is, but the body increases every day.

Therefore pointing out both these things, the immortality of the one, and the frailty of the other, He adds, "Which of you by worrying can add one cubit to his stature?" (Mt. 6:27). Thus, saying no more of the soul, since it receives not increase, He discoursed of the body only, hereby making manifest this point also, that not the food increases it, but the providence of God. Which Paul showing also in other ways, said, "So

---

[1] St. John Chrysostom, *Homily 19 on the Gospel of St. Matthew*, NPNF, s. 1, v. 10, 325-328.

then, neither is he who plants is anything, nor he who waters; but God Who gives the increase" (1 Cor. 3:7).

From what we have already, then, He urges us in this way: and from examples of other things, by saying, "Look at the birds of the air" (Mt. 6:26). So that no one would say, "We do well by taking thought" He dissuades them both by that which is greater, and by that which is less—by the greater, i.e. the soul and the body, by the less, i.e., the birds. For if of the things that are very inferior He has so much regard, how shall He not give unto you? He says. And to them on this wise, for as yet it was an ordinary multitude, but to the devil not thus; but how? "Man shall not live by bread alone, but by every word that proceeds from the mouth of God" (Mt. 4:4; Lk. 4:4).

But here He mentions the birds in order to humble them—very valuable for the purpose of admonition. However, some of the ungodly have come to so great a pitch of madness, as even to attack His illustration. Because, say they, it was not meet for one strengthening moral principle, to use natural advantages as incitements to that end. For to those animals, they add, this belongs by nature. What then shall we say to this? That even though it is theirs by nature, yet possibly we too may attain it by choice. For neither did He say, "Look at how the birds fly," which were a thing impossible to man, but that they are fed without taking thought, a kind of thing easy to be achieved by us also, if we will. And this they have proved, who have accomplished it in their actions.

Why was it so exceedingly proper to admire the consideration of our Lawgiver, in that, when He might bring forward His illustration from among men. When He could have spoken of Moses, Elijah or John, and others like them, He did not. But so He might touch them quicker, He made mention of the irrational beings. For had He spoken of those righteous men, these would have been able to say, "We have not yet become like them." But, passing over them in silence, and bringing forward the fowls of the air, He has cut off from them every excuse, imitating in this place also the old law. Yes, for the old covenant likewise sends to the bee, the ant, the turtle, and to the swallow. And neither is this a small sign of honor, when the same sort of things, which those animals possess by nature, those we are able to accomplish by an act of our choice. So, if He takes such great care of them which exist for our sakes, much more of us; if [He takes much care] of the servants, much more for the master. Therefore, He said, "Look at the birds."

But He did not say, "for they do not traffic, nor make merchandise," for these were among the things that were earnestly forbidden. But He says, "they neither sow nor reap" (Mt. 6:26). Then one says, "So, then, should we not sow?" He did not say, "we must not sow," but "we must not worry." [He did not say one] should neither work, nor be low-minded, nor to rack one's self with cares. Since He bade us also be nourished, but not in "taking thought."

David lays the foundation from old time, saying mysteriously, "You open Your hands, and fill every living thing with pleasure" (Ps. 144:16), and again, "Who gives to the cattle their food, and to the young ravens that call upon Him" (Ps. 146:9). But some may ask, "Who then have not taken thought?" Did you not hear how many of the righteous I adduced? Do you not see with them Jacob, departing from his father's house destitute of all things? Do you not hear him praying and saying, "If the Lord God...gives me bread to eat and raiment to put on" (Gen. 28:20) which was not the part of one taking thought, but of one seeking all of God? The apostles also attained this, who left all and took no thought (cf. Mt. 19:27). The same also with the "five thousand," and the "three thousand" (Acts 3:15, 4:4).

After hearing such high words, if you cannot bear to release yourself from these grievous bonds, consider the unprofitableness of the thing, and so put an end to your care. For "which of you by worrying," He says, "can add one cubit to his stature?" (Mt. 6:27; Lk. 12:25).

Do you see how by that which is evident, He has manifested that also which is obscure? So He says, "Just as you are unable to add [one cubit] by worrying, even though it is such a small [length]; neither can you gather as much food as you would like by thinking alone." Thus it is clear that it is not our diligence, but the providence of God, even when we seem to be active, effects all. So that, if He forsook us, no care, nor anxiety, nor toil, nor any other such thing, will ever appear to come to anything, but all will utterly pass away. Let us not therefore suppose His injunctions are impossible: for there are many who duly perform them, even as it is.

And if you know not of them, it is nothing marvelous, since Elijah too supposed he was alone, but was told, "And you shall leave in Israel seven thousand men" (1 Kgs. 19:18). Whence it is manifest that even now there are many who show forth the apostolic life like as the "three thousand" then, and the "five thousand" (Acts 3:15, 4:4). And if we believe not, it is not because there are none who do well, but because we are far from so doing.

So that just as the drunkard would not easily believe, that there exists any man who does not taste even water (and yet this has been achieved by many solitaries in our time), nor it is easy for he who connects himself with numberless women to live in virginity, nor he who extorts other men's goods to readily give up even his own. So neither will those, who daily melt themselves down with innumerable anxieties, easily receive this thing.

Now as to the fact, that there are many who have attained unto this, we might show it even from those, who have practiced this self-denial even in our generation. But for you, just now, it is enough to learn not to covet, and that almsgiving is a good thing, and to know that you must impart of what you have. For these things if you will duly perform, beloved, you will speedily proceed to those others also. Therefore, now let us lay aside our excessive luxury; let us endure moderation and to acquire by honest labor all that we are to have. For, even the blessed John, when he was discoursing with those who were employed upon the tribute, and with the soldiery, enjoined them to "be content" with their wages" (Lk. 3:14). Although he was anxious to lead them on to another, and a higher self-command, yet since they were still unfit for this, he speaks of the lesser things. Because, if he had mentioned what are higher than these, they would have failed to apply themselves to them, and would have fallen from the others.

For this very reason we also are instructing you in the inferior duties. Yes, because as yet, we know, the burden of voluntary poverty is too great for you, and the heaven is not more distant from the earth, than such self-denial from you. Let us then lay hold, if it be only of the lowest commandments, for even this is no small encouragement. And yet some among the heathen have achieved even this, though not in a proper spirit, and have stripped themselves of all their possessions. However, we are content in your case, if alms are bestowed abundantly by you, for we shall soon arrive at those other duties also, if we advance in this way.

But if we do not so much as this, of what favor shall we be worthy, who are hidden to surpass those under the old law, and yet show ourselves inferior to the philosophers among the heathens? What shall we say, when we should be angels and sons of God, but do not even quite maintain our being as men? For to spoil and to covet comes not of the gentleness of men, but of the fierceness of wild beast—no, worse than wild beasts are those who attack their neighbor's goods. For this comes to them naturally, but we who are honored with reason, and yet are falling away unto that unnatural vileness, what indulgence shall we receive?

Let us then, considering the measures of that discipline which are set before us, press on at least to the middle station, that we may both be delivered from the punishment which is to come, and proceeding regularly, may arrive at the very summit of all good things unto which may we all attain, by the grace and love towards mankind of our Lord Jesus Christ, to Whom be glory and dominion forever and ever. Amen

## "The Beatitudes and the Stages of Spirituality"

### *St. Augustine of Hippo*[2]

There are in all, then, these eight sentences. For now in what remains He speaks in the way of direct address to those who were present, saying: "Blessed are you when they revile you and persecute you" (Mt. 5:11). But, He addressed the former sentences in a general way: for He did not say, "Blessed are *you* poor in spirit, for *yours* is the Kingdom of heaven," but He says, "Blessed are *the* poor in spirit, for *theirs* is the Kingdom of heaven." Nor did He say, "Blessed are *you* meek, for *you* shall inherit the earth," but, "Blessed are *the* meek, for *they* shall inherit the earth." And so the others up to the eighth sentence, where He says: "Blessed are *those* who are persecuted for righteousness' sake, for *theirs* is the Kingdom of heaven."

---

[2] St. Augustine, *Our Lord's Sermon on the Mount*, bk. 1, NPNF, s. 1, v. 6, 19-26.

After that He now begins to speak in the way of direct address to those present, although what has been said before referred also to His present audience, and that which follows—which seems to be spoken specially to those present—refers also to those who were absent, or who would afterwards come into existence.

For this reason, the number of sentences before us is to be carefully considered.

(1) For the beatitudes begin with humility: "Blessed are the poor in spirit," i.e. those not puffed up, while the soul submits itself to divine authority, fearing lest after this life it goes away to punishment, although perhaps in this life it might seem to itself to be happy.

(2) Then (the soul) comes to the knowledge of the divine Scriptures, where it must show itself meek in its piety, lest it should venture to condemn that which seems absurd to the unlearned, and should itself be rendered unteachable by obstinate disputations.

(3) After that, it now begins to know in what entanglements of this world it is held by reason of carnal custom and sins. And so, in this third stage, in which there is knowledge, the loss of the highest good is mourned over, because it sticks fast in what is lowest.

(4) Then, in the fourth stage there is labor, where vehement exertion is put forth, so that the mind may wrench itself away from those things in which, by reason of their pestilential sweetness, it is entangled. Here therefore righteousness is hungered and thirsted after, and fortitude is very necessary, because what is retained with delight is not abandoned without pain.

(5) Then, at the fifth stage, to those persevering in labor, counsel for getting rid of it is given, for unless each one is assisted by a superior, in no way is he fit in his own case to extricate himself from so great entanglements of miseries. But, it is a just counsel, that he who wishes to be assisted by a stronger should assist him who is weaker in that in which he himself is stronger: therefore "Blessed are the merciful, for they shall obtain mercy" (Mt. 5:7).

(6) At the sixth stage there is purity of heart, able from a good conscience of good works to contemplate that, highest good, which can be discerned by the pure and tranquil intellect alone.

(7) Lastly, is the seventh: wisdom, itself, that is, the contemplation of the truth, tranquilizing the whole man, and assuming the likeness of God, which is thus summed up, "Blessed are the peacemakers, for they shall be called sons of God" (Mt. 5:9).

(8) The eighth, as it were, returns to the starting point, because it shows and commends what is complete and perfect. Therefore, in the first and in the eighth the Kingdom of Heaven is named, "Blessed are the poor in spirit, for theirs is the Kingdom of Heaven" and "Blessed are those who are persecuted for righteousness' sake, for theirs is the Kingdom of Heaven" (Mt. 5:10), as it is now said, "Who shall separate us from the love of Christ? Shall tribulation, or distress, or persecution, or famine, or nakedness, or peril, or sword?" (Rom. 8:35).

Seven in number, therefore, are the things which bring perfection. For the eighth brings into light and shows what is perfect, so that starting, as it were, from the beginning again, the others also are perfected by means of these stages...Moreover, the one reward, which is the Kingdom of Heaven, is variously named according to these stages:

In the first, just as should be the case, is placed the Kingdom of Heaven, which is the perfect and highest wisdom of the rational soul.

Thus, therefore, it is said: "Blessed are the poor in spirit, for theirs is the Kingdom of Heaven," just as it was said, "The fear of the Lord is the beginning of wisdom" (Ps. 110:10; Prov. 1:7, 9:10).

To the meek an inheritance is given, just as the testament of a father is given to those dutifully seeking it: "Blessed are the meek, for they shall inherit the earth."

To the mourners, comfort [is provided], just as those who know what they have lost, and in what evils they are sunk: "Blessed are those who mourn, for they shall be comforted."

To those hungering and thirsting [is granted] a full supply, just as it were a refreshment to those laboring and bravely contending for salvation:

"Blessed are those who hunger and thirst for righteousness sake, for they shall be filled."

To the merciful [is extended] mercy, as to those following a true and excellent counsel, so that this same treatment is extended toward them by one who is stronger, which they extend toward the weaker: "Blessed are the merciful, for they shall obtain mercy."

To the pure in heart is given the power of seeing God, as to those bearing about with them a pure eye for discerning eternal things: "Blessed are the pure in heart, for they shall see God."

To the peacemakers the likeness of God is given, as being perfectly wise, and formed after the image of God by means of the regeneration of the renewed man: "Blessed are the peacemakers, for they shall be called sons of God."

And those promises can indeed be fulfilled in this life, as we believe them to have been fulfilled in the case of the apostles. For that all-embracing change into the angelic form, which is promised after this life, cannot be explained in any words. "Blessed," therefore, "are those who are persecuted for righteousness' sake, for theirs is the Kingdom of Heaven."

This eighth sentence, which goes back to the starting point, and makes manifest the perfect man, is perhaps set forth in its meaning both by the circumcision on the eighth day in the Old Testament, and by the Resurrection of the Lord after the Sabbath, the day which is certainly the eighth, and at the same time the first day; and by the celebration of the eight festival days which we celebrate in the case of the regeneration of the new man; and by the very number of Pentecost.

For to the number seven, seven times multiplied, by which we make forty-nine, as it were an eighth is added, so that fifty may be made up, and we, as it were, return to the starting-point: on which day the Holy Spirit was sent, by Whom we are led into the Kingdom of Heaven, and receive the inheritance, and are comforted, fed, obtain mercy, are purified, and are made peacemakers. Being thus perfect, we bear all troubles brought upon us from without for the sake of truth and righteousness.

## "Saving Generosity"

### St. Cyril of Alexandria[3]

"No servant can serve two masters; for either he will hate the one and love the other, or else he will be loyal to the one and despise the other. You cannot serve God and mammon' (Lk. 16:13).

Let each of us then who possess earthly wealth open our hearts to those who are in need. Let us show ourselves faithful and obedient to the laws of God, and followers of our Lord's will in those things which are from without, and not our own, that we may receive that which is our own, even that holy and admirable beauty which God forms in the souls of men, fashioning them like unto Himself, according to what we originally were.

Likewise, it is impossible for a person to divide himself between contraries, and still be able to live blamelessly. He shows by saying, "No man can serve two masters; for either he will hate the one, and love the other, or else he will be loyal to the one and despise the other" (Mt. 6:24; Lk. 16:13). And this indeed is a plain and evident example, and very suitable for the elucidation of the subject before us. For that which follows is, so to speak, the conclusion of the whole argument: "for you cannot serve God and mammon" (Mt. 6:24; Lk. 16:13).

For, He says, if a man is a slave of two masters, of diverse and contrary wills, and whose minds are irreconcilable with one another, how can he please them both? For being divided in endeavoring to do that which each one approves, he is in opposition to the will of both. And so, the same person must inevitably appear bad and good. Therefore, He says if he determine to be true to the one, he will hate the other, and set him of course at nought.

Thus, it is not possible to serve God and mammon. For the unrighteous mammon, by which wealth is signified, is a thing given up to

---

[3] St. Cyril of Alexandria, *Commentary on Luke*, Sermon 109 on Luke 16:10-13, trans. P.E. Pusey (1859), 515-516.

lusts, and liable to every reproach, engendering boasting, and the love of pleasure, making men stiff-necked, the friends of the wicked, and contemptuous: yes, what base vice does it not produce in them that possess it?

But the goodwill of God renders men gentle, quiet, and lowly in their thoughts; long-suffering, merciful, and of exemplary patience; neither loving money, nor desirous of wealth; content with only food and clothing; and especially fleeing from "the love of money, which is the root of all kinds of evil" (1 Tim. 6:10). They joyfully endure toils for the sake of piety, flee from the love of pleasure, and earnestly shun every feeling of weariness in good works. They constantly value that which wins them reward: the endeavor to live uprightly and the practice of all soberness. This is that which is our own, and the true. God will bestow these things on those who love poverty and know how to distribute to those who are in need that which is another's, and comes from without, even their wealth, which also has the name of mammon.

May it then be far from the mind of each of us to be its slaves, that so we may freely and without hindrance bow the neck of our mind to Christ the Savior of us all, by Whom and with Whom to God the Father be praise and dominion, with the Holy Spirit, forever and ever, Amen

# VI

## Into the Wilderness to be Tempted

*Meditations on the Sunday of Temptation of the Great Lent*

### Gospel Reading for the Second Sunday of the Great Lent

*(Matthew 4:1-10)*

*Then Jesus was led up by the Spirit into the wilderness to be tempted by the devil. And when He had fasted forty days and forty nights, afterward He was hungry.*

*Now when the tempter came to Him, he said, "If You are the Son of God, command that these stones become bread." But He answered and said, "It is written, 'Man shall not live by bread alone, but by every word that proceeds from the mouth of God.'"*

*Then the devil took Him up into the holy city, set Him on the pinnacle of the temple, and said to Him, "If You are the Son of God, throw Yourself down. For it is written: 'He shall give His angels charge over you,' and, 'In their hands they shall bear you up, Lest you dash your foot against a stone.'" Jesus said to him, "It is written again, 'You shall not tempt the Lord your God.'"*

*Again, the devil took Him up on an exceedingly high mountain, and showed Him all the kingdoms of the world and their glory. And he said to Him, "All these things I will give You if You will fall down and worship me."*

*Then Jesus said to him, "Away with you, Satan! For it is written, 'You shall worship the Lord your God, and Him only you shall serve.'"*

## Introductory Note

*The Late Hegumen Father Pishoy Kamel*

Temptations on the road: struggle is a natural condition to a person who wishes to attain a valuable object. War is burdensome when it is an object in itself. But when the object is to progress spiritually, and to be steadfast in God, then war becomes a pleasure. It is a pleasure, because victory is certain since Christ won it for me. I, consequently, will win through Him. It is a war with a fierce enemy whom the Lord has already conquered. That evil one had used food and wealth as instruments of war against the Lord. He told Jesus to throw Himself from the top of the temple, and attempted to lure Him to choose the easy way out of the sufferings of the cross by saying: "I will give you all the kingdoms of the world if you bow down and worship me" (Mt. 4:4; cf. Lk. 4:6, 7). This seems easier than reigning over people's hearts through the Cross...throw your cross and learn to be lazy in life, but our Lord conquered and granted us victory.

Today, the Church is in a state of war; these are some of its features. For example, what can annoy Satan more than fasting? "This kind does not go out except by prayer and fasting" (Mt. 17:21; Mk 9:29). Many Western churches have neglected fasting although they continue their meetings. Some publications of the Bible have replaced the word "fast" and use "abstain from food." Satan also introduces the ways of the world into the church: love of money, dodging issues under the name of wisdom, goals validate the means, white lies.

Into such homes, Satan introduces the world through television and other vulgar images so that children absorb these rather than the sounds of hymns and prayers. The same things happen at school and in the streets: young Christian girls are surrounded by the lusts of the world. They hear everywhere about corrupt adventures besides what they read in various publications. Our children are truly entrapped in the lion's den. But, the lion's den may have been more merciful, since Daniel stopped the lion's mouth with prayer and fasting. It is a violent war.

Our safety can be assured only by prayer and fasting as well as faith. These are the weapons we carry as we undertake the journey of Lent. God told Jeremiah the Prophet, "Run about in the streets of Jerusalem and see, and know, and seek in her broad places, if you can find one…who executes judgment, and seeks faithfulness, and I will pardon him" (Jer. 5:1).

If just one person is found who observes a true fast and devotes himself, sacrificially, then God would save the whole Church. Just one person is needed—wholly consecrating his life in silence and service—to bring Satan down in shame.

War is waged on every level within the Christian family and within educational institutions. Therein exists the temptation to be an atheist or morally deprived. Faith is shaken. There are also the temptations for material or financial gain, to immigrate in search of wealth…so many temptations that turn your love for the Church to a weak or lukewarm relationship. It is a universal war waged against the Church today. Indeed, some churches in the West have been conquered and given in to the world.

During Lent, we become as trumpeters, calling everyone to enlist. For, through Jesus Christ, a powerful arsenal is placed in our hands to destroy any stronghold. We can, once and for all, subjugate every thought to obey our Lord.

Thus, the Great Fast of Lent is a general enlistment for a great war whose sure outcome is victory. The Lord is with us and He has become victorious for us. We can never agree to a peace treaty for we have to conquer. Christ is slain on the altar before us. Thus, He proclaims that we need to struggle even to the shedding of blood, for victory will be achieved through blood.

## "HIS TEMPTATION"

### *St. Jerome*[1]

Just as a soldier never ceases to train for battle and prepares in mock-warfare for the real wounds that are to come, every Christian must exercise self-restraint at all times, but especially when the enemy is near at hand with his well-trained hosts marshaled against us. It is always necessary for God's servants to fast, but it is even more imperative to acknowledge that when we fast, we are preparing for the sacrifice of the

---

[1] St. Jerome, *On Lent*, FCS, v. 2 (CUA Press, 1966), 233-236.

Lamb, for the Mystery of Baptism, for the Body and Blood of Christ. As soon as the devil is aware that his sheep are determined to withdraw from his flock, he rages in madness, and gathers all his forces against them in fury, calculating that whatever is saved for Christ is lost to him; whatever is given life for the Church is dead to his synagogue.

Consequently, dearly beloved brethren, since we are making our preparation for the Mystery of the Lord by a fast of forty days, let us fast for our sins as many days as the Lord fasted for our evil deeds. After our Lord's baptism, the devil tempted Him. He did not know that He was the Son of God and, for that reason, was off his guard. In the sequel, he questions the Lord, tempting Him: "If You are the Son of God, command that these stones become bread," (Mt. 4:3); and, "If You are the Son of God, throw Yourself down" (Mt. 4:6). Because he knows that we want to become children of God, he plots to take us by surprise, and, like a slimy serpent, coils himself about our feet to keep us from mounting to heaven. If with vile cunning he has dared to tempt the Lord, how much more boldly will he presume to deceive us? If he, a broken vessel, has fought against the Son of God and his own Potter,[2] how much more daring will he be in attacking us who are by nature inferior to him? "If the righteous one is scarcely saved, where will the ungodly and the sinner appear?" (1 Pet. 4:18; Prov. 11:31).

Not that our Lord could be deceived by the devil, but He Who took upon Himself the nature of a slave (cf. Phil. 2:7, 8) and wished to give Himself as an example in all things (cf. 1 Pet. 2:21-25) so that no one might trust in His own sanctity, since even He is tempted Whom no temptation is able to overcome.

Our motive in going over all this, dearly beloved brethren, is that we may be on our guard, for fear that, after coming out from Egypt and hastening through the desert for forty days—for forty years, as it were—to reach the Land of Promise, we should long for the fleshpots of Egypt (Ex. 16:3) and be bitten to death by the serpents (cf. Num. 21:6).

We have left Egypt; what have we to do with the food of Egypt? We who have Bread from heaven, why do we go in search of earthly foods? We

---

[2] cf. Rom. 9.21, 22; Rev. 2.28; cf. Letter 133.9, PL 22:1157 (1037).

who have left Pharaoh, let us call upon the help of the Lord so that the Egyptian king may be drowned in the baptism of those who believe. Let his horses and their riders perish there (cf. Ex. 15:1, Deut. 11:4). Let the raging army of the adversary be destroyed. Let us not murmur against the Lord lest we be struck down by Him.

Let us not talk about our priests. Let us abstain from vices rather than from food-although too much food excites greed. If when Aaron and Mariam spoke against Moses, they instantly experienced the punishment of God, coming in defense of His servant (Num. 12:1-9). How much more will anyone of you be punished by divine judgment if, with poisonous lips, he slanders his bishop?

Priests also must take care lest they be insincere, lest they doubt the power of God. If Aaron and Moses (who seemed to waver at the waters of Contradiction) (cf. Num. 20:8-13; 20:24; 27:14) did not deserve to enter the Promised Land, does it not stand to reason that we, bent under the burden of sin, shall be far less able to cross the Jordan River and reach Galgal, the place of circumcision (cf. Deut. 11:30, 31) if we shall cause one of these little ones to sin (cf. Lk. 17.2)? Since, then, the fertility of the flock is proportionate to the labor of the shepherd and the abundance of the harvest to the zeal of the farmer in preparing the Lord's granaries, let us strain every effort to be made worthy of the coming of the Pasch and the flesh of the Lamb, Christ Jesus. Amen.

## "HIS WILL IN FASTING"

### *St. Augustine of Hippo*[3]

Let the man who would follow learn the road by which he must travel. Perhaps an hour of terrible trial has come, and the choice is set before you either to sin or to endure suffering. The weak soul is troubled, on whose behalf the invincible soul [of Christ] was voluntarily troubled. Then, set the will of God before your own. For notice that it is immediately united to your Creator and Master, by Him Who made you, and became Himself, for your teaching, that which He made, for He Who

---

[3] St. Augustine, *Tracate 52 on the Gospel of St. John,* NPNF, s. 1, v. 7.

made man was made man, but He remained still the unchangeable God and transplanted manhood into a better condition.

Therefore, do not think of Him as losing hold of His own exalted position in wishing you to rise up out of the depths of your ruin. For He thought it proper to be tempted by the devil. For if He was never tempted or was not willing [to be tempted], He would never have suffered. Thus, the answers He gave to the devil are such as you also should use in times of temptation. And He, indeed, was tempted, but not endangered, that He might show you, when in danger through temptation, how to answer the tempter, so as not to be carried away by the temptation, but to escape its danger. But when He here said, "Now is My soul troubled" (Jn. 12:27); and when He said, "My soul is sorrowful, even unto death" (Mt. 26:38); and "Father, if it is possible, let this cup pass from Me" (Mt. 26:39), He assumed the infirmity of man to teach him, when thereby saddened and troubled, to say what follows: "Nevertheless, Father, not as I will, but as You will" (Mt. 26:39). For thus it is that man is turned from the human to the divine, when the will of God is preferred to his own.

## "Christ, Adam, and the Fast"

### St. Ephrem the Syrian[4]

1.

This is the fast of the First Born, the first of His victories.
    Let us rejoice in His coming; for in fasting he has overcome.
    Though He could have overcome by any means,
    He revealed for us the strength hidden in fasting,
    Overcomer of All.
    For by means of it a man can overcome that one who with
    fruit overcame Adam;
    He became greedy and gobbled it.
    Blessed is the First-Born Who encompassed

---

[4] Hymn 1, from "St. Ephrem's Hymns on Fasting: An Annotated Translation and Concordance," translated by Prof. Gary A. Anderson, Prof. Sidney Griffith, and Prof. Robin Darling Young, used with gracious permission.

Our weakness with the wall of his great fasting.
Blessed is the King Who adorned the Holy Church with fasting,
prayer and vigil.

### 2.

This is the fast which exalts; which appeared from the First Born So as to
    extol the younger ones.
    There is occasion for delight for the discerning ones in fasting;
    When one sees how much he has grown. Fasting secretly purifies
    the soul
    So it can gaze on God and grow by the vision of Him.
    For the weight that is from the earth, bends it back to the earth.
    Blessed is He Who gave us fasts,
    The sheer wings by which we fly to Him.

### 3.

Fasting is bright and beautiful for any who are bright enough
    to gaze on God. The Turbid One, stirred up by anything
    Cannot fix the eye on that Clear One. He who possesses a clear
    eye
    He can gaze upon him; as much as it is given to him to gaze.
    Instead of the clarifying wine, let us clarify our thought
    So that we will be able to see the Clear One
    Who overcame the Evil One by means of fasting, that Disturber
    of All.

### 4.

This is the fast through which greed escapes
    The peoples at the top of the mountain; clothed in fasting he
    overcame the Greedy One.
    Who had clothed himself with the food of Adam's house.
    The Lord of Victories gave us his weapon, he ascended on high
    to be an observer.
    Who would not run to the weapon by which God overcame
    It is a shameful thing, my brothers, to be bested by the weapon
    Which overcomes and causes to overcome all creation.

5.

Because the enemy is not visible, let us purge our thinking
    so that he sees that we see him.
    He is able to steal some of those whom he sees
    That they have not noticed him.
    When a soul undertakes a fast,
    The fast bears it and gives it back to its counterpart.
    Amid the volleys of sharpened arrows, hidden from view, the hidden eye
    Is polished to see from whence they come.

6.

This is the instructive fast, it teaches the athlete the ways of the contest.
    Draw near to it, study, learn to struggle shrewdly.
    Behold he instructed us to fast with our mouths and hearts,
    Let us not fast from bread and think thoughts
    In which the hidden poison of death is hidden.
    Let us confess on the fast day the First Born
    Who gave us the word of life to meditate on.

7.

Let the scriptures be for us like a mirror, let us see in them our fast
    For the Bible discriminates between fasts and prayer.
    It chooses one type of fast and rejects another
    Some fasters appease God and others anger him.
    There is a prayer which is sinful, and another which is the medicine of life
    O Lord let us rejoice in our fast
    As he rejoiced, my brothers, in his own fast.

8.

The fast is not defiling for the Holy One, for through it he descended and shone
    Another mixing made the fast defiled, though itself is pure.
    Examine nature! Are not desirable fruit Polluted by loathsome fruit?

Our thoughts are repelled by them though they be washed many times.
Blessed is the Pure One Who receives those fruits
Which all the penitent having purified them give to Him.

### 9.

The Troubler mixes filth with our Clarity,
    So as to make the first-fruits of our prayer and fasting hateful.
    It is possible by his jealousy, that our gift be rebuked.
    Take away your deceits from your fasts, remove mockery from your praise.
    May your voices wash your mouths from lies.
    Allow us, O First Born in Your mercy
    To uproot hidden weeds from our thoughts

### 10.

Do not be hindered, o simple ones, regarding that deceiver who robs fasters.
    For when he sees someone abstaining from bread,
    He is filled with anger. When he sees someone standing to pray
    He fills his mind with one distraction after another.
    He steals from his heart the prayer of his mouth,
    O Lord of ours give us an eye to see,
    How he steals the truth in deceit.

### 11.

Come be gathered, my brothers, on this fast day let us sit and marvel at how evil is the Evil One
    When he makes a transaction (gives and takes), he impoverishes us by what is his.
    And does he become wealthy through what is ours; the truth that he steals suits him not.
    The deceit he gives to us does not avail.

It is similar to the harlot,[5] his companion, who is neither ours nor his.
Judge O Lord, between us and him,
For it is through you that Solomon judged the unclean women.

### 12.

Let us seek the trace of truth on the fast day; Let us go forth by it to the place of abodes
For the blind people run, on a fast day with pride and wandering
Though there is a fast in their mouth, yet an idol is in the heart;
Prayer is on their lips, but divination in their heart
Their stomach is devoid of bread, but full of lies;
Though they wash their hands all day,
Hidden blood still screams against them.

### 13.

Blessed is he who endured and sustained and his head is crowned in exaltation.
With a bold voice, as one who deserves a payment, he demands his wage
He is not like me, who is too weak to fast, too lowly for the vigil
The first to be overcome. My enemy possesses skill
When he overcomes me, he lets me rise that he might again cast me low.
O Sea of mercies give me a handful of mercies.

## "THE MEDICINE OF SALVATION"

### *St. John Chrysostom*[6]

When was He led up? After the descent of the Spirit, after the voice that came from above, and said, "This is My Beloved Son, in

---

[5] cf. Rev. 19:2.
[6] St. John Chrysostom, *Homily 13 on the Gospel of St. Matthew*, NPNF, s. 1, v. 10, 186-189.

Whom I am well pleased" (Mt. 3:17). And marvelously, the Holy Spirit led Him up, as the Evangelist says. Intending to instruct us, He did and experienced all things.

He endures to be led up to the wilderness and to wrestle against the devil, so that if anyone who is baptized must endure greater temptations after his baptism, he may not be troubled as if the result were unexpected, but he continues to endure all nobly, as though it were happening in the natural course of things. Therefore, take up arms, not to be idle, but to fight.

God does not hold back temptations as they come in order to teach us many things. First, [He seeks to teach you] that you need to become much stronger. Second, [He demonstrates] that you should continue to be modest and not exalted by the greatness of your gifts, since the temptations have the power to repress you. Moreover, so that the wicked demon—who is for a while doubtful about your desertion of him by the touchstone of temptations—may be well assured that you have utterly forsaken and fallen from him. Fourthly, that you may in this way be made stronger and better tempered than any steel. Fifthly, that you may obtain a clear demonstration of the treasures entrusted to you.

For the devil would not have attacked you if he had not seen you brought to greater honor. Hence, for example, from the beginning, he attacked Adam because he saw him in the enjoyment of great dignity. For this reason, he arrayed himself against Job, because he saw him crowned and proclaimed by the God of all.

How then does He say, "Pray that you do not enter into temptation" (Mt. 26:41; Mk. 14:30; Lk. 22:46)? This is why [the Gospel] does not say that Jesus simply went up, but was "led up" (Mt. 4:1) according to the principle of the economy, signifying obscurely by this that we should not leap into temptation by our ourselves, but should stand courageously when dragged into it.

Notice where the Spirit led Him up, when He had taken Him: not into a city and forum, but into the wilderness. That is, He being minded to attract the devil, gives him a handle not only by His hunger, but also by the place. For the devil attacks most often when he sees men left alone and by themselves. He also did this in the beginning with the woman, after finding her alone and apart from her husband. Furthermore, he is not very confident and does not attack when he sees us with others and banded together. Therefore, because of this, we greatly need to always be together, so that we may not be open to the devil's attacks.

[The devil draws near only after he] found Him in a desolate wilderness, which is why Mark declared that He "was with the wild beasts" (Mk. 1:13). Behold, how craftily and wickedly he draws near, watching for any opportunity. For he approaches Him not during His fast, but in His hunger to teach you how important fasting is; how it is a most powerful shield against the devil; and how after the [baptismal] font, men should give themselves to fasting, not to luxury, drunkenness, and a full table.

For this is why He fasted, not as needing it Himself, but to instruct us. Since we sinned before baptism by serving the belly, He Himself brought in fasting after the font, just as if anyone who heals a sick man would forbid him from doing those things that caused the sickness. Truly, this dissatisfaction of the belly caused Adam to be cast out of Paradise, the flood to be produced in Noah's time, and thunders to be brought down on Sodom. For although there was also a charge of promiscuity, nevertheless from this grew the root of each of those punishments, which Ezekiel also signified when he said, "This was the sin of your sister Sodom: she and her daughters lived in pleasure, in fullness of bread and in abundance...and they did not aid the poor and needy" (Ezek. 16:49). Thus the Jews also perpetrated the greatest wickedness, being driven upon transgression by their drunkenness and delicacy.

On this account then even He fasts forty days, pointing out to us the medicines of our salvation. But, He proceeds no further, lest on the other hand, through the exceeding greatness of the miracle, the truth of His Economy should be discredited. For as it is, this cannot be, seeing that both Moses and Elijah, anticipating Him, could advance to so great a length of time, strengthened by the power of God. If He had preceded farther, from this among other things, His assumption of our flesh would have seemed incredible to many.

Having then fasted forty days and as many nights, "afterwards He was hungry" (Mt. 4:2; Lk. 4:2), affording Him a point to lay hold of and approach, that by actual conflict He might show how to prevail and be victorious. Wrestlers do the same. When teaching their students how to prevail and overcome, they voluntarily, in the lists, engage with others to afford these in the persons of their antagonists the means of seeing and learning the mode of conquest. The same thing occurred. Because it was His will to draw [the devil] on so far, He both made His hunger known to him, waited for his approach, and, as He waited for him, He dashed him to earth—once, twice, and three times, with such ease as became Him.

But that we may not, by hurrying over these victories, mark your profit, let us begin from the first assault, and examine each with exact care. Thus, after He was hungry, it is said, "The tempter came, [and] said, 'If You are the Son of God, command that these stones become bread'" (Mt. 4:3; cf. Lk. 4:3). For, because he had heard a voice born from above, saying, "This is My beloved Son" (Mt. 3:17). He also heard John bearing so large witness concerning Him, and after that saw Him hungry, he was confused. He could neither believe that He was a mere man, because of the things spoken concerning Him; nor could he accept that He was Son of God, seeing Him hunger. Thus, being confused he utters ambiguous sounds.

Similarly, when he first came to Adam at the beginning, he invents things that are not, that he may learn the things that are. Even so here also, not knowing clearly the unutterable mystery of the Economy and who He may be that is come, he attempts to weave other nets, whereby he thought to know that which was hidden and obscure. And what does he say?

"If You are Son of God, command that these stones become bread" (Mt. 4:3). He did not say "[Make these stones bread] because You are hungry" but "If You are the Son of God," thinking to cheat Him with his compliments. Therefore, also he was silent concerning the hunger that he might not seem to be claiming it, and blaming Him. For not knowing the greatness of the Economy which was going on, he supposed this to be a reproach to Him. Therefore flattering Him craftily, he mentions only His dignity. What then does Christ say? To put down his pride, and to signify that there was nothing shameful in what had happened, nor unbecoming His wisdom—that which the other had passed over in silence to flatter Him—He brings forward and sets it forth, saying, "Man shall not live by bread alone." Thus, He begins with the necessity of the belly.

Realize, I ask you, the craft of that wicked demon, how he begins his wrestlings, and how he does not forget his proper art. For in the same way he cast out the first man, and encompassed him with thousands of other evils, likewise he weaves his deceit here—I mean, with incontinence of the belly. So too even now one may hear many foolish ones say their bad words by thousands because of the belly.

In order to show that the virtuous man is not compelled even by this tyranny to do anything that is unseemly, Christ first hungers, then submits not to what is enjoined Him, teaching us to obey the devil in nothing. Thus, because the first man by this offended God and transgressed the law, as much and more does He teach you: that although what [the devil] commands does not [seem to be] transgression, even [still] you should not obey [him].

And why do I say, "transgression?" For one says, "Even though the devils may suggest expedient, why don't you simply give no heed to them?" Thus, for instance, He stopped the mouths of those devils who were proclaiming Him [to be the] Son of God (cf. Mk. 1:34, Lk. 4:41). Paul also rebuked them, crying this same thing and yet what they said was profitable; but he more abundantly dishonoring them and obstructing their plot against us, drove them away even when doctrines of salvation were preached by them, closing up their mouths, and bidding them to be silent.

Therefore, neither in this instance did He consent to what was said. But what does He say? "Man shall not live by bread alone." Now His meaning is like this: "God is able even by a word to nourish the hungry man," bringing him a testimony out of the ancient Scripture, and teaching us that although we hunger, yes, whatever we suffer, never to fall away from our Lord.

But if someone says, "still He should have displayed Himself," I would ask him, with what intent, and for what reason? For [the devil] did not speak so that [Christ] might believe, but that he might, as he thought, over-argue Him into unbelief. Since the first of mankind were in this way beguiled and over-argued by him, not putting earnest faith in God. For he promised them the contrary of what God had said, and puffed them up with vain hopes, and brought them to unbelief, and so eased them out of the blessings they actually possessed.

But Christ signifies Himself not to have consented, either to him then or afterwards to the Jews, his partisans, in their demand of signs—invariably instructing us that, whatever we may have power to do, nonetheless to do nothing vainly and at random, nor even when want urges us to obey the devil.

What then does this accursed one [do]? He is overcome, and unable to persuade Him to do his bidding, and that when pressed by such violent hunger, he proceeds to another thing, saying,

> "If You are Son of God, throw Yourself down; for it is written, 'He shall give His angels charge concerning You, and in their hands they shall bear You up'" (Mt. 4:6; Lk. 4:9, 10).

What can the reason be, that at each temptation He adds this, "If You are Son of God?" Much the same as he did in that former case, he does also at this time. That is, as he then slandered God, saying, "In the day you eat of it, your eyes shall be opened" (Gen. 3:5); thereby intending to signify, that they were beguiled and overreached, and had received no benefit. Even so in this case also he insinuates this same thing, saying, "In vain God has called You Son, and has cheated You by His gift. For, if this is not so, afford us some dear proof that You are of that Power."

Then, because Christ had reasoned with him from Scripture, he also brings in a testimony of the Prophet. How then does Christ do so? He is neither indignant nor provoked, but with that extreme gentleness He reasons with him again from the Scriptures, saying, "You shall not tempt the Lord your God" (Mt. 4:7; Lk. 4:12; Deut. 6:16), teaching us that we must overcome the devil, not by miracles, but by forbearance and long-suffering, and that we should do nothing at all for display and vainglory.

But mark his folly, even by the very testimony which he produced. For while both of the testimonies cited by the Lord were spoken with exceeding fitness: his, on the other hand, were chance and random sayings, neither did he bring forward on his part that which applied to the matter in hand.

Thus it is written, "He shall give His angels charge concerning You" (Mt. 4:6, Ps. 90:11), this surely is not advice to dash and toss one's self down headlong. Moreover, this was not so much as spoken concerning the Lord. However, this for the time He did not expose, although there was both insult in his manner of speech, and great inconsistency. For no man requires these things of the Son of God: but to cast one's self down is the part of the devil, and of demons. Whereas God's part is to raise up even those who have fallen.

And if He should have displayed His own power, it would not have been by casting and tossing Himself down at random, but by saving others. But to cast ourselves down cliffs, and into pits, pertains properly to his troop. Thus, for example, the juggler among them does everywhere.

But Christ, even when these things are said, does not yet reveal Himself, but as Man discourses with him for a while. For the sayings, "Man shall not live by bread alone," and "You shall not tempt the Lord your God," suited one not greatly revealing Himself, but representing Himself as one of the many.

But do not marvel [at this], if he in reasoning with Christ oftentimes turns himself about. For as wrestlers, when they have received deadly blows, roll about, drenched in much blood and blinded; even so he too, darkened by the first and the second blow, speaks at random what comes uppermost, and proceeds to his third assault.

> Again, the devil took Him up on an exceedingly high mountain, and showed Him all the kingdoms of the world and their glory. And he said to Him, 'All these things I will give You if You will fall down and worship me.' Then Jesus said to him, 'Away with you, Satan! For it is written, "You shall worship the Lord your God, and Him only you shall serve"' (Mt. 4:8-10).

Since [the devil] was now come to sinning against the Father, saying that all that is the Father's was his, and was endeavoring to make himself out to be God, as Artificer of the universe, [Christ] then rebuked him. He did so, not with vehemence, but simply, "Away with you, Satan," which itself had in it something of command rather than of rebuke. For, as soon as Christ said to him, "Away with you," He caused him to take to flight, since he did not bring any other temptations against Him.

When Luke says that, "he ended every temptation" (Lk. 4:13), it seems to me that in mentioning the chief of the temptations, he spoke about all of them, as though the rest were also included in these. These innumerable evils include: to be a slave to the belly, to do anything for vainglory, [and] to be in subjection to the madness of riches. To these, the accursed one considers greed and desire of more, to be the most powerful of all, and places it last.

And although he originally was working to come to this [temptation] from the beginning, he kept it for the end, since it was more powerful than the rest. For, in fact, this is the manner of his wrestling: to leave those things which are more likely to overthrow for the end. And he did a similar thing with Job: beginning with motives that seem to be more contemptible and weaker, he goes on to the more prevailing.

How then are we to get the better of him? In the way which Christ that taught us, by fleeing to God for refuge and not being depressed in famine, as believing in God Who is able to feed even with a word nor amidst whatever good things we may receive to tempt Him Who gave them, but to be content with the glory which is from above, making no account of that which is of men, and on every occasion to despise what is beyond our need. For nothing does so make us fall under the power of the devil, as longing for more, and loving covetousness. And this we may see even by what is done now. For now also there are those who say, "If you will worship before me, all will be Yours" (Lk. 4:7). For they indeed are men by nature, but have become his instruments. Since he at that time also approached Him, not by himself only, but also by others. Luke also was declaring this when he said, "he departed from Him until an opportune time" (Lk. 4:13), showing that after this he approached Him by his proper instruments.

"And, behold, angels came and ministered to Him" (Mt. 4:11). For when the assault was going on, He did not allow them to appear, so He might not drive away the prey by this. But after He had convicted him in all points, and caused him to take to flight, then they appear, so that you also may learn, that after your victories which are copied from His, angels will receive you also applauding you, and waiting as guards on you in all things. Thus, for example, angels take Lazarus away with them, after the furnace of poverty and of famine and of all distress. For as I have already said, Christ on this occasion exhibits many things, which we ourselves are to enjoy.

Forasmuch then as all these things have been done for you, do you emulate and imitate His victory. And should any of those who are that evil spirit's servants approach you, delighting in the things that are from him, rebuking you and saying, "If you are marvelous and great, remove the mountain," neither be troubled nor confounded. But answer with meekness, and say some such thing as you have heard your Lord say, "You shall not tempt the Lord your God" (Mt. 4:7, Deut. 6:16).

Or if he offers you glory, dominion, and an endless amount of wealth, and commands you to worship him, endure him courageously. For neither did the devil deal so with the common Lord of us all only, but every day also he brings these his machinations to bear on each of His servants, not in mountains only and in wildernesses, nor by himself: but also in cities, in marketplaces, and in courts of justice, and by means of our own kindred, even men.

Then, what should we do? Disbelieve him altogether; stop our ears against him; hate him when he flatters; and when he offers [us anything] shun him even more! Because in Eve's case also, when he was most lifting her up with hopes, then he cast her down, and did her the greatest evils. Yes, for he is a relentless enemy, and has taken up against us such war as excludes all treaty.

We are not so eager for our own salvation, as he is for our ruin. Let us then shun him—not only with words, but also with works; not in mind only, but also in deed. Let us do none of the things which he approves, for so shall we do all those which God approves. For he also makes many promises, not that he may give, but that he may take.

He promises by plunder to deprive us of the Kingdom and righteousness. He sets treasures in the earth as a kind of excitements or traps, so that he may deprive us both of these and of the treasures in heaven. He would rather have us be rich here, that we may not be rich there. If he cast us out of our inheritance there by wealth, he comes by way of poverty, as he did with Job. That is, when he saw that wealth did him no harm, he weaves his toils by poverty, expecting on that side to get the better of him. But, what could be more foolish than this? Since whoever has been able to bear wealth with moderation, much more will he bear poverty with manliness; and he who desires not riches when present, neither will he seek them when absent; even as that blessed man did not, but by his poverty, on the other hand, he became still more glorious.

For of his possessions that wicked demon had power indeed to deprive him, but his love toward God he not only could not take away, but made it even stronger. And when he had stripped him of everything, he caused him to abound with more blessings, which made him even more perplexed. For the more plagues he brought upon man, the mightier man become. Therefore, as you know, when he had gone through all, and had thoroughly tried his metal, because he made no way, he ran to his old weapon, the woman, and assumes a mask of concern, and makes a tragic picture of his calamities in most pitiable tone, and pretends that for removal of his evil he is introducing that deadly counsel. But neither so did he prevail. No, for his bait was perceived by that wondrous man, who with much wisdom stopped the mouth of the woman speaking at his instigation.

We must do the same. For if he has entered to our brother, a reliable friend, a wife, whoever nearest to us, and utters something improper, we must not receive the counsel for the person of him who so speaks. But because of the deadly counsel, turn away from the speaker. For, he does many such things and puts before him a mask of sympathy. While he seems to be friendly, he is instilling his pernicious words, more grievous than poisons. Thus, as to flatter for evil is his part, so to chastise for our good, is God's.

Let us not then be deceived, neither let us by every way seek after the life of ease. For "whom the Lord loves," it is said, "He chastens" (Heb. 12:6). Why when we enjoy prosperity, living in wickedness, then most of all should we grieve. For we should always be afraid while we sin, but especially when we suffer no ill. For when God exacts our penalties little by little, He makes our payment for these things easy to us, but when He is long-suffering for each of our negligences, He is storing us up, if we continue in such things, unto a great punishment. Since, if for the well-doers affliction be a necessary thing, much more for them that sin.

See for instance how much long-suffering Pharaoh met with, and afterwards underwent for all most extreme punishment: in how many things Nebuchadnezzar offended, yet at the end expiated all. And the rich man, because he had suffered no great ill here, for this very cause chiefly became miserable, for that having lived in luxury in the present life, he departed to pay the penalty of all these things there, where he could not obtain anything at all to soothe his calamity.

Yet for all this some are so cold and senseless, as to be always seeking only the things that are here, and uttering those absurd sayings, "Let me enjoy all things present for a time, and then I will consider about things out of sight. I will gratify my belly, I will be a slave to pleasures, I will make full use of the present life; give me today, and take tomorrow." O excess of folly! Why, then do they who talk so differ from goats and swine? For if the Prophet permits not them to be accounted men who "neigh after their neighbors wife" (Jer. 5:8), who shall blame us for esteeming these to be goats and swine, and more insensible than donkeys, by whom those things are held uncertain, which are more evident than what we see?

If you believe nothing else, why do you attend to the devils in their scourging, to those who had our hurt for their object in all their practice, both in word and deed? For you will not, I am sure, contradict this, that they do all to increase our security, and to do away with the fear of hell, and to breed disbelief of the tribunals in that world. Nevertheless, those who are so minded, by cryings and wailings do often proclaim the torments that are there. When do they so speak and utter things contrary to their own will? From no other cause, but because they are under the pressure of stronger compulsion. For they would have not been minded of their own accord to confess either that they are tormented by dead men, or those who suffer anything at all dreadful.

Why now have I said this? Because evil demons confess hell, those who would gladly have hell disbelieved. But you who enjoy so great an honor, and have been a partaker in unutterable mysteries, do not so much as imitate them, but have become more hardened even than they.

"But who," one will say, "has come from those in hell, and has declared these things?" But, who has arrived here from heaven, and told us that there is a God Who created all things? And how is it clear that we have a soul? For clearly, if you are to believe the things only that are in sight, both God and angels, and mind and soul, will be matter of doubting to you, and in this way you will find all the doctrines of the truth gone.

Yet surely, if you are willing to believe what is evident, you will believe the things invisible, rather than those which are seen. Even though what I say be a paradox, nevertheless it is true, and among men of understanding is fully acknowledged. Whereas the eyes are often deceived, not in the things unseen only (for of those they do not so much as take cognizance), but even in those which men think they actually see, distance and atmosphere, and absence of mind, and anger, and care, and ten thousand other things impeding their accuracy. The reasoning power of the soul on the other hand, if it receives the light of the Divine Scriptures, will prove a more accurate, an unerring standard of realities.

Let us not then vainly deceive ourselves, neither in addition to the carelessness of our life, which is the offspring of such doctrines as these, heap up to ourselves, for the very doctrines themselves, a more grievous fire. For if there be no judgment, and we are not to give account of our deeds, neither shall we receive rewards for our labors. Observe which way your blasphemies tend, when you say, that God, Who is righteous, and loving, and mild, overlooks so great labors and toils. And how can this be reasonable? Why, if by nothing else, at any rate by the circumstances of your own house, I bid you weigh these things, and then you will see the savage and inhuman beyond measure, and wilder than the very wild beasts, you would not choose at your death to leave the servant who had been affectionate to you without honor, but would repay him both with freedom, and with a gift of money; and forasmuch as in your own person hereafter, having departed, you will be able to do him no good, you gave charge concerning him to the future inheritors of your substance, beseeching, exhorting, doing everything, so that he may not remain unrewarded.

You, who are evil, you are so kind and loving towards your servant. Then, will the Infinite Goodness—that is, God, the Unspeakable Love to man, with His vast kindness so vast—overlook and leave uncrowned His own servants, Peter, Paul, James, and John, who every day for His sake suffered hunger, were bound, were scourged, were drowned in the sea, were given up to wild beasts, were dying, were suffering so great things that we cannot even imagine?

And whereas the Olympic judge proclaims and crowns the victor, and the master rewards the servant, and the king the soldier, and each in general him that has done him service, with what good things he can—shall God alone, after those so great toils and labors, repay them with no good thing great or small? Shall those just and pious men, who have walked in every virtue, lie in the same state with adulterers, parricides, murderers, and robbers of tombs? And in what way can this be reasonable? Since, if there is nothing after our departure from here, and our interests reach no further than things present, those are in the same. Why do they have the same end, though at a later time, as you say? Yet here, the whole of their time, the wicked have been at ease, the righteous in chastisement. And this, what sort of tyrant, what savage and relentless man did ever so devise, touching his own servants and subjects?

Did you mark the exceeding greatness of the absurdity, and in what this argument issues? Therefore, if you will not any other way, yet by these reasonings be instructed to rid yourself of this wicked thought, and to flee from vice, and cleave to the toils which end in virtue: and then will you know certainly that our concerns are not bounded by the present life. And if anyone asks you, "Who has come from there and brought word what is there?" say to him, "of men not one." For surely he would have been often disbelieved, as vaunting, and exaggerating the thing. But, the Lord of the angels has brought word with exactness of all those things. What need, then, have we of any man, seeing that He Who will demand account of us cries aloud every day that He has both made ready a hell and prepared a kingdom, and affords us clear demonstrations of these things? For if He were not hereafter to judge, neither would he have exacted any penalty here.

"Well, but as to this very point how can it be reasonable? that of the wicked some should be punished, others not? I mean, if God be no respecter of persons, as surely He is not why can it be that of one He exacts a penalty, but another He allows to go away unpunished? Why, this is again more inexplicable than the former."

Yet if you are willing to hear what we say with candor, we will solve this difficulty also. What then is the solution? He neither exacts penalty of all here, lest you should despair of the Resurrection, and lose all expectation of the Judgment, as though all were to give account here. Nor does He allow all to go away unpunished, lest on the other hand you should account all to be without His providence. But He both punishes and abstains from punishing: by those whom He punishes, signifying that in that world also He will exact a penalty of such as are unpunished here;

and by those whom He does not punish, working upon you to believe that there is some fearful trial after our departure from here.

If He were altogether indifferent about our former deeds, He neither would have punished anyone here, nor would have conferred benefits. But now you see Him for your sake stretching out the heaven, kindling the sun, establishing each, pouring forth the sea, expanding the air, and appointing for the moon her courses, setting unchangeable laws for the seasons of the years, and all other things also performing their own courses exactly at a sign from Him. For both our nature, and that of creatures irrational, of them that creep, that walk, that fly, that swim, in marshes, in springs, in rivers, in mountains, in forests, in houses, in the air, in plains; also plants, seeds, and trees, both wild and cultivated, both fruitful and unfruitful; and all things in general, moved by that unwearied Hand, make provision for our life, affording to us of themselves their ministry, not for our need only, but also for our feeling of high station.

Seeing therefore order so great and fair (and yet we have not mentioned so much as the least portion thereof), dare you say, that He Who for your sake has wrought things so many and great will overlook you in the most critical points, and suffer you when dead to lie with the donkeys and swine: and that having honored you with so great a gift, that of godliness, whereby He has even equaled you with the angels, He will overlook you after your countless labors and toils?

And how can this be reasonable? Why, these things, if we be silent "the stones will immediately cry out;" so plain are they, and manifest, and more vivid than the sunbeam itself.

Having then considered all these things, and having convinced our own soul, that after our departure from here, we shall both stand before the fearful judgment-seat, and give account of all that we have done, and shall bear our penalty, and submit to our sentence, if we continue in our negligences. But if we are willing to give a little heed to ourselves we shall receive crowns and unutterable blessings. So, let us both stop the mouths of those who contradict these things, and choose for ourselves the way of virtue, that with due confidence departing to that tribunal, we may attain unto the good things that are promised us, by the grace and love towards man of our Lord Jesus Christ, to Whom be glory and dominion, now and ever, and unto the age of ages. Amen.

## "Why Forty Days?"

### *St. Augustine of Hippo*[7]

The number "40" is a sign of that laborious period in which, under the discipline of Christ the King, we have to fight against the devil. This is also indicated by the fact that both the law and the prophets solemnized a fast of forty days—that is to say, a humbling of the soul—in the person of Moses and Elijah, who each fasted for a period of forty days. Through the fast of the Lord Himself, during which forty days He was also tempted of the devil, the gospel narrative also demonstrates that condition of temptation which appertains to us through all the space of this age, and which He bore in the flesh which He condescended to take to Himself from our mortality. After the Resurrection, it was also His will to remain with His disciples on the earth not longer than forty days, continuing to mingle for that space of time with this life of theirs in the way of human intercourse, and partaking along with them of the food needful for mortal men, although He Himself was to die no more.

All this was done with the view of signifying to them through these forty days, that although His presence should be hidden from their eyes, He would yet fulfill what He promised when He said, "Behold, I am with you, even to the end of the age" (Mt. 28:20). And in explanation of the circumstance that this particular number should denote this temporal and earthly life, what suggests itself most immediately in the meantime, although there may be another and subtler method of accounting for it, is the consideration that the seasons of the years also revolve in four successive alternations, and that the world itself has its bounds determined by four divisions, which Scripture sometimes designates by the names of the winds—East and West, North and South. But the number forty is equivalent to four times ten. Furthermore, the number ten itself is made up by adding the several numbers in succession from one up to four together.

In this way, then, as Matthew undertook the task of presenting the record of Christ as the King Who came into this world, and into this earthly and mortal life of men, to exercise rule over us who have to struggle

---

[7] St. Augustine, *Homilies on Matthew*, NPNF, s. 1, v. 4, 221-222.

with temptation, he began with Abraham, and enumerated forty men. For Christ came in the flesh from that very nation of the Hebrews with a view to the keeping of which as a people distinct from the other nations, God separated Abraham from his own country and his own kindred. And the circumstance that the promise contained an intimation of the race from which He was destined to come, served very specially to make the prediction and announcement concerning Him something all the clearer. Thus, the Evangelist did indeed mark out fourteen generations in each of three several members, stating that from Abraham until David there were fourteen generations, and from David until the carrying away into Babylon other fourteen generations, and another fourteen from that period on to the Nativity of Christ.

But he did not then calculate them all up in one sum, counting them one by one, and saying that thus they make up forty-two in all. For among these fore-fathers there is one who is named twice, namely Jechonias, with whom a kind of deflection was made in the direction of extraneous nations at the time when the transmigration into Babylon took place. When the enumeration, moreover, is thus bent from the direct order of progression, and is made to form, if we may so say, a kind of corner for the purpose of taking a different course, what meets us at that corner is mentioned twice over, namely, at the close of the preceding series, and at the head of the deflection specified. And this, also, was a figure of Christ as the One Who was, in a certain sense, to pass from the circumcision to the uncircumcision, or, so to speak, from Jerusalem to Babylon, and to be, as it were, the Cornerstone to all who believe in Him, whether on the one side or on the other. Thus was God making preparations then in a figurative manner for things which were to come in truth. For Jechonias himself, with whose name the kind of corner which I have in view was prefigured, is by interpretation the "preparation of God." In this way, therefore, there are really not forty-two distinct generations named here, which would be the proper sum of three times fourteen; but, as there is a double enumeration of one of the names, we have here forty generations in all, taking into account the fact that Christ Himself is reckoned in the number, Who, like the kingly president over this [significant] number forty, superintends the administration of this temporal and earthly life of ours.

# VII

## And He Arose and Went to His Father

*Meditations on the Sunday of the Prodigal Son of the Great Lent*

### Gospel Reading of the Third Sunday of the Great Lent

#### (Luke 15:11-32)

*Then He said: "A certain man had two sons. And the younger of them said to his father, 'Father, give me the portion of goods that falls to me.' So he divided to them his livelihood. And not many days after, the younger son gathered all together, journeyed to a far country, and there wasted his possessions with prodigal living. But when he had spent all, there arose a severe famine in that land, and he began to be in want. Then he went and joined himself to a citizen of that country, and he sent him into his fields to feed swine. And he would gladly have filled his stomach with the pods that the swine ate, and no one gave him anything.*

*But when he came to himself, he said, 'How many of my father's hired servants have bread enough and to spare, and I perish with hunger! I will arise and go to my father, and will say to him, "Father, I have sinned against heaven and before you, and I am no longer worthy to be called your son. Make me like one of your hired servants."'*

*And he arose and came to his father. But when he was still a great way off, his father saw him and had compassion, and ran and fell on his neck and kissed him. And the son said to him, "Father, I have sinned against heaven and in your sight, and am no longer worthy to be called your son."'*

*But the father said to his servants, 'Bring out the best robe and put it on him, and put a ring on his hand and sandals on his feet. And bring the fatted calf here and kill it, and let us eat and be merry; for this my son was dead and is alive again; he was lost and is found.' And they began to be merry.*

*Now his older son was in the field. And as he came and drew near to the house, he heard music and dancing. So he called one of the servants and asked what these things meant. And he said to him, 'Your brother has come, and because he has received him safe and sound, your father has killed the fatted calf.'*

*But he was angry and would not go in. Therefore his father came out and pleaded with him. So he answered and said to his father, 'Lo, these many years I have been serving you; I never transgressed your commandment at any time; and yet you never gave me a young goat, that I might make merry with my friends. But as soon as this son of yours came, who has devoured your livelihood with harlots, you killed the fatted calf for him.'*

*And he said to him, 'Son, you are always with me, and all that I have is yours. It was right that we should make merry and be glad, for your brother was dead and is alive again, and was lost and is found.'"*

## "THE GRACE OF GOD"
### *St. Athanasius the Apostolic*[1]

And that young man who went into a far country—and there wasted his goods, living in dissipation—if he receive a desire for this divine feast, and, coming to himself, shall say, "How many of my father's hired servants have bread enough to spare, and I perish with hunger!" (Lk. 15:17); and shall next arise and come to his father, and confess to him, saying, "I have sinned against heaven and before you, and am no longer worthy to be called your son. Make me like one of your hired servants" (Lk. 15:18, 19), when he shall thus confess; then he shall be counted worthy of more than he prayed for.

---

[1] St. Athanasius, *Festal Letter* 7, NPNF, s. 2, v. 4, 1256.

For the father neither receives him as a hired servant, nor does he look upon him as a stranger. But he kisses him as a son, brings him back to life as from the dead, counts him worthy of the divine feast, and gives him his former and precious robe. So that, on this account, there is singing and gladness in the paternal home. For this is the work of the Father's lovingkindness and goodness, that not only should He make him alive from the dead, but that He should render His grace illustrious through the Spirit. Therefore, instead of corruption, He clothes him with an incorruptible garment; instead of hunger, He kills the fatted calf; instead of far journeys, He watched for his return, providing shoes for his feet; and, what is most wonderful, placed a divine signet-ring upon his hand; while by all these things He created him anew according to the image of the glory of Christ. These are the gracious gifts of the Father, by which the Lord honors and nourishes those who abide with Him, and those who return to Him and repent.

## "Leaving God"

### *St. Ambrose of Milan*[2]

Appropriately, he who departed from the Church squanders his birthright. Surely, whoever separates himself from Christ is an exile from his country, a citizen of the world. But we are not "strangers and foreigners, but fellow citizens with the saints and members of the household of God" (Eph. 2:19). We, too, were in a distant land as Isaiah teaches, "The people walking in darkness behold a great light" (Is. 9:2).

This [famine] does not speak of a famine of fasts but of good works and virtues. What hunger is more wretched? Surely, whoever departs from the Word of God hungers because "man shall not live by bread alone, but by every word of God" (Lk. 4:4). Fittingly, he began to be in want, he who abandoned the treasures of wisdom and the knowledge of God and the depth of heavenly riches. Therefore, he began to want and to suffer starvation, because nothing is enough for prodigal enjoyment...

He is sent to the farm bought by the man who excused himself from the kingdom. He feeds swine, those, indeed, into which the devil should

---

[2] St. Ambrose, *Exposition on the Gospel of St. Luke*, 1.214-215.

enter, which were cast into the sea of the world as they lived in filth and foulness (Mt. 8:31, 32).

## "A Model of Repentance"
### *St. Ambrose of Milan*[3]

The Apostle does not contradict the plain teaching of Christ, Who set forth, as a comparison of a repentant sinner, one going to a foreign country after receiving all his substance from his father, wasted it in prodigal living, and later, when feeding upon waste, longed for his father's bread and then gained the robe, the ring, the shoes, and the slaying of the calf, which is a likeness of the Passion of the Lord, whereby we receive forgiveness.

Well, is it said that he went into a foreign country as one who is cut off from the sacred altar, one separated from heavenly Jerusalem, separated from the citizenship and home of the saints. This is why the Apostle says, "Therefore now you are no longer strangers and foreigners, but fellow citizens with the saints and members of the household of God" (Eph. 2:19).

"And," it is rightly said, "wasted his goods," for he whose faith ceases to bring forth good works wastes it. For "faith is the substance of things hoped for, the evidence of things not seen" (Heb. 11:1). And faith is a good substance, the inheritance of our hope.

Lacking the divine nourishment and perishing for hunger, he was forced to say, "I will arise and go to my father, and will say to him, 'Father, I have sinned against heaven, and before you.'" Don't you see it clearly declared to us, that we are urged to prayer for the sake of gaining the mystery? Do you want to take that away for the sake of which penance is undertaken?

Deprive the pilot of the hope of reaching port, and he will wander aimlessly here on the waves. Take away the crown from the athlete, and he will fail and lie on the course. Take from the fisher the power of catching

---

[3] St. Ambrose, *Concerning Repentance*, NPNF, s. 2, v. 10, 813-814.

his bounty, and he will cease to cast the nets. How, then, can he, who suffers hunger in his soul, pray more earnestly to God, if he has no hope of the heavenly food?

"I have sinned," he says, "against heaven, and before you." He confesses what is clearly a sin unto death, so that you may not think that any one doing penance is rightly shut out from pardon. For he who has sinned against heaven has sinned either against the Kingdom of Heaven, or against his own soul, which is a sin unto death, and against God, to Whom alone is said, "Against You only have I sinned, and done evil before You" (Ps. 50:6).

He gains forgiveness so quickly that, as he is coming, and is still a great way off, his father meets him and gives him a kiss, which is the sign of sacred peace. He orders the robe to be brought forth, which is the marriage garment, which if any one does not have, he is shut out from the marriage feast. He places the ring on his hand, which is the pledge of faith and the seal of the Holy Spirit; orders the sandals to be brought out, for he who is about to celebrate the Lord's Passover and is about to feast on the Lamb, should have his feet protected against all attacks of spiritual wild beasts and the bite of the serpent. He bids the calf to be slain, for "Christ our Passover has been sacrificed" (1 Cor. 5:7). Whenever we receive the Blood of the Lord, we proclaim the death of the Lord.[4] So, as He was once slain for all, whenever forgiveness of sins is granted, we receive the Mystery of His Body, that through His Blood there may be remission of sins.

Therefore most evidently we are bidden by the teaching of the Lord to confer again the grace of the heavenly mystery on those guilty even of the greatest sins, if they with open confession bear the penance due to their sin.

---

[4] St. Cyril's words are reflected beautifully in the Coptic liturgical tradition in which the priest prays, "For every time you shall eat of this bread and drink of this cup you proclaim My death, confess My Resurrection, and remember Me till I come."

## "The Patience of the Father"
### *The Scholar Tertullian*[5]

There is a breadth of patience in our Lord's parables, the patience of the shepherd that makes him seek and find the straying sheep. Impatience would readily take no account of a single sheep, but patience undertakes the wearisome search. He carries it on his shoulders as a patient bearer of a forsaken sinner.

In the case of the Prodigal Son, it is the patience of his father that welcomes, clothes, feeds and finds an excuse for him in the face of the impatience of his angry brother. The one who perished is rescued, because he embraced repentance. Repentance is not wasted because it meets up with patience!

## "Returning to the Father"
### *St. Cyril of Alexandria*[6]

I hear one of the holy prophets trying to win to repentance those who are far from God, and saying, "Return, O Israel, to the Lord your God: for have become weak in your iniquity. Take with you words, and return to the Lord our God" (Hos. 14:1). What sort of words, therefore, did he, under the influence of the Spirit, command them to take with them? Or were they not such as what is appropriate for those who wish to repent; such namely, as would appease God, Who is gentle, and loves mercy? For He even said by one of the holy prophets, "Return you returning children, and I will heal your bruises" (Jer. 3:22). And yet, again, by the voice of Ezekiel, "Return you altogether from your wickedness, O house of Israel. Cast away from you all your ungodliness which you have sinned against Me, that it may not become to you the punishment of iniquity...For I do not desire the death of the sinner, but that he should turn from his evil way and live" (Ezek. 18:29-32).

---

[5] Tertullian, *On Patience*, 12, FCS 40:214-5.
[6] St. Cyril of Alexandria, *Commentary on the Gospel of St. Luke* (n.p.: Studion Publishers, 1983), 427-434.

Christ also teaches this same truth by this most beautifully composed parable, which I will now, to the best of my ability, endeavor to discuss, briefly gathering up its broad statements and explaining and defending the ideas which it contains.

It is the opinion of some that the two sons signify the holy angels, and us, the dwellers upon earth. The elder one [they say], who lived soberly, represents the company of the holy angels while the younger and reckless son is the human race. But there are some among us who give it a different explanation, arguing that the elder and well conducted son signifies Israel after the flesh while the other, whose choice it was to live in the lust of pleasures, and who removed himself far from his father, depicts the company of the Gentiles.

I do not agree with these explanations. But I would have him who loves instruction search after that which is true and unobjectionable. What, then, I say is "giving occasions to the wise...and instruct a just man" (Prov. 9:9), as Scripture commands. For they will examine for a fitting meaning the explanations proposed to them.

If, then, the upright son refers to the person of the holy angels, we do not find him speaking such words as are appropriate to them, nor sharing their feelings towards repentant sinners, who turn from an impure life to that conduct which is worthy of admiration. For the Savior of all and Lord says that "there is joy in the presence of the angels of God over one sinner who repents" (Lk. 15:10). But the son, who is described to us in the present parable as being acceptable unto his father and leading a blameless life is represented as being angry, and as even having continued so far in his unloving sentiments as to find fault with his father for his natural affection for him who was saved. For he would not, it says, go into the house, being angry at the reception of the penitent almost before he had come to his senses, and even because they killed the calf in his honor and his father made for him a feast.

But this, as I said, is at variance with the feelings of the holy angels, for they rejoice and praise God when they see the inhabitants of the earth being saved. When the Son submitted to be born in the flesh of a woman at Bethlehem, they carried the joyful news to the shepherds, saying, "Do not be afraid, for behold, I bring you good tidings of great joy which will be to all people. For there is born to you this day in the city of David a

Savior, Who is Christ, the Lord" (Lk. 2:10, 11). And crowning Him Who was born with lauds and praises, they said, "Glory to God in the highest, and on earth peace, good will toward men!" (Lk. 2:14).

Neither can we say that the virtuous and sober son symbolizes Israel according to the flesh, because it is in no way whatsoever proper to say of the Israelites that they chose a blameless life, since throughout the inspired Scripture we see them accused of being rebellious and disobedient. They were told by the voice of Jeremiah, "What trespasses have your fathers found in Me, that they have revolted far from Me, and have gone after vanities, and become vain?" (Jer. 2:5). Similarly, God spoke by the voice of Isaiah, saying, "This people draw near to Me with their mouth and honor Me with their lips, but their heart far from Me; but in vain do they worship Me, teaching the commandments and doctrines of men" (Is. 29:13).

And how then can anyone apply to those who are thus blamed the words used in the parable of the virtuous and sober son? For he said, "Lo, these many years I have been serving you; I never transgressed your commandment at any time" (Lk. 15:29). But they would not have been blamed for their mode of life had it not been that, transgressing the divine commandments, they took themselves to a careless and polluted mode of life.

Also, some would refer that fatted calf, which the father killed when his son was called to repentance, to the Person of our Savior. But how, then, could the virtuous son—who is described as wise and prudent, constant in his duty, and whom some even refer to the person of the holy angels—treat the slaying of the calf as a reason for anger and vexation? For one can find no proof of the powers above being grieved when Christ endured death in the flesh, and, so to speak, was slain on our behalf. Rather they rejoiced, as I said, in seeing the world saved by His holy Blood. Also, why did the virtuous son say, "You never gave me a young goat" (Lk. 15:29)? For what blessing do the holy angels need, inasmuch as the Lord of all has bestowed upon them with beneficent hand a plentiful supply of spiritual gifts? Or what sacrifice are they in need of —for there was no necessity for Emmanuel to suffer also on their behalf?

But if anyone imagines, as I have already said before, that the carnal Israel is meant by the virtuous and sober son, how can he say with truth,

"You never gave me a young goat?" For whether we call it a calf or a goat, Christ is to be understood as the sacrifice offered for sin. He was sacrificed, not for the Gentiles only, but that He might also redeem Israel, who by reason of his frequent transgression of the law had brought upon himself great blame. And the wise Paul bears witness to this, saying, "Therefore Jesus also, that He might sanctify the people with His own Blood, suffered outside the gate" (Heb. 13:12).

What, then, is the object of the parable? Let us examine the occasion which led to it, for we shall learn the truth through it. The blessed Luke, therefore, had himself said a little before of Christ the Savior of us all, "Then all the tax collectors and the sinners drew near to Him to hear Him. And the Pharisees and scribes complained, saying, 'This Man receives sinners and eats with them'" (Lk. 15:1, 2). Therefore, as the Pharisees and Scribes made this outcry at His gentleness and love to man, and wickedly and impiously blamed Him for receiving and teaching men whose lives were impure, Christ very necessarily set before them the present parable, to show them clearly this very thing that the God of all requires even him who is thoroughly steadfast and firm, and who knows how to live righteously, and has attained to the highest praise for sobriety of conduct, to be earnest in following His will, so that when any are called to repentance, even if they are men highly blamable, they must rejoice and not give way to an unloving vexation on their account.

For we also sometimes experience something of this sort. For there are some who live a perfectly honorable and consistent life, practicing every kind of virtuous action and abstaining from every thing disapproved by the law of God, and crowning themselves with perfect praises in the sight of God and of men. While another is perhaps weak, trampled, and humbled by every kind of wickedness, guilty of base deeds, loving impurity, given to covetousness, and stained with all evil. Yet such a person often in old age turns to God and asks the forgiveness of his former offenses. He prays for mercy, and putting away his readiness to fall into sin, sets his affection on virtuous deeds. Or even perhaps when about to close his mortal life, he is admitted to divine baptism, and puts away his offenses, God being merciful unto him.

Also, sometimes persons are indignant at this, and even say, "This man, who has been guilty of such and such actions, and has spoken such and such words, has not paid unto the judge the retribution of his conduct, but has been counted worthy of a grace thus noble and admirable. He has been inscribed among the sons of God, and honored with the glory of the saints." Such complaints men sometimes give utterance too from an empty narrowness of mind, not conforming to the purpose of the universal Father.

For He greatly rejoices when He sees those who were lost obtaining salvation, and raises them up again to that which they were in the beginning, giving them the dress of freedom, and adorning them with the chief robe, and putting a ring upon their hand, even the orderly behavior which is pleasing to God and suitable to the free.

It is our duty, therefore, to conform ourselves to that which God wills, for He heals those who are sick. He raises those who are fallen. He gives a helping hand to those who have stumbled. He brings back him who has wandered. He forms anew unto a praiseworthy and blameless life those who were wallowing in the mire of sin. He seeks those who were lost. He raises as from the dead those who had suffered the spiritual death.[7] Let us also rejoice. Let us, in company with the holy angels, praise Him as being Good and Lover of mankind; as gentle, and not remembering evil. For if such is our state of mind, Christ will receive us, by Whom and with Whom, to God the Father be praise and dominion with the Holy Spirit, unto ages of ages. Amen.

---

[7] This last paragraph correlates well with the later Coptic Litany of the Sick, "You are the One Who looses the bound and uplifts the fallen, the hope of those who have no hope, the help of those who have no helper, the comfort of the faint-hearted, the harbor of those in the storm..." The following also reminds us of the ancient Morning Prayer, "Let us praise with the angels, saying, 'Glory to God in the highest,'" which St. Cyril cites above.

## "THE FEAST ABOVE THE CLOUDS"
### *St. Clement of Alexandria and Another Writer*[8]

#### 1.

What choral dance and high festival is held in heaven, if there is one that has become an exile and a fugitive from the life led under the Father, knowing not that those who put themselves far from Him shall perish; if he has squandered the gift, and substance, and inheritance of the Father; if there is one whose faith has failed, and whose hope is spent, by rushing along with the Gentiles into the same profligacy of debauchery and then, famished and destitute, not even filled with what the swine eat, has arisen and come to his father!

But the kind father does not wait until the son comes to him! For perhaps he would never be able or venture to approach, if he had not found him gracious. Therefore, when he merely wishing, when he immediately made a beginning, when he took the first step, while he was yet a great way off, [the father] was moved with compassion, and ran, and fell upon his neck and kissed him. And then the son, taking courage, confessed what he had done.

Therefore the father bestows on him the glory and honor that was worthy and proper, putting on him the best robe, the robe of immortality; and a ring, a royal signet and divine seal, the impress of consecration, the signature of glory, the pledge of testimony—for it is said, "He has set to his seal that God is true" (Jn. 3:33)[9]—and shoes, not those perishable ones which he who has set his foot on holy ground is bidden take off, nor such as he who is sent to preach the Kingdom of Heaven is forbidden to put on, but those that do not wear, and are suited for the journey to heaven,

---

[8] *Oration on Luke 15: Parable of the Prodigal Son,* translated by Rev. William Wilson. This fragment of a longer work by St. Clement has survived because it is quoted in an oration on Luke 15 by Macarius Chrysocephalus. The second part, however, starting at section 4, is in a different style and refers directly to the Novatian schism which took place after St. Clement's departure. The second unknown author is however very close to St. Clement in his general exegetical approach.

[9] The New King James translation reads "He who has received His testimony has certified that God is true" (Jn. 3:33).

becoming and adorning the heavenly path, such as unwashed feet never put on, but those which are washed by our Teacher and Lord.[10] Many, truly, are the shoes of the sinful soul, by which it is bound and cramped. For each man is cramped by the cords of his own sins. Accordingly, Abraham swears to the king of Sodom, "I will not take anything from all your goods, from a string to a shoelace" (Gen. 14:23). As a result of these being defiled and polluted on the earth, every kind of wrong and selfishness engrosses life. As the Lord reproves Israel by Amos, saying, "For three sins of Israel, yes, for four, I will not turn away from him; because they sold the righteous for silver, and the poor for sandals, with which to tread on the dust of the earth" (Am. 2:6, 7).

### 2.

Now the shoes which the Father bids the servant give to the repentant son who has taken himself to Him do not impede or drag to the earth (for the earthly tabernacle weighs down the anxious mind). But they are buoyant, and ascending, are carried to heaven, and serve as such a ladder and chariot as he requires who has turned his mind towards the Father. After being first beautifully adorned with all these things without, he beautifully enters into the gladness within.

For "Bring out" was said by Him Who had first said, "when he was still a great way off...[he] ran and fell on his neck." For it is here that all the preparation for entrance to the marriage to which we are invited must be accomplished. He, then, who has been made ready to enter will say, "Therefore this joy of Mine is fulfilled" (Jn. 3:29). But the unlovely and unsightly man will hear, "Friend, how did you come in here without a wedding garment?' And he was speechless" (Mt. 22:12). And the fat and humble food—the delicacies abundant and satisfying of the blessed—the fatted calf is killed. This is also spoken of as a lamb (not literally), that no one may suppose it small, but it is the great and greatest. For not small is "the Lamb of God Who takes away the sin of the world!" (Jn. 1:29), Who

---

[10] St. Ambrose of Milan comments on the attribute of protection afforded by the shoes given to the Prodigal Son by his father, saying, "[The father] orders the shoes to be brought out, for he who is about to celebrate the Lord's Passover, about to feast on the Lamb, ought to have his feet protected against all attacks of spiritual wild beasts and the bite of the serpent." *Concerning Repentance*, 2.3.18. NPNF, s. 2, v. 10.

"was led as a sheep to the slaughter" (Is. 53:7; Acts 8:32). The sacrifice full of marrow, all whose fat, according to the sacred law, was the Lord's. For He was wholly devoted and consecrated to the Lord; so well grown, and to such excessive size, as to reach and extend over all, and to fill those who eat Him and feed upon Him. For He is both flesh and bread, and has given Himself as both to us to be eaten.

To the sons, then, who come to Him, the Father gives the Calf, and it is slain and eaten. But those who do not come to Him He pursues and disinherits, and is found to be a most powerful bull. Here, by reason of His size and prowess, it is said of Him, "His glory is as that of a unicorn[11]" (Num. 23:22). And the Prophet Habakkuk sees Him bearing horns, and celebrates His defensive attitude: "horns in His hands" (Hab. 3:4). Therefore the sign shows His power and authority—horns that pierce on both sides, or rather, on all sides, and through everything. And those who eat are so strengthened and retain such strength from the life-giving food in them that they themselves are stronger than their enemies and are all but armed with the horns of a bull, as it is said, "In You we will push down our enemies" (Ps. 43:5).

### 3.

There is gladness, music and dancing (Lk. 15:25), although the elder son, who had always been completely obedient to the father, takes it unfavorably, when he who himself had never been away or profligate sees the guilty one made happy.

Accordingly, the father calls him, saying, "Son, you are always with me" (Lk. 15:31). And what greater joy, feast, and festivity can be than being continually with God, standing by His side and serving Him? "And all that I have is yours" (Lk. 15:31). And so, blessed is the heir of God, for whom the Father holds possession, the faithful, to whom the whole world of possessions belongs.

"It was right that we should make merry and be glad; for your brother was dead, and is alive again" (Lk 15:32). For, our kind Father gives all things life and raises the dead. "And was lost, and is found." And "blessed

---

[11] Some translations read "wild ox."

is he whom You have chosen and adopted" (Ps. 64:4), and whom having sought, You do find. "Blessed are they whose transgressions are forgiven and whose sins are covered" (Ps. 31:1).

It is man's duty to repent of his sins. But let this be accompanied by a change that will not be checked. For he who does not act so shall be put to shame, because he has acted not with his whole heart, but in haste. It is our duty also to flee to God. And let us endeavor after this ceaselessly and energetically. For He says, "Come to Me, all you who labor and are heavy laden, and I will give you rest" (Mt. 11:28). And prayer and confession with humility are voluntary acts. Therefore, it is commanded, "First confess your transgressions, that you may be justified" (Is. 43:26). But it is not right for us to judge what we shall obtain afterwards and what we shall be.

4.[12]

Such is the strict meaning of the parable. The repentant son came to the pitying Father, never hoping for these things—the best robe, and the ring, and the shoes—or to taste the fatted calf, or to share in gladness, or enjoy music and dances; but he would have been contented with obtaining what in his own estimation he deemed himself worth. "Make me," he had made up his mind to say, "like one of your hired servants" (Lk. 15:19). But when he saw the father's welcome meeting him, he did not say this, but said what he had in his mind to say first, "Father, I have sinned against heaven and in your sight" (Lk. 15:21). And so both his humility and his accusation became the cause of justification and glory. For the righteous man condemns himself in his first words.

Thus, the publican departed justified rather than the Pharisee. Then, the son did not know either what he was to obtain or how to take or use or put on himself the things given him, since he did not take the robe himself, and put it on. But it is said, "Put it on him" (Lk. 15:22). He did not himself put the ring on his finger, but those who were bidden "Put a ring on his hand." Nor did he put the shoes on himself, but it was they who heard "and sandals on his feet." These things were perhaps incredible

---

[12] Another author appears to have completed this work from this section.

to him and to others, and unexpected before they took place, but gladly received and praised were the gifts with which he was presented.

### 5.

The parable shows that the exercise of the faculty of reason has been accorded to each man. Therefore, the Prodigal is introduced, demanding from his father his portion, that is, of the state of mind, endowed by reason. For the possession of reason is granted to all, to the pursuit of what is good, and the avoidance of what is bad. But many who are furnished by God with this make a bad use of the knowledge that has been given them, and land in the profligacy of evil practices, and wickedly waste the substance of reason—the eye on disgraceful sights, the tongue on blasphemous words, the smell on offensive lustful excesses of pleasures, the mouth on swinish[13] gluttony, the hands on thefts, the feet on running into plots, the thoughts on impious counsels, the inclinations on indulgence on the love of ease, the mind on brutish pastime. They preserve nothing of the substance of reason unwasted.

Such a one, therefore, Christ represents in the parable, as a rational creature with his reason darkened and asking from the Divine Being what is suitable to reason. Then, as obtaining from God, and making a wicked use of what had been given, and especially of the benefits of baptism, which had been vouchsafed to him; whence also He calls him a prodigal; and then, after the dissipation of what had been given him, and again his restoration by repentance, [He represents] the love of God shown to him.

### 6.

For He says, "And bring the fatted calf here and kill it, and let us eat and be merry; for my son..." (Lk. 15:23, 24)—a name of nearest relationship, and indication of what is given to the faithful—"...was dead...and lost," an expression of the most extreme alienation. For what is more alien to the living than the lost and dead? For neither can be possessed anymore. But having from the nearest relationship fallen to the

---

[13] Sensual, brutish, or ill-mannered like swine.

most extreme alienation, again by repentance he returned to near relationship. For it is said, "Bring out the best robe" (Lk. 15:22), which was his at the moment he obtained baptism. I mean the glory of baptism, the remission of sins, and the communication of the other blessings, which he obtained immediately when he had touched the font. "And put a ring on his hand" (Lk. 15:22). Here is the mystery of the Trinity, which is the seal impressed on those who believe. "And put shoes on his feet," for "the preparation of the gospel of peace" (Eph. 6:15) and the whole course that leads to good actions.

### 7.

But whom Christ finds lost due to sins committed after baptism, Novatus, the enemy of God, resigns to destruction.[14] Do not let us then consider any fault if we repent; guarding against falling, let us, if we have fallen, retrace our steps. And while dreading to offend, let us, after offending, avoid despair and be eager to be confirmed; and on sinking, let us haste to rise up again. Let us obey the Lord, Who calls to us, "Come to Me, all you who labor...and I will give you rest" (Mt. 11:28). Let us employ the gift of reason for actions of prudence. Let us learn now abstinence from what is wicked, that we may not be forced to learn in the future. Let us employ life as a training school for what is good; and let us be roused to the hatred of sin. Let us bear about a deep love for the Creator; let us cleave to Him with our whole heart; let us not wickedly waste the substance of reason, like the Prodigal. Let us obtain the joy laid up, in which Paul exulting, exclaimed, "Who shall separate us from the love of Christ?" (Rom. 8:35).

To Him belongs glory and honor, with the Father and the Holy Spirit unto the age of ages. Amen.

---

[14] The Church during the days of St. Clement was plagued by the schismatic Novantus (i.e., Novatian, or Nauatus), a Roman priest who declared himself antipope. He was declared a heretic by the Church because he and his followers taught the inefficacy of repentance on the part of the apostates who denied Christ and sacrificed to pagan gods.

## "Do Not Love the World"

### St. Augustine of Hippo[15]

#### 1.

The Lord's command that "whoever desires to come after Me, let him deny himself" (Mk. 8:34) seems to be hard and grievous. But what He commands is not hard or grievous, Who aids us that what He commands may be done. For it is true which is said to Him in the Psalm, "By the words of Your lips I have observed hard ways" (Ps. 16:4). And it is true which He said Himself, "My yoke is easy, and My burden is light" (Mt. 11:30).

For whatever is hard in what is commanded us, love makes easy. We know what great things love itself can do. Very often is this love even abominable and impure. But how great hardships have men suffered? What indignities and intolerable things have they endured, to attain to the object of their love —whether it be a lover of money who is called covetous; or a lover of honor, who is called ambitious; or a lover of beautiful women, who is called lustful. And who can enumerate all types of loves? Yet consider what labor all lovers undergo, and are not conscious of their labors; and then does any such one most feel labor when he is hindered from labor?

Since, then, the majority of men are such as their loves are, and there should be no other care for the regulation of our lives than the choice of that which we should love, why do you wonder, if he who loves Christ and who wishes to follow Christ, for the love of Him denies himself? For if by loving himself man is lost, surely by denying himself he is found.

#### 2.

The first destruction of man was the love of himself. For if he had not loved himself, if he had preferred God to himself, he would have been willing to be ever subject unto God and would not have been turned to the

---

[15] St. Augustine, *Sermons on Selected Lessons of the New Testament,* Sermon 46, NPNF, s. 1, v. 6.

neglect of His will and the doing his own will. For to wish to do one's own will is to love oneself. Prefer instead God's will. Learn to love yourself by not loving yourself. So you may learn that it is a vice to love oneself, the Apostle speaks saying, "For men will be lovers of themselves" (2 Tim. 3:2).

But, can he who loves himself have any sure trust in himself? No, for he begins to love himself by forsaking God and is driven away from himself to love those things which are beyond himself to such a degree that, when the Apostle had said, "Men shall be lovers of themselves," he subjoined immediately, "lovers of money." Already you see that you are without. You have begun to love yourself; stand in yourself if you can. Why do you go outside? Have you, as being rich in money, become a lover of money? You have begun to love what is outside of you; you have lost yourself.

When a man's love, then, goes even away from himself to those things which are outside himself, he begins to share the vanity of his vain desires, and prodigal, as it were, to spend his strength. He is dissipated, exhausted, without resource or strength; he feeds swine, and wearied with this office of feeding swine, he at last remembers what he was and says, "How many of my father's hired servants have bread enough and to spare, and I perish with hunger!" (Lk. 15:17).

When the son in the parable says this, what is said about him who had squandered all he had on harlots, who wished to have in his own power what was being well kept for him with his Father, who wished to have it at his own disposal, who squandered all and was reduced to indigence? What is said about him? "But when he came to himself" (Lk. 15:17). If "he came to himself," he had gone away from himself. And since he had fallen from himself and had gone away from himself, he returns first to himself so that he may return to that state from which he had fallen away in falling from himself. For by falling away from himself, he remained in himself; so by returning to himself, he should not remain in himself, lest he again go away from himself.

Returning, then, to himself, that he might not remain in himself, what did he say? "I will arise and go to my Father" (Lk. 15:18). See, when he had fallen away from himself, he had fallen away from his Father. He had fallen away from himself, he had gone away from himself to those things which are outside. He returns to himself and goes to his Father, where he may keep himself in all security. So, if he had gone away from himself, let him also in returning to himself, from Whom he had gone away that he may "go to his Father," deny himself.

What does it mean to "deny himself?" Let him not trust in himself, let him feel that he is a man, and have respect for the words of the prophet, "Cursed is the man who trusts in man" (Jer. 17:5). Let him withdraw himself from himself, but not toward things below. Let him withdraw himself from himself, that he may cleave to God.

Whatever good he has, let him commit it to Him by Whom he was made; whatever of evil he has, he has made it for himself. The evil that is in him God did not make. Let him destroy what he himself has done, who has been thereby undone. "Let him deny himself," He says, "and take up his cross, and follow Me" (Mk. 8:34).

### 3.

And to where must the Lord be followed? We know where He has gone, [for it has been only] a very few days since we celebrated its solemn memorial. For He has risen again and ascended into heaven. To there must He be followed. Undoubtedly we must not despair of heaven, because He has Himself promised us. Not that man can do anything [to gain haven]. For heaven was far away from us before our Head had gone into heaven. But now why should we despair, if we are members of that Head? To there, then, He must be followed.

And who would be unwilling to follow Him to such a dwelling, especially since we are in so great travail on earth with fears and pains? Who would be unwilling to follow Christ there, where there is supreme joy, supreme peace, and perpetual security? It is good to follow Him there, but we must see by what way we are to follow. For the Lord Jesus did not say the words we are engaged in, when He had now risen from the dead.

He had not yet suffered. He had still to come to the Cross, to His dishonoring. He came to the outrages, the scourging, the thorns, the wounds, the mockeries, the insults, and death. The way is indeed rough; it slows you down so that you have no desire to follow. But follow on! Rough is the way which man has made for himself, but what Christ has tread in His passage is worn smooth.

Who does not desire exaltation? It is pleasing to all, but humility is the step toward it. Why do you put out your foot ahead of you? You have a mind to fall, not to ascend. Begin by the step, and so you have ascended. This is the step of humility to which those two disciples were unwilling to see, who said, "Grant us that we may sit, one at Your right hand, and the other at the left, in Your glory" (Mk. 10:37). They sought for exaltation, they did not see the step. But the Lord showed them this step. For what did He answer them? "You who seek the hill of exaltation, can you drink the cup of humiliation?" And therefore He does not say simply, "Let him deny himself, and follow Me," however, but He said more, "Let him take up his cross, and follow Me."

4.

What does it mean to say, "Let him take up his cross?" Let him bear whatever trouble he has, let him follow Me. For when he shall begin to follow Me in conformity to My life and precepts, he will have many to contradict him, he will have many to hinder him, he will have many to dissuade him, and that from those who are even, as it were, Christ's companions. They who hindered the blind men from crying out were walking with Christ (Mt. 20:31).

Therefore, whether they are threats or caresses, or whatsoever hindrances, if you wish to follow, turn them into your cross and bear it, carry it, do not give way beneath it. There seems to be an exhortation to martyrdom in these words of the Lord. If there is persecution, shouldn't all things be despised in consideration of Christ?

The world is loved, but let Him be preferred by Whom the world was made. Great is the world, but greater is He by Whom the world was made.

Beautiful is the world, but more beautiful is He by Whom the world was made. Sweet is the world, sweeter is He by Whom the world was made. Evil is the world, and good is He by Whom the world was made.

How shall I be able to explain and unravel what I have said? May God help me! For what have I said? Why have you applauded? See, it is but a question, and yet you have already applauded. How is the world evil, if He by Whom the world was made is good? Did not God make all things, "and behold they were very good" (Gen. 1:31)? Does not Scripture at each several work of creation testify that God made it good, by saying, "And God saw that it was good" (Gen. 1:8, 10, 12, 18, 21, 24) and at the end summed them all up together thus how that God had made them, "And, behold, they were very good?" (Gen. 1:31).

5.

How then is the world evil, and He good by Whom the world was made? How? Since, "the world was made through Him, and the world did not know Him" (Jn. 1:10). The world was made by Him, the heaven and earth and all things that are in them. "The world did not know Him," for the lovers of the world and the despisers of God truly do not know Him.

So, then, the world is evil, because they are evil who prefer the world to God. And He is good Who made the world, the heaven, and earth, the sea, and those who love the world. For this only, that they love the world and do not love God, He did not make in them. But He made everything that pertains to their nature, and whatever pertains to guiltiness, He did not make. This is what I said a little while ago, "Let man destroy what he has made so he will be well-pleasing to Him Who made him."

6.

For there is among men themselves a good world also, but one that has been made good from being evil. For he who first sinned made the whole world—if you take the word "world" for men, putting aside (what we call the world) the heaven and earth and all things that are in them—evil. The whole mass was corrupted in the root. God made man good, as the Scripture says, "God made man upright; but they have sought out many devices" (Eccl. 7:30).

Run from these "many" to One; gather up your scattered things into One; flow on together, fence yourself in, abide with One; go not to many things. There is blessedness. But we have flowed away, have gone on to perdition. We were all born with sin, and we added to this ancestral sin our evil living, and the whole world has become evil.

But Christ came, and He chose that which He made, not what He found, for He found all evil, and by His grace He made them good. And so another "world" was made which now persecutes the "world."

### 7.

What is the "world" which persecutes? That of which it is said to us, "Do not love the world, neither the things that are in the world. If anyone loves the world, the love of the Father is not in him. For all that is in the world— the lust of the flesh, the lust of the eyes, and the pride of life—is not of the Father, but of the world. And the world is passing away, and the lust of it: but he who does the will of God abides forever" (1 Jn. 2:15-17), even as God abides forever.

Behold, I have spoken of two "worlds:" the "world" which persecutes, and that which it persecutes. What is the "world" which persecutes? "All that is in the world—the lust of the flesh, and the lust of the eyes, and the pride of life —is not of the Father, but of the world" and "the world passes away" (1 Jn. 2:15). Behold, this is the "world" which persecutes. What is the "world" which it persecutes? "He who does the will of God abides forever," even as God abides forever.

### 8.

But see, that which persecutes is called the "world." Let us prove whether that also which suffers persecution is called "the world." What! Are you deaf to the voice of Christ who speaks, or rather to Holy Scripture, which testifies, "God was in Christ reconciling the world to Himself" (2 Cor. 5:19)? "If the world hates you, know that it first hated Me" (Jn. 15:18). See, the "world" hates. What does it hate but the "world?" What "world?"

"God was in Christ reconciling the world to Himself." The condemned "world" persecutes, the reconciled "world" suffers persecution. The condemned "world" is all that is without the Church, the reconciled "world" is the Church. For He says, "The Son of Man did not come to judge the world, but that the world through Him might be saved" (Jn. 3:17).

### 9.

Now in this world, holy, good, reconciled, saved, or rather to be saved, and now saved in hope, "for we are saved in this hope" (Rom. 8:24, KJV). in this world, I say, that is in the Church which wholly follows Christ, He has said as of universal application, "Whoever desires to come after Me, let him deny himself" (Mk. 8:34).

For it is not that the virgins should give ear to this, and the married women should not; or that the widows should, and the women who still have their husbands should not; or that monks should, and the married men should not; or that the clergy should, and the laymen should not. But let the whole Church, the whole Body, all the members, distinguished and distributed throughout their several offices, follow Christ. Let the whole Church follow Him, that only Church, let the Dove follow Him, let the Spouse follow Him, let Her who has been redeemed and endowed with the Bridegroom's Blood, follow Him. There, virgin purity has its place. There, widowed continence has its place. There, married chastity has its place. But adultery has no place of its own there and there is no room for lust, [which is] unlawful and indictable.

Let these several members which have their place there, in their kind and place and measure, "follow Christ." Let them "deny themselves," that is, let them presume nothing of themselves. Let them "take up their cross," that is, let them in the world endure for Christ's sake whatever the world may bring upon them. Let them love Him Who, alone, does not deceive and Who, alone, is not deceived. Let them love Him, for He promises what is true. But, because He does not give at once, faith wavers. Hold on, persevere, endure, bear delay, and you have borne the Cross.

### 10.

Let not the virgin say, "I shall alone be there." For Mary shall not be there alone but the widow, Anna, shall be there also. Let not the woman who has a husband say, "The widow will be there, not I." For it is not that Anna will be there, and Susanna will not be there. But, by all means, let them who would be there prove themselves hereby, that those who have a lower place here may not envy, but love in others the better place.

For example, my brethren (so that you may understand me), one man has chosen a married life, another a life of celibacy. If he who has chosen the married life has adulterous lusts, he has "looked back" if he has lusted after that which is unlawful. Also, he who would wish afterwards to return from celibacy to a married life, has "looked back." He has chosen what is in itself lawful, yet he has "looked back." Is marriage then to be condemned? No. Marriage is not to be condemned, but see where he had come from who has chosen it. He had already got before it. When he was living as a young man in voluptuousness,[16] marriage was before him and he was making his way towards it. But when he had chosen celibacy, marriage was behind him.

"Remember," says the Lord, "Lot's wife" (Lk. 17:32). Lot's wife, by looking behind, remained motionless. Then, to whatever point anyone has been able to reach, let him fear to "look back" from there and let him walk in the way, let him "follow Christ." "Forgetting those things which are behind and reaching forward to those things which are ahead," let him by an earnest inward intention "press toward the goal for the prize of the upward call of God in Christ Jesus" (Phil. 3:13, 14). Let those that are married regard the unmarried as above themselves; let them acknowledge that they are better; let them love in them what they themselves do not have; and let them in them love Christ.

---

[16] Gluttony, sensuality and luxury.

## A Prayer of Return to our Heavenly Father

O my dear Lord, You Who are my Heavenly Father, Who have seen me walk away in arrogance, defiance and ingratitude, Who were patient with me when I disobeyed Your law, and merciful when I return, Who accept me in my every return, although I do not deserve Your loving kindness, help me always to return to You, no matter how far I have travelled, how much I have wasted, or how long I have been absent. Help me to return to myself, to return to my Way, to return to You. For in Your presence is fullness of joy, and any second spent outside of Your precious embrace is wasted. Draw me, O Lord, unto You, so that I may experience the heavenly grace, and abide with You forever in Your heavenly mansion. Amen.

# VIII

## Give Me this Water that I May Not Thirst

*Meditations on the Sunday of the Samaritan Woman of the Great Lent*

### Gospel Reading of the Fourth Sunday of the Great Lent

#### (John 4:1-42)

*Therefore, when the Lord knew that the Pharisees had heard that Jesus made and baptized more disciples than John (though Jesus Himself did not baptize, but His disciples), He left Judea and departed again to Galilee. But He needed to go through Samaria.*

*So He came to a city of Samaria which is called Sychar, near the plot of ground that Jacob gave to his son Joseph. Now Jacob's well was there. Jesus therefore, being wearied from His journey, sat thus by the well. It was about the sixth hour.*

*A woman of Samaria came to draw water. Jesus said to her, "Give Me a drink." For His disciples had gone away into the city to buy food. Then the woman of Samaria said to Him, "How is it that You, being a Jew, ask a drink from me, a Samaritan woman?" For Jews have no dealings with Samaritans.*

*Jesus answered and said to her, "If you knew the gift of God, and Who it is Who says to you, 'Give Me a drink,' you would have asked Him, and He would have given you living water."*

*The woman said to Him, "Sir, You have nothing to draw with, and the well is deep. Where then do You get that living water? Are You greater than our father Jacob, who gave us the well, and drank from it himself, as well as his sons and his livestock?"*

*Jesus answered and said to her, "Whoever drinks of this water will thirst again, but whoever drinks of the water that I shall give him will never thirst. But the water that I shall give him will become in him a fountain of water springing up into everlasting life."*

*The woman said to Him, "Sir, give me this water, that I may not thirst, nor come here to draw."*

*Jesus said to her, "Go, call your husband, and come here." The woman answered and said, "I have no husband."*

*Jesus said to her, "You have well said, 'I have no husband,' for you have had five husbands, and the one whom you now have is not your husband; in that you spoke truly."*

*The woman said to Him, "Sir, I perceive that You are a prophet. Our fathers worshipped on this mountain, and you Jews say that in Jerusalem is the place where one ought to worship."*

*Jesus said to her, "Woman, believe Me, the hour is coming when you will neither on this mountain, nor in Jerusalem, worship the Father. You worship what you do not know; we know what we worship, for salvation is from the Jews. But the hour is coming, and now is, when the true worshipers will worship the Father in spirit and truth; for the Father is seeking such to worship Him. God is Spirit, and those who worship Him must worship in spirit and truth."*

*The woman said to Him, "I know that Messiah is coming" (Who is called Christ). "When He comes, He will tell us all things."*

*Jesus said to her, "I Who speak to you am He."*

*And at this point His disciples came, and they marveled that He talked with a woman; yet no one said, "What do You seek?" or, "Why are You talking with her?"*

*The woman then left her waterpot, went her way into the city, and said to the men, "Come, see a Man Who told me all things that I ever did. Could this be the Christ?" Then they went out of the city and came to Him.*

*In the meantime His disciples urged Him, saying, "Rabbi, eat." But He said to them, "I have food to eat of which you do not know." Therefore the disciples said to one another, "Has anyone brought Him anything to eat?"*

*Jesus said to them, "My food is to do the will of Him Who sent Me, and to finish His work. Do you not say, 'There are still four months and then comes the harvest?' Behold, I say to you, lift up your eyes and look at the fields, for they are already white for harvest! And he who reaps receives wages, and gathers fruit for eternal life, that both he who sows and he who reaps may rejoice together. For in this the saying is true: 'One sows and another reaps.' I sent you to reap that for which you have not labored; others have labored, and you have entered into their labors."*

*And many of the Samaritans of that city believed in Him because of the word of the woman who testified, "He told me all that I ever did." So when the Samaritans had come to Him, they urged Him to stay with them; and He stayed there two days. And many more believed because of His own word.*

*Then they said to the woman, "Now we believe, not because of what you said, for we ourselves have heard Him and we know that this is indeed the Christ, the Savior of the world."*

## INTRODUCTORY NOTE

The approximate location of the village from which the Samaritan Woman came is clear: the vicinity of Jacob's well in the narrow valley between Mount Ebal and Mount Gerizim on the direct route between Galilee and Jerusalem. Over the well stands an unfinished Greek Orthodox Church, begun during the Czarist regime and abandoned when the Communists took over in Russia.[1]

Jacob's well was dug by the patriarch Jacob when he came to Shechem (Gen. 33:18). With strict water laws for people and their herds, this was a wise thing to do. It has a narrow opening, wide enough for a man to fit tightly and tunneled about 105 feet into the earth. Today, the well is dried up, and is only 75 feet deep due to trash that has been placed in the well

---

[1] H. F. Vos, *Nelson's New Illustrated Bible Manners & Customs: How the People of the Bible Really Lived* (Nashville: Thomas Nelson, 1999).

over the years. The site of Jacob's well is acknowledged by Jews, Muslims, and Christians.

## "To Save Us"

### St. John Chrysostom[2]

He indeed did not baptize, but they who carried the news, desiring to excite their hearers to envy, so reported. Why, then, did He depart [for Samaria]? Not from fear, but to take away their malice and to soften their envy. He was indeed able to restrain them when they came against Him, but this He would not do continually, that the Dispensation of the Flesh might not be disbelieved. For had He often been seized and escaped, this would have been suspected by many. Therefore, for the most part, He rather orders matters after the manner of a man. And as He desired it to be believed that He was God, so also that, being God, He bore the flesh. Therefore even after the Resurrection, He said to the disciple, "Handle Me and see, for a spirit does not have flesh and bones" (Lk. 24:39). Therefore also He rebuked Peter when He said, "Far be it from You, Lord; this shall not happen to You!" (Mt. 16:22). So much was this matter an object of care to Him.

For this is no small part of the doctrines of the Church; it is the chief point of the salvation wrought for us, by which everything has come to be, and has had success, for it was thus that the bonds of death were loosed, sin taken away, and the curse abolished, and ten thousand blessings introduced into our life. And therefore He especially desired that the Dispensation should be believed, as having been the root and fountain of innumerable goods to us. Yet while acting thus in regard of His Humanity, He did not allow His Divinity to be overcast. And so, after His departure He again employed the same language as before. For He went not away into Galilee simply, but to effect certain important matters, those among the Samaritans; nor did He dispense these matters simply, but with the wisdom that belonged to Him, and so as not to leave to the Jews any pretense even of a shameless excuse for themselves.

---

[2] St. John Chrysostom, *Commentary on John*, NPNF s. 1, v. 14, 251-252.

## "The Living Water as Daily Renewal"

### The Scholar Origen[3]

Consider therefore whether it may be as follows. Although, on the one hand, the Lord Jesus is "the Bread of Life" (Jn. 6:35, 48), and He Himself feeds the hungry souls, on the other hand, He admits that He hungers when He says, "I was hungry, and you gave Me food" (Mt. 25:35). Again, on the one hand, although He is "the living water" (Jn. 7:38) and gives drink to all who thirst, on the other hand, He says to the Samaritan woman, "Give Me to drink" (Jn. 4:7). So also, although the prophetic word gives drink to the thirsting, it is nevertheless said to be given a drink by these when it receives the exercises and vigilances of the zealous. A soul such as this, then, which does all things patiently, which is so eager and is secured with so much learning, which has been accustomed to draw streams of knowledge from the depths, can be united in marriage with Christ.

Therefore, unless you come daily to the wells, unless you daily draw water, not only will you not be able to give a drink to others, but you yourself also will suffer "a thirst for the Word of God" (Am. 8:11, NKJV). Hear also the Lord saying in the gospels, "If anyone thirsts, let him come to Me and drink" (Jn. 7:37). But, as I see it, you neither hunger nor thirst for righteousness (Mt. 5:6). So, how will you be able to say, "As the deer pants after the fountains of water, so my soul pants after You, O God. My soul has thirsted after the living God; when shall I come and appear before His presence" (Ps. 41:2, 3)?

## "Encountering the Beloved"

### St. Augustine of Hippo[4]

#### 1.

It is nothing new to your ears, beloved, that the Evangelist John, like an eagle, takes a loftier flight, and soars above the dark mist of earth,

---

[3] Origen, *Homilies on Genesis 10.3*, FCS 71:161, 62.
[4] St. Augustine, *Tracates on John*, Tracate 15, NPNF, s. 1, v. 7.

to gaze with steadier eyes upon the light of truth. From his gospel much has already been treated and discussed through our ministry, with the Lord's help; and the passage which has been read today follows in due order. What I am about to say, with the Lord's permission, many of you will hear in such a way that you will be reviewing what you know, rather than learning what you do not know. Yet, for all that, your attention should not be slack, because it is not an acquiring, but a reviewing, of knowledge. This has been read, and we have in our hands to discourse upon this passage—that which the Lord Jesus spoke with the Samaritan woman at Jacob's well. The things spoken there are great mysteries, and the resemblance of great things: feeding the hungry, and refreshing the weary soul.

### 2.

Now, "When the Lord knew that the Pharisees had heard that Jesus made and baptized more disciples than John (though Jesus Himself did not baptize, but His disciples), He left Judea and departed again to Galilee" (Jn. 4:1-3). We must not discourse of this too long, lest, by dwelling on what is manifest, we shall lack the time to investigate and lay open what is obscure.

Certainly, if the Lord saw that the fact of their coming to know that He made more disciples, and baptized more, would so avail to salvation to the Pharisees in following Him, as to become themselves His disciples, and to desire to be baptized by Him, then He would not have left Judea, but would have remained there for their sakes. But because He knew their knowledge of the fact, and at the same time knew their envy, and that they learned this, not to follow, but to persecute him, He departed from there.

Indeed, if He did not want to be taken from them, He could have prevented this, even when He was present. He had it in His power not to be put to death, if He did not want to, since He had the power not to be born, if He did not want to. But because, in everything that He did as man, He was showing an example to those who were to believe in Him. That is, any servant of God does not sin if he retires into another place, when he might sees the rage of his persecutors, or of those who seek to bring his soul into evil. But if a servant of God did this he might appear to commit sin, had not the Lord led the way in doing it. Thus, that good Master did this to teach us, not because He feared it.

### 3.

It may perhaps surprise you why it is said that "Jesus baptized more than John," and after this was said, it is subjoined, "although Jesus baptized not, but His disciples" (Jn. 4:1, 2). What, then? Was the statement made false, and then corrected by this addition? Or are both true, i.e., that Jesus both did and did not baptize? He did in fact baptize, because it was He that cleansed; and He did not baptize, because it was not He that touched. The disciples supplied the ministry of the body; He afforded the aid of His majesty. Now, when could He cease from baptizing, so long as He ceased not from cleansing? Of Him it is said by the same John, in the person of the Baptist, who says, "This is He Who baptizes" (Jn. 1:33). Jesus, therefore, is still baptizing, and so long as we continue to be baptized, Jesus baptizes. Let a man come without fear to the minister below; for he has a Master above.

### 4.

But one may say, "Christ does indeed baptize, but in Spirit, not in Body." As if, indeed, it were by the gift of another than Him that any is blessed even with the mystery of corporal and visible baptism. Would you know that it is He Who baptizes, not only with the Spirit, but also with water? Hear the Apostle: "Just as Christ," he says, "loved the Church, and gave Himself for Her, that He might sanctify and cleanse Her with the washing of water by the word, that He might present Her to Himself a glorious Church, not having spot or wrinkle or any such thing" (Eph. 5:25-27). How does He sanctify Her? "With the washing of water by the Word." What is the baptism of Christ? The washing of water by the Word. Take away the water, it is not baptism; take away the Word, it is not baptism.

### 5.

This much, then, on the preliminary circumstances, by occasion of which He came to a conversation with that woman. Now, let us look at the matters that remain, matters full of mysteries. "But He needed to go through Samaria. So He came to a city of Samaria which is called Sychar, near the plot of ground that Jacob gave to his son Joseph. Now Jacob's well was there" (Jn. 4:4-6). It was a well, but every well is a fountain, yet not every fountain a well. For where the water flows from the earth and offers itself for use to them that draw it, it is called a fountain; but if accessible, and on the surface, it is called only a fountain; if, however, it be deep and far down, it is called a well, but in such way as not to lose the name of fountain.

6.

"Jesus therefore, being wearied from His journey, sat thus by the well. It was about the sixth hour" (Jn. 4:6). Now begin the mysteries. For it is not without a purpose that Jesus is weary; not indeed without a purpose that the strength of God is weary; not without a purpose that He is weary, by Whom the wearied are refreshed; not without a purpose is He weary, by Whose absence we are wearied, by Whose presence we are strengthened. Nevertheless Jesus is weary, and weary with His journey; and He sits down, and that, too, near a well; and it is at the sixth hour that, being wearied, He sits down. All these things hint something, are intended to intimate something; they make us eager, and encourage us to knock. May He open to us and to you, He Who has condescended to exhort us, saying, "Knock, and it will be opened to you" (Lk. 11:9).

It was for you that Jesus was wearied with His journey. We find Jesus to be strength, and we find Jesus to be weak. We find a strong and a weak Jesus: strong, because "In the beginning was the Word, and the Word was with God, and the Word was God: He was in the beginning with God" (Jn. 1:1, 2). Would you see how this Son of God is strong? "All things were made through Him, and without Him was nothing made that was made" (Jn. 1:3), and they were also made without labor. Then what can be stronger than He, by Whom all things were made without labor? Do you know Him to be weak? "The Word became flesh, and dwelt among us" (Jn. 1:14). The strength of Christ created you; the weakness of Christ created you anew. The strength of Christ caused that to be which was not; the weakness of Christ caused that what was should not perish. He fashioned us by His strength; He sought us by His weakness.

### 7.

As weak, then, He nourishes the weak, as a hen her chicks, for He likened Himself to a hen: "How often," He says to Jerusalem, "I wanted to gather your children together, as a hen gathers her brood under her wings; but you were not willing!" (Lk. 13:34, Mt. 23:37). And you see, brethren, how a hen becomes weak with her chicks. No other bird, when it is a mother, is recognized at once to be so. We see all kinds of sparrows building their nests before our eyes; we see swallows, storks, and doves, every day building their nests, but we do not know them to be parents, except when we see them on their nests. But the hen is so enfeebled over her brood, that even if the chickens are not following her, if you see not the young ones, yet you immediately know she is a mother. With her wings drooping, her feathers ruffled, her tone hoarse, in all her limbs she becomes so sunken and abject, that, as I have said, even though you do not see young, yet you perceive her to be a mother. In such manner was Jesus weak, wearied from His journey. His journey is the flesh assumed for us. For how can He, Who is present everywhere, have a journey, He Who is nowhere absent?

Where does He go, or from where, but that He could not come to us, except He had assumed the form of visible flesh? Therefore, as He condescended to come to us in such manner, that He appeared in the form of a servant by the flesh assumed, that same assumption of flesh is His journey. Thus, "wearied from His journey," what else is it but wearied in the flesh? Jesus was weak in the flesh, but for you, do not become weak, but be strong in His weakness, because what is "the weakness of God is stronger than men" (1 Cor. 1:25).

### 8.

Under this image of things, Adam, who was the figure of Him Who was to come, afforded us a great indication of this mystery. Rather, God afforded it in him. For he was deemed worthy to receive a wife while he slept, and that wife was made for him of his own rib; since from Christ, sleeping on the Cross, was the Church to come—from His side, namely, as He slept. For it was from His side, pierced with the spear, as He hung on the Cross, that the Mysteries of the Church flowed forth.

But why have I chosen to say this, brethren? Because it is the weakness of Christ that makes us strong. A remarkable figure of this went before in the case of Adam. God could have taken flesh from the man to make of it a woman, and it seems that this might have been the more suitable.

[For if it was] the weaker gender that was being made, then weakness should have been made of flesh rather than of bone, for the bones are the stronger parts it the flesh. [But] He did not take flesh to make from it a woman, but took a bone, and from the bone the woman was shaped. And flesh was filled in into the place of the bone. He could have restored bone for bone; He could have taken, not a rib, but flesh, for the making of the woman. What, then, did this signify? Woman was made, as it were, strong, from the rib; Adam was made, as it were, weak, from the flesh. It is Christ and the Church; His weakness is our strength.

### 9.

But why at "the sixth hour?" Because [it represents] the sixth age of the world. In the Gospel, count up as an hour each, the first age from Adam to Noah; the second, from Noah to Abraham; the third, from Abraham to David; the fourth, from David to the removing to Babylon; the fifth, from the removing to Babylon to the baptism of John. Then, the sixth is enacted.

Why do you marvel? Jesus came, and, by humbling Himself, He came to a well. He came wearied, because He carried weak flesh. At the sixth hour, in the sixth age of the world. To a well, because to the depth of this our habitation. For which reason it is said in the Psalm: "Out of the depths I have cried out to You, O Lord" (Ps. 129:1). He sat, as I said, because He was humbled.

### 10.

And there came "a woman"—the figure of the Church not yet justified. But now, she is about to be justified: for this is the subject of the discourse. She comes ignorant, she finds Him, and there is a dealing with her. Let us see how and why.

"A woman of Samaria came to draw water" (Jn. 4:7). The Samaritans did not belong to the nation of the Jews. They were foreigners, although they inhabited neighboring lands. It would take a long time to relate the origin of the Samaritans; that we may not be detained by long discourse of this, and leave necessary matters unsaid, suffice to say, then, that we regard the Samaritans as foreigners.

And, lest you should think that I have said this with more boldness than truth, hear the Lord Jesus Himself. He said about that Samaritan, one of the ten lepers whom He had cleansed, who alone returned to give thanks, "Were there not ten cleansed? But where are the nine? Were there not any found who returned to give glory to God except this foreigner?" (Lk. 17:17).[5] It is pertinent to the image of the reality, that this woman, who bore the type of the Church, comes of strangers: for the Church was to come of the Gentiles, a foreigner from the race of the Jews. In that woman, then, let us hear ourselves, and in her, acknowledge ourselves, and in her, give thanks to God for ourselves. For she was the figure, not the reality; for she both first showed forth the figure and became the reality. For she believed on Him Who, of her, set the figure before us. She had come, then, "to draw water," as people were accustomed, whether they are men or women.

### 11.

"Jesus said to her, 'Give Me a drink.'" For His disciples had gone away into the city to buy food. Then the Samaritan woman said to Him, 'How is it that You, being a Jew, ask a drink of me, a Samaritan woman?' For the Jews have no dealings with Samaritans" (Jn. 4:7-9). You see that they were foreigners. Indeed, the Jews would not use their vessels. And as the woman brought with her a vessel with which to draw the water, it made her wonder that a Jew sought drink from her—a thing which the Jews were

---

[5] St. Augustine is in harmony with other Fathers, such as St. Cyril of Alexandria, who stress the same point using the miracle of our Lord healing the ten lepers in Luke 17:1-19: "The stranger, a Samaritan, was of foreign race brought from Assyria...It shows that the Samaritans were grateful but that the Jews, even when they benefited, were ungrateful." St. Cyril of Alexandria, *Commentary on the Gospel of St. Luke*, trans. R. Payne Smith (n.p.: Studion Publishers, 1983). Out of the ten lepers who were healed, only one-the Samaritan, the foreigner-returned to thank our Lord Jesus Christ and give glory to Him, reflecting our Lord's words, "For many are called, but few are chosen" (Mt. 22:14), and elsewhere, "for many, I say to you, will seek to enter and will not be able" (Lk. 13:24, 25).

not accustomed to do. But He Who was asking for drink was thirsting for the faith of the woman herself.

### 12.

At length, hear Who it is Who asks a drink: "Jesus answered and said unto her, 'If you knew the gift of God, and Who it is Who said to you, "Give Me to drink," you would, it may be, have asked of Him, and He would have given you living water'" (Jn. 4:10). He asks to drink, and promises to give drink. He longs as one about to receive; He abounds as one about to satisfy.

"If you knew," He says, "the gift of God." The gift of God is the Holy Spirit. Yet, He speaks to the woman guardedly, and enters into her heart by degrees. It may be He is now teaching her. For what can be sweeter and kinder than that exhortation? "If you knew the gift of God..." Thus far, He keeps her in suspense. That is commonly called living water which issues from a spring; that which is collected from rain in pools and cisterns is not called living water. And it may have flowed from a spring. But, if it should stand collected in some place, not admitting to it that from which it flowed, but, with the course interrupted, separated, as it were, from the channel of the fountain, it is not called "living water," but that is called living water which is taken as it flows. Such water there was in that fountain. Why, then, did He promise to give that which He was asking?

### 13.

The woman, however, being in suspense, says to Him, "Sir, You have nothing to draw with, and the well is deep" (Jn. 4:11). See how she understood the living water, simply the water which was in that fountain. "You will give me living water? But I carry that with which to draw, and You do not. The living water is here; how are You going to give it me?" Understanding another thing, and taking it physically, she does in a manner knock, that the Master may open up that which is closed. She was knocking in ignorance, not with earnest purpose; she is still an object of pity, not yet of instruction.

14.

The Lord speaks somewhat more clearly of that living water. Now the woman had said, "Are You greater than our father Jacob, who gave us the well, and drank of it himself, his children, and his cattle?" (Jn. 4:12). You cannot give me of the living water of this well, because You have nothing to draw with: perhaps You promised another fountain? Can You be better than our father, who dug this well, and used it himself? Let the Lord, then, declare what He called living water.

"Jesus answered and said unto her, 'Every one who drinks of this water will thirst again, but whoever drinks of the water that I shall give him, will never thirst. But the water that I shall give him will become in him a fountain of water, springing up into everlasting life'" (Jn. 4:13, 14). The Lord has spoken more openly: "It shall become in him a fountain of water, springing up into everlasting life. He that drinks of this water shall not thirst forever." He promises something not visible, but invisible water. How clear is it that He was speaking, not in a physical, but in a spiritual sense?

15.

Still, however, the woman has her mind on the flesh. She is delighted with the thought of thirsting no more, and fancies that this was promised to her by the Lord after a physical sense; which it will be indeed, but in the Resurrection of the dead. She desired this now. God had indeed granted once to His servant Elijah, that during forty days he neither hungered nor thirsted. Could not He give this always, seeing He had power to give it during forty days? She, however, sighed for it, desiring to have no want, no toil. To be always coming to that fountain, to be burdened with a weight with which to supply her want, and, when that which she had drawn is spent, to be obliged to return again. This was a daily toil to her, because that want of hers was to be relieved, not extinguished. Such a gift as Jesus promised delighted her; she asks Him to give her living water.

16.

Nevertheless, let us not overlook the fact that it is something spiritual that the Lord was promising. What does, "Whoever shall drink of this water shall thirst again" (Jn. 4:13) mean? It is true as to this water and what the water signified. Since the water in the well is the pleasure of the world in its dark depth: from this, men draw it with the vessel of lusts. Stooping forward, they let down the lust to reach the pleasure fetched from the depth of the well and enjoy the pleasure and the preceding lust let down to fetch it. For whoever has not dispatched his lust in advance cannot reach the pleasure.

Consider lust, then, as the vessel and pleasure as the water from the depth of the well. When one has reached for the pleasure of this world, it is food for him, it is drink, it is a bath, a show, an affair. Can it be that he will not thirst again? Therefore, He says, "Whoever shall drink of this water will thirst again." But if he shall receive water from Me, "he shall never thirst." "We shall be filled," it says, "with the good things of Your house" (Ps. 64:5). Of what water, then, is He to give, but of that of which it is said, "With You is the fountain of life" (Ps. 35:10)? For how shall they thirst, who "shall be satisfied with the fatness of Your house" (Ps. 35:8)?

### 17.

What He was promising them was a certain feeding and abundant fullness of the Holy Spirit. But the woman did not yet understand, and not understanding, how did she answer? "The woman said to Him, 'Sir, give me this water, that I may not thirst, nor come here to draw'" (Jn. 4:15). Want forced her to labor and her weakness was pleading against the toil. Perhaps she heard the invitation, "Come to Me, all you who labor and are heavy laden, and I will give you rest" (Mt. 11:28). This is, in fact, what Jesus was saying to her, that she might no longer labor. But she did not yet understand.

### 18.

At length, wishing her to understand, "Jesus said to her, 'Go, call your husband, and come here'" (Jn. 4:16). What does this mean, "Call your husband?" Was it through her husband that He wished to give her that water? Or, because she did not understand, did He wish to teach her through her husband? Perhaps it was as the Apostle says concerning women, "If they want to learn something, let them ask their own husbands at home" (1 Cor. 14:35). But this the Apostle says of that where there is no

Jesus present to teach. It is said, in short, to women whom the Apostle was forbidding to speak in the Church (1 Cor. 14:34). But when the Lord Himself was at hand, and in person speaking to her, what need was there that He should speak to her by her husband? Was it through her husband that he spoke to Mary, while sitting at His feet and receiving His word; while Martha, wholly occupied with much serving, murmured at the happiness of her sister (Lk. 10:40)?

Therefore, my brethren, let us hear and understand what it is that the Lord says to the woman, "Call your husband." For it may be that He is saying also to our soul, "Call your husband." Let us inquire also concerning the soul's husband. Why is not Jesus Himself already the soul's real husband? Let the understanding be present, since what we are about to say can hardly be apprehended except by attentive hearers. Therefore, let the understanding be present to apprehend, and perhaps that same understanding will be found to be the husband of the soul.

### 19.

Now Jesus, seeing that the woman did not understand, and willing her to understand, says to her, "Call your husband."

"For the reason why you know not what I say is, because your understanding is not present. I am speaking after the Spirit, and you are hearing after the flesh. The things which I speak relate neither to the pleasure of the ears, nor to the eyes, nor to the smell, nor to the taste, nor to the touch. By the mind alone are they received; by the understanding alone are they drawn up. That understanding is not with you, how can you understand what I am saying? 'Call your husband' [means] bring your understanding forward. What is it for you to have a soul? It is not much, for a beast has a soul. In what way are you better than the beast? In having understanding, which the beast has not."

"Then what is 'Call your husband'?"

"You do not apprehend Me, you do not understand Me. I am speaking to you of the gift of God, and your thought is of the flesh. You do not wish to thirst in a carnal sense. I, Myself, am addressing to the Spirit. Your understanding is absent. Call your husband. Do not be as the horse and mule, which have no understanding."

Therefore, my brethren, to have a soul, and not to have understanding, that is, not to use it, not to live according to it, is a beast's life. For we have somewhat in common with the beasts, that by which we live in the flesh, but it must be ruled by the understanding. For the motions of the soul, which move after the flesh, and long to run unrestrainedly loose after carnal delights, are ruled over by the understanding.

Which is to be called the husband: that which rules, or that which is ruled? Without doubt, when the life is well ordered the understanding rules the soul, for itself belongs to the soul. For the understanding is not something other than the soul, but a thing of the soul: as the eye is not something other than the flesh, but a thing of the flesh. But while the eye is a thing of the flesh, yet it alone enjoys the light; and the other fleshy members may be steeped in light, but they cannot feel the light. The eye alone is both bathed in it, and enjoys it. Thus, in our soul there is something called understanding. This something of the soul, which is called understanding and mind, is enlightened by the higher light. Now that higher light, by which the human mind is enlightened, is God. For "That was the true Light Which gives light to every man coming into the world" (Jn. 1:9).

Such a light was Christ, such a light was speaking with the woman yet she was not present with the understanding, to have it enlightened with that light; not merely to have it shed upon it, but to enjoy it. Therefore the Lord said, "Call your husband," as if He were saying, "I wish to enlighten, and yet there is not here whom I may enlighten. Bring here the understanding through which you may be taught, by which you may be ruled." Thus, consider the soul without the understanding is the "woman," and having the understanding is having "the husband."

But this husband does not rule the wife well, except when he is ruled by a Higher [One]. For "the head of every man is Christ, the head of woman is man" (1 Cor. 11:3). The Head of the man was talking with the woman, and the man was not present. And so the Lord, as if He said, "Bring here your head, that he may receive his head," says, "Call your husband, and come here"—that is, be here, be present. For you are as absent, while you do not understand the voice of the Truth present here. Be present here, but not alone. Be here with your husband.

### 20.

Since the husband was not yet called, she still does not understand, still she minds the flesh, for the man is absent. She says, "I have no husband" (Jn. 4:17), and the Lord proceeds and utters mysteries. You may understand that this woman really had no husband then. She was living with some man, not a lawful husband, rather a paramour.[6] And the Lord said to her, "You have well said, 'I have no husband'" (Jn. 4:17, 18). How then did You say, "Call your husband"?

Now hear how the Lord knew well that she had no husband "He says to her..." In case the woman might suppose that the Lord had said, "You have well said, 'I have no husband,'" just because He had learned this fact from her, and not because He knew it by His own divinity, He speaks something which she has not said, "For you have had five husbands, and the one whom you now have is not your husband; in that you spoke truly" (Jn. 4:18).

### 21.

Again, He urges us to investigate the matter somewhat more exactly concerning these five husbands. Many have in fact understood (not indeed absurdly, nor so far improbably) the five husbands of this woman to mean the five books of Moses. For the Samaritans' made use of these books, and were under the same law: for it was from it they had circumcision.

But since we are hemmed in by what follows, "And the one whom you now have is not your husband," it appears to me that we can more easily take the five senses of the body to be the five former husbands of the soul. For when one is born, before he can make use of the mind and reason, he is ruled only by the senses of the flesh. In a little child, the soul seeks for or shuns what is heard, seen, smells, tastes, touches. It seeks for whatever soothes, and shuns whatever offends, those five senses. At first, the soul lives according to these five senses, as five husbands, because it is ruled by them.

---

[6] The illicit lover of a woman.

But why are they called husbands? Because they are lawful and right, made indeed by God, and are the gifts of God to the soul. The soul is still weak while ruled by these five husbands, and living under these five husbands. But when she comes to years of exercising reason, if she is taken in hand by the noble discipline and teaching of wisdom, these five men are succeeded in their rule by no other than the true and lawful husband, and one better than they, who both rules better and rules for eternity, who cultivates and instructs her for eternity. For the five senses rule us, not for eternity, but for those temporal things that are to be sought or shunned.

But when the understanding, imbued by wisdom, begins to rule the soul, it knows now not only how to avoid a pit, and to walk on even ground—a thing which the eyes show to the soul even in its weakness; nor merely to be charmed with musical voices and to repel harsh sounds; nor to delight in agreeable scents and to refuse offensive smells; nor to be captivated by sweetness and displeased with bitterness; nor to be soothed with what is soft and hurt with what is rough. For all these things are necessary to the soul in its weakness.

Then what rule is made use of by that understanding? Not for one to discern between black and white, but between just and unjust, between good and evil, between the profitable and the unprofitable, and between chastity and impurity—so that it may love the one and avoid the other—between charity and hatred, to be in the one, not to be in the other.

### 22.

This husband had not yet succeeded to those five husbands in that woman. And where he does not succeed, error sways. For when the soul has begun to be capable of reason, it is ruled either by the wise mind or by error: but yet error does not rule but destroys. Thus, after these five senses was that woman still wandering, and error was tossing her to and fro. And this error was not a lawful husband, but a paramour: for that reason the Lord says to her, "You have well said, I have not a husband. For you have had five husbands."

The five senses of the flesh ruled you at first; you are come to the age of using reason, and yet you are not come to wisdom, but are fallen into error. Therefore, after those five husbands, "this whom you now have is not your husband." And if not a husband, what was he but a paramour? And so, "Call," not the paramour, but "your husband," that you may receive Me with the understanding, and not by error have some false notion of Me.

For the woman was still in error, as she was thinking of that water; while the Lord was now speaking of the Holy Spirit. Why was she erring, but because she had a paramour, not a husband? Put away, therefore, that paramour who corrupts you, and "Go, call your husband." Call, and come so that you may understand Me.

### 23.

"The woman said unto Him, 'Sir, I perceive that You are a prophet'" (Jn. 4:19). The husband begins to come, but he has not yet fully arrived. She considered the Lord a prophet; and a prophet indeed He was, for it was of Himself He said that "a prophet is not without honor, except in his own country" (Mt. 13:57). Again, of Him it was said to Moses, "I will raise up for them a Prophet of their brethren like you" (Deut. 18:18). "Like," here, relates to the form of the flesh, but not in the eminence of His majesty. Accordingly, we find the Lord Jesus called a prophet. Hence this woman is now not far wrong. "I perceive," she says, "that you are a prophet." She begins to call the husband, and to shut out the paramour; she begins to ask about a matter that is accustomed to disturb her.

For there was a contention between the Samaritans and the Jews, because the Jews worshipped God in the temple built by Solomon; but the Samaritans, being situated at a distance from it, did not worship there. For this reason the Jews, because they worshipped God in the temple, boasted themselves to be better than the Samaritans. "For the Jews have no dealings with the Samaritans" because the latter said to them, "How can you boast and account yourselves to be better than we, just because you have a temple which we do not have? Did our fathers, who were pleasing to God, worship in that temple? Was it not in this mountain where we are they worshipped? We then do better," they say, "who pray to God in this mountain, where our fathers prayed." Both peoples contended in ignorance because they did not have the husband. They were inflated against each other, on the one side on behalf of the temple, on the other on behalf of the mountain.

## 24.

What, however, does the Lord teach the woman now, as one whose husband has begun to be present? "The woman said to Him, 'Sir, I perceive that you are a prophet. Our fathers worshipped in this mountain; and you say that in Jerusalem is the place where men should worship.' Jesus said to her, 'Woman, believe Me'" (Jn. 4:19, 20). For the Church, as it is said in the Song of Songs, "will come, and will pass over from the beginning of faith" (Song 4:8). She will come to pass through, but she cannot pass through except from the beginning of faith. Now, she rightly hears since the husband is present: "Woman, believe Me. For there is that in you now which can believe, since your husband is present. You have begun to be present with the understanding when you called Me a prophet. Woman, believe Me; for if you do not believe, you will not understand (cf. Is. 7:9). Therefore, 'Woman, believe Me, for the hour will come when you shall neither in this mountain nor in Jerusalem worship the Father. You worship you do not know; we know what we worship; for salvation is from the Jews'" (Jn. 4:21, 22).

"But the hour is coming." When? "And now is." Well, what hour? "When the true worshippers will worship the Father in spirit and in truth," neither on this mountain, nor in the temple, but in spirit and in truth. "For the Father is seeking such to worship Him" (Jn. 4:23). Why does the Father seek such to worship Him, neither on a mountain, not in the temple, but in spirit and in truth? "God is Spirit." If God were body, it would be right that He should be worshipped on a mountain, for a mountain is corporeal; it would be right that He should be worshipped in the temple, for a temple is corporeal. But, "God is Spirit; and those who worship Him must worship in spirit and in truth" (Jn. 4:24).

## 25.

We have heard, and it is manifest. We had gone outside of the doors, and we were sent back in. "I would have thought that I need to find, as You said, some high and lofty mountain! For I thought that, because God is on high, He would hear me better from a high place." Do you imagine that because you are on a mountain that your are closer to God, and that He will quickly hear you, as if calling to Him from the nearest place? He dwells on high, but regards the lowly. "The Lord is near." To whom? To the high, perhaps? "To those who are contrite of heart" (Ps. 33:19).

It is a wonderful thing: He dwells on high, and yet is near to the lowly; "He regards the lowly things, but lofty things He knows from afar" (Ps. 138:6). He sees the proud afar off, and He is the less near to them the higher they appear to themselves to be. Did you seek a mountain, then? Come down, that you may come near Him. But, would you ascend? Ascend, but do not seek a mountain. "The ascents," it says, "are in his heart, in the valley of weeping" (Ps. 83:6). The valley is humility. Therefore do all within. Even if perhaps you seek some lofty place, some holy place, make yourself a temple for God within time. "For the temple of God is holy, which temple you are" (1 Cor. 3:17). Would you pray in a temple? Pray in yourself. But, first, be a temple of God, for He in His temple hears him who prays.

### 26.

"The hour is coming when you will neither on this mountain, nor in Jerusalem, worship the Father. You worship what you do not know; we know what we worship, for salvation is from the Jews" (Jn. 4:21, 22). A great thing has He attributed to the Jews; but do not understand Him to mean those spurious Jews. Understand that wall to which another is joined, that they may be joined together, resting on the cornerstone, which is Christ. For there is one wall from the Jews, another from the Gentiles; these walls are far apart, only until they are united in the Corner. Now the aliens were strangers and foreigners from the covenants of God (cf. Eph. 2:11, 22). According to this, it is said, "We worship what we know." It is said, indeed, in the person of the Jews, but not of all Jews, not of reprobate Jews, but of such as were the apostles, as were the prophets, as were all those saints who sold all their goods, and laid the price of their goods at the apostles' feet. "For God has not cast away His people whom He foreknew" (Rom. 11:2).

### 27.

The woman heard this, and proceeded. She had already called Him a prophet; she observes that He with Whom she was speaking uttered such things as still more pertained to the prophet; and what answer did she make? See: "The woman said to Him, 'I know that Messiah is coming' (Who is called Christ). 'When He comes, He will tell us all things'" (Jn. 4:25). What is this? Just now she says, the Jews are contending for the temple, and we for this mountain. When He has come He will despise the mountain, and overthrow the temple. He will teach us all things, that we may know how to worship in spirit and in truth. She knew who could teach her, but she did not yet know Him that was now teaching her. But now she was worthy to receive His manifestation. Now *Messiah* means "anointed;" and "anointed" in Greek is *Christ;* in Hebrew, *Messiah;* and in Punic, *messe* means "anoint." For the Hebrew, Punic and Syriac are cognate and neighboring languages.

### 28.

Then, "The woman said to Him, 'I know that Messiah is coming' (Who is called Christ). 'When He comes, He will tell us all things.' Jesus said to her, 'I Who speak to you am He'" (Jn. 4:25, 26). She called her husband; he is made the head of the woman, and Christ is made the head of the man. Now, the woman is constituted in faith, and ruled, as about to live rightly. After she heard, "I Who speak to you am He," what else could she say? For, the Lord Jesus willed to manifest Himself to the woman, to whom He had said, "Believe Me?"

### 29.

"And at this point His disciples came, and they marveled that He talked with a woman." That He was seeking her who was lost, He Who came to seek that which was lost (Lk. 19:10). They marveled at this. They marveled at a good thing; they were not suspecting an evil thing. "Yet no one said, 'What do You seek?' or, 'Why are You talking with her?'" (Jn. 4:27).

### 30.

"The woman then left her waterpot" (Jn. 4:28), having heard, "I Who speak to you am He" (Jn. 4:26). And having received Christ the Lord into her heart, what could she do but now leave her waterpot, and run to preach the gospel? She cast out lust, and hastened to proclaim the truth. Let those who would preach the gospel learn; let them throw away their waterpot at the well. Remember what I said before about the waterpot: it was a vessel with which the water was drawn, called *hydria*, from its Greek name, because water is *hydor* in Greek; just as if it were called "aquarium," from the Latin. She threw away her waterpot then, which was no longer of use, but a burden to her. Such was her enthusiasm to be satisfied with that water. Throwing her burden away, to make known Christ, "The woman then left her waterpot, went her way into the city, and said to the men, 'Come, see a Man Who told me all things that I ever did.'" Step by step, lest those men should get angry and indignant, and should persecute her. "'Could this be the Christ?' Then they went out of the city and came to Him" (Jn. 4:28-30).

### 31.

"In the meantime His disciples urged Him, saying, 'Rabbi, eat.'" For they had gone to buy food, and had returned. "But He said to them, 'I have food to eat of which you do not know.' Therefore the disciples said to one another, 'Has anyone brought Him anything to eat?'" (Jn. 4:31-33). What wonder if that woman did not understand about the water? See; the disciples do not yet understand the meat. But He heard their thoughts, and now as a Master instructs them, not in a roundabout way, as He did the woman while He still sought her husband, but openly and immediately: "My food," says He, "is to do the will of Him Who sent Me" (Jn. 4:34). Therefore, in the case of that woman, it was even His drink to do the will of Him that sent Him. That was why He said, "I thirst, give Me to drink," namely, to work faith in her, and to drink of her faith, and to transplant her into His own body; for His Body is the Church. Therefore He says, "My food is to do the will of Him Who sent Me."

### 32.

"Do you not say, 'There are still four months and then comes the harvest?'" (Jn. 4:35). He was aglow for the work, and was arranging to send forth laborers. You count four months to the harvest; I show you another harvest, white and ready. "Behold, I say to you, lift up your eyes and look at the fields, for they are already white for harvest!" Therefore He is going to send forth the reapers. "For in this the saying is true: 'One sows and another reaps.' I sent you to reap that for which you have not labored; others have labored, and you have entered into their labors" (Jn. 4:35-38).

What then? He sent reapers; sent He not the sowers? Where are the reapers? Where others labored already. For where labor had already been bestowed, surely there had been sowing; and what had been sown had now become ripe, and required the sickle and the threshing. Where, then, were the reapers to be sent? Where the prophets had already preached before; for they were the sowers. Had they not been the sowers, how had this come to the woman, "I know that Messiah will come"?

That woman was now ripened fruit, and the harvest fields were white, and sought the sickle. "I sent you," then. Where? "To reap what you have not sown: others sowed, and you are entered into their labors." Who labored? Abraham, Isaac, and Jacob. Reap their labors; in all their labors there is a prophecy of Christ, and for that reason they were sowers. Moses, and all the other patriarchs, and all the prophets, how much they suffered in that cold season when they sowed! Therefore was the harvest now ready in Judea. Justly was the corn there said to be as it were ripe, when so many thousands of men brought the price of their goods, and, laying them at the apostles' feet, having eased their shoulders of this worldly baggage, began to follow the Lord Christ. Truly, the harvest was ripe. What was made of it? Of that harvest a few grains were thrown out, and sowed the whole world; and another harvest is rising which is to be reaped in the end of the world. Of that harvest it is said, "Those who sow in tears shall reap with joy" (Ps. 125:5). But to that harvest not apostles, but angels, shall be sent forth. "The reapers," He says, "are the angels" (Mt. 13:39). That harvest, then, is growing among tares, and is awaiting to be purged in the end of the world. But that harvest to which the disciples were sent first, where the prophets labored, was already ripe. But, brethren, observe what was said, "both he who sows and he who reaps may rejoice together" (Jn.4:36). They had dissimilar labors in time, but the rejoicing they shall enjoy alike equally; they shall receive for their wages together eternal life.

### 33.

"And many of the Samaritans of that city believed in Him because of the word of the woman who testified, 'He told me all that I ever did.' So when the Samaritans had come to Him, they urged Him to stay with them; and He stayed there two days. And many more believed because of His own word. Then they said to the woman, 'Now we believe, not because of what you said, for we ourselves have heard Him and we know that this is indeed [the Christ], the Savior of the world" (Jn. 4:39-42). This also must be slightly noticed, for the lesson has come to an end. The woman first announced Him, and the Samaritans believed her testimony; and they besought Him to stay with them, and He stayed there two days, and many more believed. And when they had believed, they said to the woman, "Now we believe, not because of what you said, for we ourselves have heard Him and we know that this is indeed [the Christ], the Savior of the world." First by report, then by His presence. So it is today with those that are outside, and are not yet Christians. Christ is made known to them by Christian friends; and just upon the report of that woman, that is, the Church, they come to Christ, they believe through this report. He stays with them two days, that is, gives them two precepts of charity; and many more believe, and more firmly believe, on Him, because He is in truth the Savior of the world.

## "Worshiping the Father"

### St. Ambrose of Milan[7]

It is objected by heretics that Christ offered worship to His Father. But instead it is shown that this must be referred to His humanity, as is clear from an examination of the passage. However, it also offers fresh witness to His Godhead, as we often see it happening in other actions that Christ did.

But if any one were to say that the Son worships God the Father, because it is written, "You worship what you do not know; we know what we worship" (Jn. 4:22), let him consider when it was said, and to whom, and to whose wishes it was in answer. In the earlier verses of this chapter it was stated, not without reason, that Jesus, being weary with the journey, was sitting down, and that He asked a woman of Samaria to give

---

[7] St. Ambrose, *The Christian Faith*, 5.4, NPNF s. 2, v. 10, 687, 688.

Him drink. He spoke as man; but as God He could neither weary nor thirst.

When this woman addressed Him as a Jew and thought Him to be a prophet, He answered her as a Jew who spiritually taught the mysteries of the law. "You worship what you do not know; we know what we worship." He says, "We," for He joined Himself with men. But how is He joined with men, but according to the flesh? And to show that He answered as being incarnate, He added, "for salvation is from the Jews." Immediately after this He put aside His human feelings, saying: "But the hour is coming, and now is, when the true worshippers will worship the Father." He did not say, *"We* will worship." He certainly would have said this if He had a share in our obedience. When we read that Mary worshipped Him, we should learn that it is not possible for Him under the same nature both to worship as a servant, and to be worshipped as Lord. Rather, that as man He is said to worship among men, and that as Lord, He is worshipped by His servants.

Many things therefore we read and believe, considering the mystery of the Incarnation. But even in the very feelings of our human nature we may behold the Divine Majesty. Jesus is wearied from His journey, that He may refresh the weary; He desires to drink, when about to give spiritual drink to the thirsty; He was hungry, when about to supply the food of salvation to the hungry; He dies, to live again; He is buried, to rise again; He hangs upon the dreadful tree, to strengthen those in dread; He veils the heaven with thick darkness, that He may give light; He makes the earth to shake, that He may make it strong; He rouses the sea, that He may calm it; He opens the tombs of the dead, that He may show they are the homes of the living; He is born of a Virgin, that men may believe He is begotten of God; He pretends not to know, that He may make the ignorant to know; as a Jew He is said to worship, that the Son may be worshipped as true God.

## "He Restored Our Nature"
### *St. Gregory of Nyssa*[8]

Since our nature has deteriorated and become as hard as stone due to the worship of idols, and has become frozen in the cold of atheism and unable to progress; therefore the Sun of Righteousness arose (Mal. 4:2). In this bitter cold, the coming of the spring appeared, and the warm southern winds erased all traces of the cold, while the shining rays of the Sun brought warmth to the whole world. Consequently, the human race that had turned into stone because of the cold became embraced by the warmth through the Holy Sprit Who is the rays of the Word of God. It is in this manner that the Holy Spirit once more becomes like the water that grants eternal life (Jn. 4:14)...' Who turned the rock into a pool of water, the flint into a fountain of waters" (Ps 113:8).

## "The Husband of Souls"
### *The Scholar Origen*[9]

What a skillful divine healer! He uncovers the infirmity in the woman, and with His divine blade, begins to attack the body with skill, power and love. This leads her to confess what no other woman would pronounce, "I have no husband" (Jn. 4:17). Her confession is not the result of painful reprimand or confronting her with her shameful self. It is the result of His love. This arouses her conscience and reveals to her the reality of the Lord. Consequently, she becomes trustful and admits the truth about her personal life as she realizes that He can heal her wounds and restore her spiritual health.

We have mentioned earlier that the law controls the soul; that everyone submits himself to it; and that in the case of marriage the husband represents the law. To support this, we will quote from the Apostle who writes to the Romans and says: "Or do you not know, brethren (for I speak to those who know the law), that the law has dominion over a man as long as he lives? For the woman who has a

---

[8] St. Gregory of Nyssa, *Homilies on the Song of Songs*, Sermon 5.
[9] Origen, *Commentary on John*, bk. 13:43-51, 181, 206-217.

husband is bound by the law to her husband as long as he lives" (Rom. 7:1, 2). So the husband impersonates the law as long as he lives. However, once he dies, she no longer is obligated to fulfill the duties a wife has towards her husband.

The Apostle, in this context, says, "But if the husband dies, she is released from the law of her husband" (Rom. 7:2). Now that the law is dead in its literal sense, the soul is no longer considered adulterous if it gives itself to another man. In other words, the soul can now associate itself with the law according to the spirit. It is possible to say that the wife has died also since she leaves her dead husband, once a man dies and leaves his wife. We understand this statement through logical deduction as follows: "Therefore, my brethren, you also have become dead to the law through the body of Christ, that you may be married to another, even to Him Who was raised from the dead, that we should bear fruit to God" (Rom. 7:4).

Therefore if the husband represents the law, and the Samaritan woman has a husband, then she has subjugated herself to some strange law based on a misunderstanding of the correct law. It is a fabricated law that is embraced by those who wish to live by it. In such a situation the Divine Word requires the fabricating soul to uncover its shame by confessing the law that controls it. As the woman faces and despises herself because she does not belong legally to any husband, she looks for another bridegroom. The Lord wishes her to belong to another One: to the Word Who has been raised from the dead, Who will not be conquered or destroyed, but will endure forever (Is. 40:8; 1 Pet. 1:25); and Who controls and dominates all His enemies (Ps. 8:7; Eph. 1:22). This is because "Christ having been raised from the dead, dies no more. Death has no longer dominion over Him. For the death that He died, He died to sin once for all, but the life that He lives He lives to God" (Rom. 6:9, 10). He sits at the right hand of God (Heb. 10:12), and all His enemies are subjugated under His feet (1 Cor. 15:25). That is why the Lord tells her: "Go, call your husband." By replying: "I have no husband" (Jn. 4:17), she convicts herself on account of her wrongful association with a man who is not her husband in such a manner.

I think that every soul that embraces the Christian religion does so through the reading of the Holy Books. She begins by taking in matters that can be comprehended through the senses and are known as physical matters. These have five husbands, one for every sense. However, after the soul keeps company with matters that are comprehended by the senses, it desires later on to transcend above them and rush towards matters comprehended by the spirit. At this point, the soul collides with corrupt teachings based on symbolic spiritual meanings. Consequently, she draws near to another husband, other than the five to whom she sends divorce documents. It is as though she has decided to live with that sixth one. We too live with that sixth husband until the Lord Jesus Christ arrives and enables us to discover the character of such a husband. When the Word of the Lord arrives and enters into a conversation with us, we reject that husband and say, "I have no husband." Then, the Lord will respond saying, "You have well said, 'I have no husband'" (Jn. 4:17).

**"The woman then left her waterpot, went her way into the city..."**

When the Samaritan woman received the divine truth, she abandoned her waterpot and forgot the reason that had brought her to the well. So she returned without getting water. However she returned to offer the water of truth to the people of the city. She left her waterpot because she did not want it to impede her from running to the city and giving testimony to the truth. She informed everyone in the streets that she had found the treasure she has been looking for, and that she has found the Source of her inner joy.

Earlier on, the Lord had asked her to call her husband, and here she is calling all the men of the city and succeeding in her task. She does not inform them that He discussed with her serious religious matters concerning worship and the manner in which it should be conducted. Instead, she informs them of how He has touched her heart truly because He knows her secrets, how He attracted her to Him by His powerful words, and consequently how this led her to recognize His person and that He is the Messiah. She could have abandoned her waterpot which was in a deep well. She took pride in its depth; in other words she took pride in the teachings. However, she has come to despise the thoughts she had accepted previously. Now she accepts a better pot than the earlier waterpot for it contains water "springing up into everlasting life" (Jn. 4:14).

Here is a woman who proclaims the Messiah to the Samaritans. At the end of the gospels there is also another woman who is the first one to see Him and who informs the disciples about the Resurrection of the Lord Jesus Christ (Jn. 20:18). This is all what this Samaritan woman had done. She had a relationship with five husbands, then she got involved with a sixth man who was not her legal husband, and finally she renounced that last man, abandoned her waterpot, and rested reverently on a Saturday. Besides, she brought great benefits to those who lived with her in the same city. Considering her old beliefs, they shared incorrect teachings with her. This was the fault that led them to leave the city and come to the Lord Jesus Christ.

**"But He said to them, 'I have food to eat of which you do not know.'"**

The body requires food that is different from that of the spirit. And just as the bodies themselves have different needs regarding the kind and quantity of food, so, too, do the spirits and souls have different requirements.

The Lord Jesus Christ seizes every chance to lift the minds and hearts of the disciples to matters beyond time and to the heavens themselves. He reveals to them the extent of His joy that arises from the redemption of souls. This represents His delicious food. He finds his satisfaction and comfort in toiling for every soul and in fulfilling His Father's plan. He will not rest and will persevere in the task until He leaves this world.

Indeed, the same nourishing words, meditative thoughts and the actions relevant in accompanying them are not suitable for all souls. Truly, there are vegetables and there is food for the strong (Rom. 14:2; Heb. 5:2), which may not promote progress to the needy souls if they are offered at the same time.

In this context, St. Peter says, "as newborn babes, desire the pure milk of the world, that you may grow thereby" (1 Pet. 2:2). The same thing applies to some who are like children as in the case of the Corinthians and to whom St. Paul says, "I fed you with milk and not solid food" (1 Cor. 3:2). May those who are weak eat vegetables since they do not believe (Rom. 14:2). This is what St. Paul is teaching when he says: "For one believes he may eat all things, but he who is weak eats only vegetables" (Rom. 14:2).

Truly, there is a time when "better is a dinner of herbs where love is, than a fatted calf with hatred" (cf. Prov. 15:17). "But solid food belongs to those who are of full age, that is, who by reason of use have their senses exercised to discern both good and evil" (Heb. 5:14). However, there is also food that is hateful as we learn in the Book of Kings when the men told Elisha, "O man of God, there is death in the pot!" (2 Kgs. 4:40).

It is appropriate to lift our thoughts from the level of unreasoning creatures and mankind to that of the angels who are refreshed by food. They are not completely self-sufficient as the Psalmist says, "Men ate the bread of angels" (Ps. 77:25).

Now we need to return to the statement before us concerning the food of the Lord Jesus Christ with which the disciples were not familiar until that moment. The Lord truly says, "I have food to eat of which you do not know" (Jn. 4:31) because the disciples are not aware of what the Lord was doing. He was obeying the will of He Who sent Him and fulfilling His perfect work (Jn. 4:34). He performs the will of God which is one and the same as His own will.

## "THE SPRING OF YOUR LOVE WATERS THE DEPTH OF MY SPIRIT"

### *A Prayer by Hegumen Father Tadros Malaty*[10]

1.

Your wonderful love defies all rules
    No difficulty or obstacle stands in its way.
    For the sake of a poor, disreputable Samaritan woman
    You went to Samaria on foot and fasting!
    You Whom the heavenly beings long to carry.
    Your tender body was exhausted;

---

[10] Fr. Tadros Malaty, *Patristic Commentary on the Gospel of John*, 300, 301.

But Your spirit was thirsty for the woman's salvation.

### 2.

The Samaritan woman was ashamed to go in the morning, fearing she would meet someone.
She had neither servant nor maid to fetch water for her.
She found You, alone, at noon seeking her,
Bringing to her the spring of living water.
Whoever drinks of it will never thirst.

### 3.

Your modesty, love and gentleness made her forget the hostility between the Samaritans and the Jews.

Seeing You kindled her heart to worship God.
She trusted You and talked at length about worship!
She recognized You and gradually knew You,
For she searched for You faithfully and You declared Yourself to her!

### 4.

O how wonderful, she never saw a miracle or sign, But Your words attracted her wholly to enjoy redemption.
She confessed her secrets, because she found her soul's Bridegroom.
The five men she had and the man she then had did not satisfy her.
She realized that the five Books of Moses and the teachings she had could not quench her thirst.
You alone are the Bridegroom of her soul.

### 5.

She possessed You within herself so her heart expanded with love for all mankind.
She left her waterpot and without permission ran to her city.
With her heart aflame she was not ashamed to wisely proclaim,

"A man told me all things that I ever did. Could this be the Christ?"

The whole city went out toward the wonderful Bridegroom.

6.

She was not ordered to preach; she was not trained in witnessing.
> But she did what no apostle or disciple did!
> With her love, she attracted the whole city.
> When they met You they refused to learn from any other but You.
> They announced firmly what Your disciples did not.
> "We know that this is indeed the Christ, the Savior of the world."

7.

You are truly the Savior of the world; You grant healing and life.
> O You Who raised the nobleman's son as from death,
> Raise my poor spirit to enjoy You, the Source of life and joy!

# IX

## RISE, TAKE UP YOUR BED AND WALK

*Meditations on the Sunday of the Paralytic Man of the Great Lent*

### GOSPEL READING OF THE FIFTH SUNDAY OF THE GREAT LENT

#### (John 5:1-18)

*After this there was a feast of the Jews, and Jesus went up to Jerusalem. Now there is in Jerusalem by the Sheep Gate a pool, which is called in Hebrew, Bethesda, having five porches. In these lay a great multitude of sick people, blind, lame, paralyzed, waiting for the moving of the water. For an angel went down at a certain time into the pool and stirred up the water; then whoever stepped in first, after the stirring of the water, was made well of whatever disease he had.*

*Now a certain man was there who had an infirmity thirty-eight years. When Jesus saw him lying there, and knew that he already had been in that condition a long time, He said to him, "Do you want to be made well?" The sick man answered Him, "Sir, I have no man to put me into the pool when the water is stirred up; but while I am coming, another steps down before me."*

*Jesus said to him, "Rise, take up your bed and walk." And immediately the man was made well, took up his bed, and walked.*

*And that day was the Sabbath. The Jews therefore said to him who was cured, "It is the Sabbath; it is not lawful for you to carry your bed." He answered them, "He Who made me well said to me, 'Take up your bed and* walk.'" Then they asked him, "Who is the Man who said to you, 'Take up your bed and walk'?" But the one who was healed did not know who it was, for Jesus had withdrawn, a multitude being in that place.

*Afterward Jesus found him in the temple, and said to him, "See, you have been made well. Sin no more, lest a worse thing come upon you."*

*The man departed and told the Jews that it was Jesus who had made him well. For this reason the Jews persecuted Jesus, and sought to kill Him, because He had done these things on the Sabbath. But Jesus answered them, "My Father has been working until now, and I have been working." Therefore the Jews sought all the more to kill Him, because He not only broke the Sabbath, but also said that God was His Father, making Himself equal with God."*

## INTRODUCTORY NOTE

**What is the Symbolism behind this story?**

This passage, as many in Scripture, is laden with symbols related to our salvation.[1] Bethsaida is known as the "house of mercy." The only mention of it is in John 5:2. It may have taken its name from God's mercies that were revealed in the healing of those who stepped down into it. The Sheep Gate was probably so called because the priests used to wash the sacrificial lambs before taking them into the Temple. The pool is a type of the baptismal font in which believers enjoy a new birth and healing from sin. The five porches represent the law recorded in the five Books of Moses, the Pentateuch. The sick enter through them to the pool so that those who enter realize they are in need of a Heavenly Physician. Thus, the water enclosed by the five porches is the Jewish nation controlled by the five Books of the Law. The angel coming down from heaven typifies the Incarnate Logos of God, the Heavenly Physician. The healing of one man symbolizes the One Church that enjoys healing from sin.

The stirring up of the water symbolizes: 1) the suffering of Christ when the crowd rose against Him; 2) the conversion of the water into

---

[1] For additional explanation, see Fr. Tadros Malaty's *Commentary on the Gospel of John*.

healing, living water, as the Holy Spirit changes simple water to life-giving springs in the Mystery of Baptism, creating him anew as he emerges from the womb of the Church (Jn. 3); and 3) the gift of the Lord Jesus Christ, as the Lord says to the Samaritan woman that whoever drinks of that water will never thirst.

**Where is the Pool of Bethsaida today?**

Tradition is varied concerning the location of the site. In the third century, Eusebius, describes the pool as consisting of two pools and named Bezatha (answering to the northeastern suburb of Bezetha in the gospel times). Some have suggested that "the pool of the Virgin" is "the pool of Bethsaida," or "the king's pool" in Nehemiah. Others identify it with the church of Anne, mother of Mary, Beit Hanna, or Bethsaida, the "house of grace.[2]

In the fourth to the thirteenth century, one pool was believed to be the location, which was northwest of the present St. Stephen's Gate. It was part of a twin pool and over it were erected, at two successive periods, two Christian churches. Afterwards, this site was entirely lost and the great Birket Israel, just north of the Temple area, was pointed out as the site.[3] Within 30 years or so, the older traditional site, now close to the Church of St. Anne, had been rediscovered, excavated and popularly accepted. This pool is a rock-cut, rain-filled cistern, 55 feet long and 12 feet wide, and is approached by a steep and winding flight of steps. The floor of the rediscovered early Christian church roofs over the pool, being supported upon five arches in commemoration of the five porches. At the western end of the church, where probably the font was situated, there was a fresco, now much defaced and fast fading, representing the angel troubling the waters.

Although public opinion supports this site, others believe that the pool was at the "Virgin's Fount" (Gihon), which is today an intermittent spring whose "troubled" waters are still visited by Jews for purposes of cure. As the only source of "living water" near Jerusalem, it is a likely spot for there

---

[2] "Bethsaida," *Fausset's Bible Dictionary*.
[3] E.W.G. Masterman, "Bethsaida," *International Standard Bible Encyclopedia*.

to have been a "sheep pool" or "sheep place" for the vast flocks of sheep coming to Jerusalem in connection with the temple ritual.[4]

The pool had two chambers separated by a twenty-foot-wide pathway. The two pools together form a trapezoid about 165 feet across the northern and over 215 feet on its southern side. They have a long side measuring over 300 feet. The reference in John 5 mentions five porches, porticoes or colonnaded walkways. There were colonnades around the four sides of the two pools and in between them, making a total of five.

Nevertheless, the Church today acknowledges the pool of Bethsaida as the baptismal font our regeneration, where we encounter the Holy Trinity.

## "Christ, Our Rescue from Despair"
### *The Late Hegumen Father Pishoy Kamel*

This gospel warns us that there is despair along our journey to Christ. But there can be no failure or despair after our encounter with the Lord Jesus Christ. The paralytic rose and carried his bed after being ill for 38 years —38 years of paralysis, 38 years of sin, 38 years lost!

But our Lord Jesus Christ does not count the years. When we get to know Him, He renews our strength as the eagles. As we pray each day to the Lord, "Count us among the fellows of the eleventh hour," our life with Christ is renewed each day. It is neither dull, boring, nor routine.

When tribulations and trials face us, Christ becomes our great bulwark. St. Paul the Simple began his relationship with Christ after he was sixty years old, after he had had a fight with his young and unfaithful wife. He went to St. Anthony the Great and became an ascetic. After 60 years, he learned and achieved a high level of fasting and worship!

In Christianity, there is no place for senility or despair...but we experience a constant renewal of hope. This is the law governing our journey of fasting: hope and renewed life in Christ; joy, courage, optimism and spiritual flight and growth—it is a journey that knows no end!

---

[4] See *Biblical World*, 25, 80ff.

## "Do You Want to be Made Well?"
### *St. Cyril of Alexandria*[5]

Jesus departs from Jerusalem after the killing of the sheep and goes to the Samaritans and Galileans, preaching among them the word of salvation. What else will this mean except His actual withdrawal from the Jews after His sacrifice and death at Jerusalem upon the Precious Cross, when He at length began to freely give Himself to them of the Gentiles and foreigners, bidding it to be shown to His Disciples after His Resurrection, that "He will go before them to Galilee" (Mt. 28:7). However, His return at the fulfillment of the weeks of Holy Pentecost to Jerusalem signifies in types that there will be, out of His loving kindness, a return of our Savior to the Jews in the last ages of the present world, in which those who have been saved through faith in Him, shall celebrate the all-holy feasts of the saving Passion.

The healing of the paralytic before the full time of the law signifies again (in a type) that Israel having blasphemously raged against Christ, will be infirm and paralytic, and will spend a long time without doing anything. Yet, [Israel] will not depart to complete punishment, but will have some visitation from the Savior and will also be healed at the pool through obedience and faith.

**"He said to him, "Do you want to be made well?"**

[This is] evident proof of the extreme goodness of Christ, [for] He does not wait for the request of the sick, but He runs, as you see, to him that lies, has compassion on him that was sick without comfort. But the question whether he would like to be relieved from his infirmity was not that of one asking out of ignorance a thing manifest and evident to all, but one of stirring up to more earnest desire and inciting to most diligent entreaty. The question whether he wanted to obtain what he longed for is big, with a kind of fore and expression that He has the power to give, and is even now ready to do so, and only waits for the request of him who receives the grace.

---

[5] St. Cyril of Alexandria, *Commentary on St. John*, v. 1, bk. 2, ch. 5, 236-246.

**"The sick man answered Him, ' Sir, I have no man to put me into the pool when the water is stirred up; but while I am coming, another steps down before me.'"**

Around the day of the Holy Pentecost, angels coming down from heaven used to trouble the water of the pool. Then, they would stir the waters as a sign of their presence. The water would be sanctified by the holy angel, and whoever was previously sick when entering the water would rise up without the suffering that troubled him. Yet this power of healing was allowed only the first one who seized it and entered. This, too, was a sign of the benefit of the law by the hands of angels, which extended to the one race of the Jews alone, and healed none others except them.

For from Dan so also called even to Bethsheba the commandments given by Moses were spoken, ministered by angels in Mount Sinai in the days afterwards marked out as the Holy Pentecost. For this reason, the water of the pool also was not stirred at any other time, signifying the decent of the holy angels on it. The paralytic, then not having anyone to throw him into the water with the disease that binds him, was bewailing the want of healers, saying, "I have no man" to let me down into the water—for he fully expected Jesus to tell and advise him of this.

**"Jesus said to him, 'Rise, take up your bed and walk.' And immediately the man was made well, took up his bed, and walked. And that day was the Sabbath."**

Christ heals the man on the Sabbath day. Once he is healed, he is commanded by [Christ] immediately to break the custom of the law and walk on the Sabbath with his bed—even though God clearly cries aloud by one of the holy prophets, "Do not carry a burden out of your houses on the Sabbath day" (Jer. 17:22). I suppose no one who is sober-minded would say that the man was despising or disobedient to the divine commands, but that as in a type Christ was making known the Jews that they should be healed by obedience and faith in the last times of the world—which, I think, signifies the Sabbath, since it is the last day of the week.

But that having once received the healing through faith and having been remodeled unto newness of life, it was necessary that the oldness of the letter of the law should become of no effect, and that the typical worship should be rejected—since it was in shadows and in the vain observance of Jewish custom. Therefore, I think, the blessed Paul, also writes to those who were returning to the Law after [they converted] to the Faith, "Indeed I, Paul, say to you that if you become circumcised, Christ will profit you nothing" (Gal. 5:2), and again "You have become estranged from Christ, you who attempt to be justified by law; you have fallen from grace" (Gal. 5:4).

**"The Jews therefore said to him who was cured, "It is the Sabbath; it is not lawful for you to carry your bed...""**

Most reasonably, I think, He cries over them, "Hear now these things, O foolish and senseless people, who have eyes, but do not see, who have ears, but do not hear" (Jer. 5:21). For what can be more ignorant that such people, or what greater foolishness? They do not even admit into their mind that they should wonder at the Power of the Healer. But being bitter critics, and skilled in this alone, they accuse one who has just recovered from a long disease the charge of with breaking the law. Foolishly, they bid him to lie down again, as he needed to be ill in order to honor the Sabbath.

**"He answered them, 'He Who made me well said to me, "Take up your bed and walk.""**

The sentence is replete with wisest meaning and repulsive of the stubbornness of the Jews. For, they said it was not lawful to take up his bed and go home on the Sabbath day, devising an accusation of breaking the law against him that was healed. Thus, he needed a more resolved defense, saying that he had been ordered to walk by Him, Who was manifested to him as the Giver of health. He says something like, "Most honorable [gentlemen] I will tell You Who He is. Even though He commanded me to violate the honor of the Sabbath, Who has so great power and grace as to drive away my disease? For since such excellence in these things does not belong to just any man, but is befitting of God's power and might, how can the worker of these things do wrong? Or how shall He Who is possessed of God-befitting Power advise against what is well-pleasing to God?" So, the speech has within itself some strong meaning.

>"Then they asked him, 'Who is the Man Who said to you, "Take up your bed and walk?"' But the one who was healed did not know who it was, for Jesus had withdrawn, a multitude being in that place."

The mind of the Jews is unyielding unto bloodshed. For they search out who it was who had commanded this, and intended to involve Him together with the miraculously healed. For it seems that he was irritated them in respect of the Sabbath, for he escaped impassable toils and snares and had been drawn away from the very gates of death. But he could not entreat his Physician, although they make diligent inquiries. For Christ concealed Himself skillfully and in His Economy to escape the present heat of their anger. He escapes because He could not suffer unless He willed to suffer. So He makes Himself an example to us in this also.

>"Afterward Jesus found him in the temple, and said to him, 'See, you have been made well. Sin no more, lest a worse thing come upon you.'"

After hiding economically, He appears again economically, observing the proper time for each. For it was not possible that this should be done by Him Who knew no sin, which should not recall have its proper season. He then gave him a message for his soul's health, saying that it is required of him to transgress no more, lest he be tormented by worse evils than those past. In this, He teaches not only that God treasures up man's transgressions unto the judgment to come (Rom. 2:5) but afflicts those living in their bodies in various ways, even before the "great and glorious day" of Him Who shall judge all (Acts 2:20). Because we are oftentimes struck down when we stumble and grieve God, the most-wise Paul will testify, crying "For this reason many are weak and sick among you, and many sleep. For if we would judge ourselves, we would not be judged. But when we are judged, we are chastened by the Lord, that we may not be condemned with the world" (1 Cor. 11:30-32).

>"The man departed and told the Jews that it was Jesus Who had made him well."

He makes Jesus known to the Jews, not that they by daring to do anything against Him should be found to be blasphemers, but in order that if they also should be willing to be healed by Him, they might know the wondrous Physician. For observe how this was his aim. For he does not come like one of the accusers and say that it was Jesus Who had commanded him to walk on the Sabbath day, but "Who had made him well." For this was partly how his Physician would be revealed.

**"For this reason the Jews persecuted Jesus, and sought to kill Him, because He had done these things on the Sabbath."**

The narrative does not contain the simple relation of the madness of the Jews. For the Evangelist does not only show that they persecute Him, but why they do not blush from doing this, saying most emphatically, "Because He was doing these things on the Sabbath." For they persecute Him foolishly and blasphemously, as though the law forbade [anyone] to do good on the Sabbath, as though it was not lawful to pity and sympathize with the sick; as though it behooved [them] to put off the law of love, the praise of brotherly kindles, and the grace of gentleness. For the Jews failed to do many good things on the Sabbath, and instead rejected it by observing it in an empty way, not knowing the true aim of the Lawgiver in respecting the Sabbath.

For Christ, Himself, said, "Does not each of you on the Sabbath loose his ox or donkey from the stall, and lead it away to water it?" (Lk. 13:15), and that, "a man receives circumcision on the Sabbath so that the Law of Moses should not be broken." So when they are angry because a man "was made completely well on the Sabbath" (Jn. 7:23), it is because of their exceeding stubbornness alike and disorder of their habits, not even to brutes [to reject] Him Who is made in the Divine Image. Instead they think that one should pity a sheep on the Sabbath and free to release it from famine and thirst, yet that they are open to the charge of transgressing the law to the last degree, who are gentle and good to their neighbor on the Sabbath.

But we may see that they were senseless beyond measure, and therefore deserved to hear with justice, "You are mistaken, not knowing the Scriptures nor the power of God" (Mt. 22:29). Come, let us take from the Divine Scriptures to show clearly that Jesus was long ago depicted as in a type taking no account of the Sabbath.

When the all-wise Moses reached a great age (as it is written), he departed from things of men and was removed to the mansions above, by the judgment and decree of God that rules all. Then, Joshua the son of

Nun obtained and inherited the command over Israel (Josh. 6). When he set in an array of ten thousand heavy, armed soldiers around Jericho and devised to overthrow it, he arranged with the Levites to take the ark around for about six whole days. But on the seventh day, that is the Sabbath, he commanded the innumerable multitude of the host to shout along with trumpets, and thus the wall collapsed. They, rushing in, took the city, not observing the unseasonable rest of the Sabbath; nor refusing their victory, by reason of the law restraining them. Nor did they then withstand the leadership of Joshua, but wholly free from reproach did they keep the command of man. In this is the type.

But when the Truth came, that is Christ—Who destroyed and overcame the corruption set up against man's nature by the devil—and is seen doing this on the Sabbath, as in preface and commencement of action, in the case of the paralytic, they foolishly take it wrongly, and condemn the obedience of their fathers, not allowing nature to conquer sickness on the Sabbath, to such an extent that they were zealous in persecuting Jesus Who was working good on the Sabbath.

**"But Jesus answered them, 'My Father has been working until now, and I have been working.'"**

Christ is speaking, as it were, on the Sabbath. For the word, "until" signifies this. But, the Jews who were untutored and did not know Who the Only-Begotten is by nature. They attributed to God the Father alone the appointing of the law through Moses, and asserted that we should obey Him alone. He attempts to clearly convince them that He works all things together with the Father and that—having the nature of Him Who begot Him in Himself by reason of His not being other than He, as far as pertains to the sameness of essence—He will never think something other than that which seems good to Him Who begot Him. As being the same essence, He will also will the same things. Yes, being Himself the living Will and the Power of the Father, He works all things in all with the Father.

In order to repel the vain murmuring of the Jews and shame those who were persecuting Him because they thought it was right to be angry, as though He despised the honor due to the Sabbath, He says, "My Father has been working until now, and I have been working." For He only wished to explain to them something like this: "If you believe, O man, that God having created and compacted all things by His command and will order the creation on the Sabbath day also, so that the sun rises; the rain-giving fountains are set loose; fruits spring from the earth, not refusing their increase by reason of the Sabbath; fire works its own work, ministering to the necessities of man permissibly...confess and know that the Father works God-befitting operations on the Sabbath also."

Why then does He say, do you foolishly accuse Him through Whom He works all things? For God the Father will work in no other way, except through the Son, His Power and Wisdom. Therefore He says, "He and I work." He continuously shames the unrestrained mind of His persecutors with arguments, showing that they are not opposing [Christ] any more than they are speaking against the Father, to Whom alone they were zealous to ascribe the honor of the Law, not yet knowing the Son Who is of Him and through Him by nature. For this reason He uniquely calls God His own Father, leading them most skillfully to this most excellent and precious lesson.

**"Therefore the Jews sought all the more to kill Him, because He not only broke the Sabbath, but also said that God was His Father, making Himself equal with God."**

The mind of the Jews is wound up unto cruelty and whereby they should have been healed, they are more sick, that they may justly hear, "How can you say, 'We are wise and the law of the Lord is with us?'" (Jer. 8:8). For when they should have been softened in disposition and transformed by suitable reasoning unto piety, they even devise slaughter against Him Who proves by His deeds that He has in no way transgressed the Divine Law by healing a man on the Sabbath. They weave in with their wrath on account of the Sabbath, the truth as a charge of blasphemy, trapping themselves in nets of their own transgressions unto binding wrath (cf. Prov. 5:22). For they seemed to be pious in their distress, that He being a Man, should say that God was His Father.

They did not know that He Who was for our sakes made in the form of a servant, is God the Logos, the Life springing forth from God the Father, that is the Only-Begotten, to Whom alone God is rightly and truly inscribed and is Father. But it is not the same for us at all, for we are adopted, mounting up to excellence above nature through the will of Him Who honored us, and gaining the title of gods and sons because of Christ that dwells in us through the Holy Spirit.

Looking therefore to the flesh alone, and not acknowledging God Who dwells in the flesh, they do not endure His springing up to measure beyond the nature of man, through His saying, that God was His Father. For in saying, "My Father," He would with reason induce this idea. But they reasoned that He Whose Father God properly is, must be equal with Him in nature. In this alone they rightly conceived, for so it is and no otherwise. Since then the word introduces with it this meaning, they perverted the upright word of truth are more angry.

## "The Baptismal Font"
### The Scholar Tertullian[6]

An Angel, by His intervention, came to stir the pool at Bethsaida. Those complaining of ill-health used to watch for him; for whoever had been the first to descend into them, after his washing, ceased to complain. This figure of corporeal healing sang of a spiritual healing, according to the rule by which things carnal are always antecedent as figurative of things spiritual. Thus, when the grace of God advanced to higher degrees among men, an accession of efficacy was granted to the waters and to the angel.

Those who needed to remedy bodily defects, now heal the spirit; those who used to work temporal salvation now renew eternal; those who left only once in the year, now save peoples in a body daily, death being done away through ablution of sins. Once the guilt was removed, the penalty was also removed. Thus man will be restored for God to His "likeness," who previously was conformed to "the image" of God. (The "image" is considered to be in His form: the "likeness" in His eternity) for he receives again that Spirit of God which he had then first received from His divine inspiration, but had afterward lost through sin.

---

[6] Tertullian, *Treatise on Baptism*, ANF v. 3, ch. 5.

### The Baptismal Formula

Not that in the waters we obtain the Holy Spirit; but in the water, under (the witness of) the Angel, we are cleansed, and prepared for the Holy Spirit. In this case also a type has preceded, for thus was John beforehand the Lord's forerunner, "preparing His ways." Thus, too, does the Angel, the witness of baptism, "make the paths straight" for the Holy Spirit, Who is about to come upon us, by the washing away of sins, which faith, sealed in (the Name of) the Father, and the Son, and the Holy Spirit, obtains. For if "in the mouth of three witnesses every word shall stand"—while, through the benediction, we have the same (Three) as witnesses of our faith whom we have as sureties of our salvation too, how much more does the number of the divine Names suffice for the assurance of our hope likewise! Moreover, after the pledging both of the attestation of faith and the promise of salvation under "three witnesses," there is added, of necessity, mention of the Church; inasmuch as, wherever there are Three, (that is, the Father, the Son, and the Holy Spirit) there is the Church, which is a body of Three.

### Chrismation

After this, when we have issued from the font, we are thoroughly anointed with a blessed unction—(a practice derived) from the old discipline, in order to enter the priesthood, men had to be anointed with oil from a horn —which is how Aaron was anointed by Moses. Aaron is called "Christ" because the "chrism," is the spiritual "unction" or "anointing" that provided an appropriate name to the Lord, because He was "anointed" with the Spirit by God the Father. As it is written in the Acts, "For truly against Your holy Servant Jesus, Whom You anointed.[they] were gathered together" (Acts 4:27). Thus, too, in our case, the unction becomes a physical anointing (on our body) but we benefit spiritually. Similarly, as the act of baptism is also physical act, since we are immersed in water, but the effect is spiritual, since we are freed from sins.

### The Imposition of Hands, Typified by the Flood and the Dove

In the next place the hand is laid on us invoking and inviting the Holy Spirit through benediction. Shall it be granted possible for human ingenuity to summon a spirit into water, and, by the application of hands from above, to animate their union into one body with another spirit of so clear sound; and shall it not be possible for God, in the case of His own organ, to produce, by means of "holy hands," a sublime spiritual modulation?

But this, as well as the former, is derived from the old sacramental rite in which Jacob blessed his grandsons, born of Joseph, Ephraim, and Manasseh; with his hands laid on them and interchanged, and indeed so transversely slanted one over the other, that, by delineating Christ, they even foreshadowed the future benediction into Christ. Then, over our cleansed and blessed bodies that Holiest Spirit willingly descends from the Father.

He rests over the waters of baptism, recognizing as it were His ancient seat. [He Who] glided down on the Lord "in bodily form like a dove" (Lk. 3:22), in order that the nature of the Holy Spirit might be declared by means of the creature (the emblem) of simplicity and innocence, because even in her bodily structure the dove is without literal gall. And accordingly He says, be "harmless as doves" (Mt. 10:16).

Even this is not without the supporting evidence of a preceding figure. For after the waters of the deluge—by which the old iniquity was purged after the baptism, so to say, of the world—a dove was the herald which announced to the earth the alleviation of heavenly wrath. When she had been sent her way out of the ark, and had returned with the olive-branch, a sign which even among the nations is the type of peace. By the self-same law of heavenly effect, the dove of the Holy Spirit flies to earth (that is, to our flesh) as it emerges from the font, after its old sins [are removed]. [This Dove] brings us the peace of God, sent out from the heavens; the Church also typified by the ark.

But the world returned to sin; in which point baptism would be ill-compared to the Flood. And so it is destined to fire, just as the man, too, is, who after baptism renews his sins: so that this also should be accepted as a sign for our admonition.

## "Water of Renewal"

### *St. John Chrysostom*[7]

And as now in this time of spring the earth brings forth roses, violets, and other flowers; and the rains make the fields yet more lovely, you do not think that the rains cause the flowers to spring up, nor that the earth of its own power brings forth, but that it is by God's command the seed brings forth. In the beginning, water brought forth also animals that moved; for Scripture says, "Let the waters bring forth reptiles having life, and winged creatures flying above the earth in the firmament of heaven" (Gen. 1:20). And the command was fulfilled, and the substance without life brought forth living creatures. So now the waters bring forth, not reptiles however, but divine spiritual gifts. The waters have brought forth fish that were dumb and void of reason; now they bring forth spiritual fish endowed with reason. First as the Apostle taught, "Follow Me," Jesus said, "and I will make you fishers of men" (Mt. 4:19). This is the fishing He spoke of. A new kind indeed; for they who need fish draw fish out of the water. But we throw them into the water; and that is how we fish!

Once under the Jewish Law there was a pool. Listen to what the pool could do, so as to learn of the poverty of the Law, and understand the richness of the Church. The pool was full of water, and at certain times an angel would descend and move the waters. And at the moving of the waters, one sick man would enter the pool and be healed. And only one person was healed each year, and then the grace ended—not because of the poverty of the One Who bestowed the grace, but because of the infirmity of those who received it. Then an angel descended into the pond, and moved its waters, and one person was healed. The Lord of the angels descended into the Jordan and moved the waters, and healed the whole world.

In the first case, he who next descended into the pool, after the first, received no healing; for grace was first given to the sickened Jews. Here, after the first, the second is healed, and after the second, the third, and after the third the fourth, and even ten, or a hundred, or ten thousand.

---

[7] St. John Chrysostom, *The Fruits of Christ's Resurrection*, PG 50, "On the Pasch," SSGF, vol. 2, 223-225.

Even if you had immersed the whole world into the pool, you would not consume the grace, nor exhaust the gift, nor soil the stream. A new way of purification! For it is not of the body. For in bodily purification, the more the water cleanses, the more it becomes soiled. Here, the more the water washes, the cleaner it becomes.

Consider how great a gift this is! Treasure the greatness of this gift, O man! It is not lawful for you to live indifferently. Seek with all diligence to know the law to which you are subject. This life is a struggle and a warfare, and one who is fighting restrains himself in everything.

Do you want me to tell you a good and worthy way of doing what is just? Erase from your mind the things which seem to you to be of no importance but which bring about sin. For among our actions some are sinful and some are not sinful in themselves, yet are the cause of sin. So, laughter is not a sin, in and of itself. But it becomes sinful if indulged in beyond measure. For from laughter comes coarse jesting, from jesting arises obscenity in word, from that comes obscenity in deeds, and from evil deeds comes punishment and retribution.

Therefore, first take out the root that you may then remove the whole disease.

## "HEAL ME O LORD!"

### *St. John Chrysostom*[8]

### 1.

"He said to him, "Do you want to be made well? The sick man answered Him, "Sir, I have no one to put me into the pool..."

Great is the profit of the divine Scriptures, and all-sufficient is the aid which comes from them. And Paul declared this when he said, "For whatever things were written before were written for our admonition, that we through the patience and comfort of the Scriptures might have

---

[8] St. John Chrysostom, Homily 37 on John 5:6, 7, NPNF, s. 1, v. 14.

hope" (Rom. 15:4; 1 Cor. 10:11). For the divine oracles are a treasury of all manner of medicines, so that whether it be needful to quench pride, to lull desire to sleep, to tread under foot the love of money, to despise pain, to inspire confidence, to gain patience, from them one may find abundant resource.

For what kind of person who is struggling with long poverty or is held by a grievous disease, will not, when he reads the passage before us, receive much comfort? Since this man who had been paralytic for thirty and eight years, and who saw each year others delivered, and himself bound by his disease, not even so fell back and despaired, though in truth not merely despair for the past, but also hopelessness for the future, was sufficient to throw him down.

Hear now what he says, and learn the greatness of the tragedy. For when Christ had said, "Do you want to be made well?" he said, "Yes, Lord. But, I have no man to put me into the pool when the water is stirred up."

What can be more pitiable than these words? What is more sad than these circumstances? Do you see a heart crushed through long sickness? Do you see all violence subdued? He uttered no blasphemous word, nor such as we hear the many use in defeat. He cursed not his day, he was not angry at the question, nor did he say, "Have You come to mock me and joke, that You ask whether I want to be made well?" But he replied gently, and with great mildness, "Yes, Lord."

Yet, he knew not Who it was that asked him, nor that He would heal him, but still he mildly relates all the circumstances and asks nothing further, as though he were speaking to a physician, and desired merely to tell the story of his sufferings. Perhaps he hoped that Christ might be so far useful to him as to put him into the water, and desired to attract Him by these words. What then does Jesus say?

**"Arise, take your bed and walk..."**

Now some suppose that this is the man in Matthew who was "lying on a bed" (Mt. 9:2); but it is not so, as is clear in many ways. First, from his wanting persons to stand forward for him. That man had many to care for and to carry him, this man not a single one. Therefore he said, "I have no man."

Secondly, from the manner of answering: the other uttered no word, but this man relates his whole case. Thirdly, from the season and time: this man was healed at a feast and on the Sabbath, that other on a different day. The places also were different: one was cured in a house, the other by the pool. The manner also of the cure was altered: there Christ said, "Your sins are forgiven you" (Mt. 9:2), but here He secured the body first, and then cared for the soul. In that case there was remission of sins, for He said, "Your sins are forgiven." But in this case, there are warning and threats to strengthen the man for the future: "Sin no more, lest a worse thing come unto you" (Jn. 5:14). The charges also of the Jews are different: here they object to Jesus, His working on the Sabbath, there they charge Him with blasphemy.

Consider now, I ask you, the exceeding wisdom of God. He did not immediately raise up the man, but first makes him familiar by questioning, making way for the coming faith. Nor does He only raise him, but bids him to "take up" his bed, as to confirm the miracle that had been worked so that none might suppose what was done to be illusion or a piece of acting. For unless his limbs had been firmly and thoroughly compacted, he would not have been able to carry his bed.

And Christ often does this to effectually silence those who would be so insolent. In the case of the loaves, He allowed there to be many fragments of the loaves so that no one might assert that the men had been merely satisfied, and that what was done was an illusion. So He said to the leper who was cleansed, "Go your way, show yourself to the priest" (Mt. 8:4), instantly providing most certain proof of the cleansing, and stopping the shameless mouths of those who asserted that He was legislating in opposition to God.

In a similar way, He acted in the case of the wine. For He did not merely show it to them, but also caused it to be borne to the governor of the feast, in order that one who knew nothing of what had been done, by his confession might bear to Him unsuspected testimony. Therefore, the Evangelist said that the ruler of the feast "did not know where it came from" (Jn. 2:9) thus showing the impartiality of his testimony.

And in another place, when He raised the dead, "He commanded that she be given something to eat" (Lk. 8:55), supplying this proof of a real resurrection, and by these means persuading even the foolish that He was no deceiver, no dealer in illusions, but that He had come for the salvation of the common nature of mankind.

2.

But why did Jesus not require faith from this man, as He did in the case of others, saying, "Do you believe that I am able to do this?" (Mt. 9:28)?[9] It was because the man did not yet clearly know Who He was. For, we find Him doing this after He works miracles, not before. For persons who had beheld His power exerted on others would reasonably have this said to them. From those who had not yet learned Who He was, but who were to know afterwards by means of signs, it is *after* the miracles that faith is required. And therefore Matthew does not introduce Christ as having said this at the beginning of His miracles, but when He had healed many, to the two blind men only.

However, observe in this way the faith of the paralytic. When he had heard, "Take up your bed and walk," he neither mocked nor said, "What can this mean? An angel comes down and troubles the water, and heals only one, and do You, a man, by a simple command and word hope to be able to do greater things than angels? This is mere vanity, boasting, and mockery!" He neither said nor imagined anything like this. Once he heard he was not disobedient to Him Who gave the command. But he immediately arose, for he was immediately made whole, and "took up his bed and walked." What followed was even far more admirable.

That he believed at first, when no one troubled him, was not so marvelous, but that afterwards, when the Jews were full of madness and pressed upon him on all sides, accusing and besieging him and saying, "It is not lawful for you to take up your bed," that then he gave no heed to their madness. But he most boldly in the midst of the assembly proclaimed his Benefactor and silenced their shameless tongues. This, I say, was an act of great courage. For when the Jews arose against him, and said in a reproachful and insolent manner to him:

---

[9] Other manuscripts add here the following, "as in the case of the blind men, saying, 'Do you believe?' (Mt. 9:28)."

"'It is the Sabbath; it is not lawful for you to carry your bed'...[But he answered them,] 'The Man who made me well said to me, "Take up your bed and walk."'"

All but saying, "You are silly and mad who bid me not to take Him for my Teacher Who has delivered me from a long and grievous malady, and not to obey whatever He may command." Had he chosen to act in an unfair manner, he might have spoke differently, saying, "I do not do this of my own will, but at the bidding of another. If this is a matter of blame, blame Him Who gave the order, and I will set down the bed." And he might have concealed the cure, for he well knew that they were vexed not so much at the breaking of the Sabbath, as at the curing of his infirmity. Yet he neither concealed this, nor said that, nor asked for pardon, but with a loud voice he confessed and proclaimed the benefit. Thus did the paralytic. But consider how unfairly they acted. For they did not remain silent after asking, "Who is it Who has made you well?" but kept bringing forward the seeming transgression.

"Then they asked him, 'Who is the Man who said to you, "Take up your bed and walk?"' But the one who was healed did not know who it was, for Jesus had withdrawn, a multitude being in that place."

And why did Jesus conceal Himself? First, that while He was absent, the testimony of the man might be unsuspected, for he who now felt himself whole was a credible witness of the benefit.

Secondly, [He hid Himself so] that He might not cause the fury of the Jews to be yet more inflamed, for the very sight of one whom they envy is accustomed to kindle not a small spark in malicious persons. On this account, He retired, and left the deed by itself to plead its cause among them, that He might not say anything in person respecting Himself, but that they might do so who had been healed, and with them also the accusers. Even these last for a while testify to the miracle. For they did not say, "Why have You commanded these things to be done on the Sabbath day?" but, "Why do You do these things on the Sabbath day?" not being displeased at the transgression, but envious at the restoration of the paralytic.

Regarding human labor, what the paralytic did was rather a work, for the other was a saying and a word. Here then He commands another to break the Sabbath, but elsewhere He does the same Himself, mixing clay and anointing a man's eyes. Yet He did these things not transgressing, but going beyond the Law. We shall speak about this afterwards. For we must carefully observe that when He was accused by the Jews respecting the Sabbath, He does not always defend Himself in the same terms.

### 3.

Let us consider for awhile how great an evil is envy, how it disables the eyes of the soul to endanger the salvation of one who is possessed by it. For as madmen often thrust their swords against their own bodies, so also malicious persons looking only to one thing, the injury of him they envy, care not for their own salvation. Men like these are worse than wild beasts; they when wanting food, or having first been provoked by us, arm themselves against us. But when these men have received kindness, they have often repaid their benefactors as though they had wronged them. They are worse than wild beasts, like the devils, or perhaps even worse—for they truly have an unceasing hostility against us, but do not plot against those of their own nature. And by this Jesus silenced the Jews when they said that He cast out devils by Beelzebub. But these men neither respect their common nature, nor spare their own selves. For before they vex those whom they envy, they vex their own souls, filling them with all manner of trouble and despondency, fruitlessly and in vain.

For why do you grieve, O man, at the prosperity of your neighbor? We should grieve at the ills we suffer, not because we see others in good repute. Therefore this sin is stripped of all excuse. The fornicator may allege his lust, the thief his poverty, the man-slayer his passion—frigid and unreasonable excuses, still they have these to allege. But what reason, tell me, will you name? None other at all, but that of intense wickedness. If we are commanded to love our enemies, what punishment shall we suffer if we hate our very friends?

And if he who loves those that love him will be in no better a state than the heathen, what excuse, what cloak shall he have who injures those that have done him no wrong? Listen to what Paul says, "Though I give my body to be burned, but have not love, it profits me nothing" (1 Cor. 13:3). Now, it is clear to everyone that where envy and malice are, there is not love. This feeling is worse than fornication and adultery, for these go no farther than him who does them. But, the tyranny of envy has overturned entire churches, and has destroyed the whole world.

Envy is the mother of murder. Through this Cain slew Abel, his brother. Through this, Esau (would have slain) Jacob, and his brethren, Joseph. Through this, the devil slew all mankind. You indeed now do not kill, but you do many things worse than murder, desiring that your brother may act improperly, laying snares for him on all sides, paralyzing his labors on the side of virtue, grieving that he pleases the Master of the world. Yet you do not war with your brother, but with Him Whom he serves. Him you insult when you prefer your glory to His. And what is truly worst of all, is that this sin seems to be an unimportant one, while, in fact, it is more grievous than any other. For although you show mercy, watch and fast, you are more accursed than any if you envy your brother. This is clear from this circumstance also.

A man of the Corinthians was once guilty of adultery, yet he was charged with his sin and soon restored to righteousness. Cain envied Abel, but he was not healed. Although God Himself continually charmed the wound, he became more pained and wave-tossed, and was hurried on to murder. Thus, this passion is worse than that other, and does not easily permit itself to be cured except when we give it heed.

Let us, then, by all means tear it up by the roots, considering this, that as we offend God when we waste with envy at other men's blessings, so when we rejoice with them, we are well pleasing to Him, and render ourselves partakers of the good things laid up for the righteous. Therefore Paul exhorts us to "Rejoice with those who rejoice, and weep with those who weep" (Rom. 12:15), that on either hand we may reap great profit. Considering then that even when we labor not, by rejoicing with him who labors, we become sharers of his crown, let us cast aside all envy, and implant love in our souls, that by applauding those of our brethren who are well pleasing unto God, we may obtain both present and future good things, through the grace and loving-kindness of our Lord Jesus Christ, by Whom and with Whom, to the Father and the Holy Spirit, be glory, now and ever, world without end. Amen.

## "Spiritual Paralytics"

### *The Scholar Origen*[10]

"And when they had come to the multitude, a man came to Him, kneeling down to Him and saying, 'Lord, have mercy on my son.'"

Those who are suffering, or the relatives of the sufferers, are along with the multitudes. Therefore, when He has dispensed the things that were beyond the multitudes, He descends to them, so that those who were not able to ascend because of the sicknesses that repressed their soul, might be benefited when the Word descended to them from the loftier regions.

But should inquire in respect of what diseases the sufferers believe and pray for their own healing, and in respect of what diseases others do this for them, as, for example, the centurion for his servant, and the nobleman for his son, and the ruler of the synagogue for a daughter, and the Canaanite woman for her female child who was vexed with a demon, and now the man who kneels to Him on behalf of his epileptic son. Along with these you will investigate when the Savior heals of Himself and unasked by any one, as for example, the paralytic. For these cures, when compared with one another for this very purpose, and examined together, will exhibit to him who is able to hear the "wisdom of God hidden in a mystery" (1 Cor. 2:7) many dogmas concerning the different diseases of souls, as well as the method of their healing.

But since our present object is not to make inquiry about every case, but about the passage before us, let us, adopting a figurative interpretation, consider who we may say the epileptic was, and who was his father who prayed for him, and what is meant by the sufferer falling not constantly but oftentimes, sometimes into the fire, and sometimes into the water, and what is meant by the fact that he could not be healed by the disciples but by Jesus Himself. For if every sickness and every infirmity, which our Savior then healed among the people, refers to different disorders in souls, it is also in accordance with reason that by the paralytics are symbolized the palsied in soul, who keep it lying paralyzed in the body. Those who are

---

[10] Origen, *Commentary on Matthew*, 13.3-4.

blind symbolized those who are blind in respect of things seen by the soul alone, and these are really blind. And by the deaf are symbolized those who are deaf in regard to the reception of the word of salvation.

On the same principle it will be necessary that the matters regarding the epileptic should be investigated. Now this affection attacks the sufferers at considerable intervals, during which he who suffers from it seems in no way to differ from the man in good health, at the season when the epilepsy is not working on him. Similar disorders you may find in certain souls, which are often supposed to be healthy in point of temperance and the other virtues. Then, sometimes, as if they were seized with a kind of epilepsy arising from their passions, they fall down from the position in which they seemed to stand, and are drawn away by the deceit of this world and other lusts. Perhaps, therefore, you would not err if you said, that such persons, so to speak, are epileptic spiritually, having been cast down by "the spiritual hosts of wickedness in the heavenly places" (Eph. 6:12) and are often ill, at the time when the passions attack their soul. At one time falling into the fire of burnings, when, according to what is said in Hosea, they become adulterers, like a pan heated for the cooking from the burning flame (Hos. 7:4); and, at another time, into the water, when the king of all the dragons in the waters casts them down from the sphere where they appeared to breath freely, so that they come into the depths of the waves of the sea of human life.

This interpretation of ours in regard to the lunatic will be supported by him who says in the Book of Wisdom with reference to the even temperament of the just man, "The discourse of a pious man is always wisdom, but, in regard to what we have said, the fool changes as the moon" (Sir. 27:11). Sometimes even in the case of such you may see impulses which might carry away in praise of them those who do not attend to their want of ballast, so that they would say that it was as full moon in their case, or almost full moon. And you might see again the light that seemed to be in them diminishing—as it was not the light of day but the light of night— fading to so great an extent, that the light which appeared to be seen in them no longer existed. But whether or not those who first gave their names to things, on account of this gave the name of lunacy to the disease epilepsy, you will judge for yourself.

## "The Great Physician"
### *St. Cyril of Jerusalem*[11]

Jesus means "Savior" in Hebrew, but in Greek, it means "Healer" for He is the Physician of the spirits and bodies. He is the healer of the spirits. He opened the eyes of the born blind, and He guided the minds to the light. He cures the visibly paralyzed and leads the sinners to the path of repentance. He says to the paralytic: "Sin no more" (Jn. 5:14), and "Take up your bed and walk" (Jn. 5:8), for the body was paralyzed because of the spirit's sin. Christ served the soul first so that the healing extends to the body. Therefore, if one of you suffers in his self because of his sins, he will find Christ is his physician, and if one of you has little faith, he must say, "Help my unbelief!" (Mk. 9:24). And if one of you feels physical pain, he must not be an unbeliever, he must rather come closer to Jesus who cures such an illness; and he must know that Jesus is the Christ.

## "I Have No Man"
### *A Prayer by Hegumen Father Tadros Malaty*[12]

My spirit groans with the paralytic man of Bethesda. I entered with him as through the five porches, the five books of Moses. I fell under the Law that exposed my weakness. I discovered I was sick, in need of a heavenly Physician!

My life passed like 38 years, during which I lacked true love!
I have no man to put me into the water of divine love to get cured!
Who may grant me true love for my God and brethren?
Who will support me to perfect the law of love that I may be healed?

You often passed, O Physician of the souls,
As though You left everybody to search for me, the first among sinners!
With love You continuously repeated, "Do you want to be made well?"

Because of my foolishness I did not hear Your voice!
I loved the noise of the world and was preoccupied with it.

---

[11] St. Cyril of Jerusalem, *Catechetical Lecture* 10.13.
[12] Fr. Tadros Malaty, *Patristic Commentary on the Gospel of John*.

I do not have two ears to hear the voice of heavenly Love!
Your sweet voice, but because of my deafness I did not listen to it!

Your wonderful Holy Spirit attracted my heart to You.
I heard Your sweet voice;
And I rejoiced in Your face that is more beautiful than the sons of men!
I have confessed to You my need for One Who will heal me.

At Your mighty word I rose from my bed
In obedience to Your command I took up my bed and walked home!
I took up the bed of my illness;
I see it and remember my weakness and death.

I remember Your authority, You Who grants forgiveness and life.
I walk, and walk until I enter my house.
I shall not rest until I reach the Bosom of Your Father,
My eternal dwelling place!

# X

## Go, Wash in the Pool of Siloam

*Meditations on the Sunday of the Man Born Blind of the Great Lent*

### Gospel Reading of the Sixth Sunday of the Great Lent

#### (John 9:1-41)

*Now as Jesus passed by, He saw a man who was blind from birth. And His disciples asked Him, saying, "Rabbi, who sinned, this man or his parents, that he was born blind?" Jesus answered, "Neither this man nor his parents sinned, but that the works of God should be revealed in him. I must work the works of Him Who sent Me while it is day; the night is coming when no one can work. As long as I am in the world, I am the Light of the world."*

*When He had said these things, He spat on the ground and made clay with the saliva; and He anointed the eyes of the blind man with the clay. And He said to him, "Go, wash in the pool of Siloam" (which is translated, Sent).*

*So he went and washed, and came back seeing.*

*Therefore the neighbors and those who previously had seen that he was blind said, "Is not this he who sat and begged?" Some said, "This is he." Others said, "He is like him." He said, "I am he."*

*Therefore they said to him, "How were your eyes opened?" He answered and said, "A Man called Jesus made clay and anointed my eyes and said to me, 'Go to the pool of Siloam and wash.' So I went and washed, and I received sight."*

*Then they said to him, "Where is He?" He said, "I do not know." They brought him who formerly was blind to the Pharisees.*

*Now it was a Sabbath when Jesus made the clay and opened his eyes. Then the Pharisees also asked him again how he had received his sight. He said to them, "He put clay on my eyes, and I washed, and I see."*

*Therefore some of the Pharisees said, "This Man is not from God, because He does not keep the Sabbath." Others said, "How can a man who is a sinner do such signs?" And there was a division among them.*

*They said to the blind man again, "What do you say about Him because He opened your eyes?" He said, "He is a prophet."*

*But the Jews did not believe concerning him, that he had been blind and received his sight, until they called the parents of him who had received his sight. And they asked them, saying, "Is this your son, who you say was born blind? How then does he now see?" His parents answered them and said, "We know that this is our son, and that he was born blind; but by what means he now sees we do not know, or who opened his eyes we do not know. He is of age; ask him. He will speak for himself." His parents said these things because they feared the Jews, for the Jews had agreed already that if anyone confessed that He was Christ, he would be put out of the synagogue. Therefore his parents said, "He is of age; ask him."*

*So they again called the man who was blind, and said to him, "Give God the glory! We know that this Man is a sinner." He answered and said, "Whether He is a sinner or not I do not know. One thing I know: that though I was blind, now I see."*

*Then they said to him again, "What did He do to you? How did He open your eyes?" He answered them, "I told you already, and you did not listen. Why do you want to hear it again? Do you also want to become His disciples?" Then they reviled him and said, "You are His disciple, but we are Moses' disciples. We know that God spoke to Moses; as for this fellow, we do not know where He is from." The man answered and said to them, "Why, this is a marvelous thing, that you do not know where He is from; yet He has opened my eyes! Now we know that God does not hear sinners; but if anyone is a worshiper of God and does His will, He hears him. Since the world began it has been unheard of that anyone opened the eyes of one who was born blind. If this Man were not from God, He could do nothing." They answered and said to him, "You were completely born in sins, and are you teaching us?"*

*And they cast him out. Jesus heard that they had cast him out; and when He had found him, He said to him, "Do you believe in the Son of God?" He answered and said, "Who is He, Lord, that I may believe in Him?"*

*And Jesus said to him, "You have both seen Him and it is He Who is talking with you." Then he said, "Lord, I believe!" And he worshipped Him.*

*And Jesus said, "For judgment I have come into this world, that those who do not see may see, and that those who see may be made blind."*

*Then some of the Pharisees who were with Him heard these words, and said to Him, "Are we blind also?" Jesus said to them, "If you were blind, you would have no sin; but now you say, 'We see.' Therefore your sin remains.*

## "Making Clay"
### St. Irenaeus of Lyons[1]

The Lord most plainly manifested Himself and the Father to His disciples, so that they would not seek after another God besides Him Who formed man, and Who gave him the breath of life; and so that men might not rise to such a pitch of madness as to invent another father above the Creator. Therefore, He also healed by a word all the others who were in a weakly condition because of sin, to whom also He said, "See, you have been made well. Sin no more, lest a worse thing come upon you" (Jn. 5:14). By this, He pointed out that because of the sin of disobedience, infirmities have come upon men.

To that man, however, who had been blind from his birth, He gave sight, not by means of a word, but by an outward action. He did this not without a purpose, or because it so happened, but that He might show forth the hand of God, that which at the beginning had molded man. Therefore, when His disciples asked Him why the man had been born blind—whether for his own or his parents' fault—He replied, "Neither this

---

[1] St. Irenaeus, *Against the Heresies*, Book V, ANF v. 1, 1122, 1123.

man nor his parents sinned, but that the works of God should be revealed in him" (Jn. 9:3).

Now the work of God is the fashioning of man. For, as the Scripture says, He made man by a kind of process: "And God formed the man from dust of the earth" (Gen. 2:7). The Lord spat on the ground, made clay, and smeared it upon the eyes, pointing out the original fashioning [of man], how it was effected, and manifesting the hand of God to those who can understand by what [hand] man was formed out of the dust. For that which the Artificer, the Word, had omitted to form in the womb, [viz., the blind man's eyes], He then supplied in public, that the works of God might be manifested in him, in order that we might not be seeking out another hand by which man was fashioned, nor another Father; knowing that this hand of God which formed us at the beginning, and which does form us in the womb, has in the last times sought us out who were lost, winning back His own, and taking up the lost sheep upon His shoulders, and with joy restoring it to the fold of life.

Now, that the Word of God forms us in the womb, He says to Jeremiah, "Before I formed you in the belly, I knew you; and before you came forth from the womb, I sanctified you; I appointed you a prophet to the nations" (Jer. 1:5). Likewise Paul says, "God, Who separated me from my mother's womb... that I might preach Him among the Gentiles" (Gal. 1:15, 16). Therefore, as we are by the Word formed in the womb, this very same Word formed the visual power in him who had been blind from his birth.

This openly shows who it is that fashions us in secret, since the Word Himself had been made manifest to men, and declaring the original formation of Adam, and the manner in which he was created, and by what hand he was fashioned, indicating the whole from a part. For the Lord Who formed the visual powers is He Who made the whole man, carrying out the will of the Father. And inasmuch as man, with respect to that formation which, was after Adam, having fallen into transgression, needed the layer of regeneration, [the Lord] said to him [upon whom He had conferred sight], after He had smeared his eyes with the clay, "Go to the pool of Siloam, and wash" (Jn. 9:11), thus restoring to him both [his perfect] confirmation, and that regeneration which takes place by means of the laver. And for this reason when he was washed he came seeing, that he might both know Him Who had fashioned him, and that man might learn [to know] Him Who has conferred upon him life.

## "The Light of the World"

### St. Gregory Nazianzen[2]

Again my Jesus, and again a mystery; not deceitful, nor disorderly, nor belonging to Greek error or drunkenness (for so I call their solemnities, and so I think will every man of sound sense); but a mystery lofty and divine, and allied to the glory above. For the Holy Day of the Lights, to which we have come, and which we are celebrating today, has for its origin the Baptism of my Christ, "the True Light Who gives light to every man who comes into the world" (Jn. 1:9), and effects my purification, and assists that light which we received from the beginning from Him from above, but which we darkened and confused by sin.

Therefore listen to the Voice of God, which sounds so exceeding clearly to me, who am both disciple and master of these mysteries, as would to God it may sound to you, "I am The Light of the World" (Jn. 8:12). Therefore approach Him and be enlightened. Do not let your faces be ashamed being signed with the true Light. It is a season of new birth, let us be born again. It is a time of reform, let us receive again the first Adam. Let us not remain what we are, but let us become what we once were. The light shines in darkness (Jn. 1:5), in this life and in the flesh, and is chased by the darkness, but is not overtaken by it—I mean the adverse power leaping up in its shamelessness against the visible Adam, but encountering God and being defeated—in order that we, putting away the darkness, may draw near to the Light, and may then become perfect Light, the children of perfect Light. See the grace of this day; see the power of this mystery. Are you not lifted up from the earth? Are you not clearly placed on high, being exalted by our voice and meditation? And you will be placed much higher when the Word shall have prospered the course of my words.

---

[2] St. Gregory Nazianzen, *Oration 39*, NPNF s. 2, v. 7, 685.
This oration was preached on the Feast of Theophany, also called the Feast of Lights since the baptized carried candles or torches after their baptism, in 381. A discussion of the Lord's baptism is most appropriate for this, the "Sunday of Baptism."

## "Does God Listen to Sinners?"

### *St. Augustine of Hippo*[3]

#### 1.

The Lord Jesus, as we heard when the holy gospel was being read, opened the eyes of a man who was born blind. Brethren, if we consider our hereditary punishment, the whole world is blind. And therefore came Christ the Enlightener, because the devil had been the blinder. He made all men to be born blind, who seduced the first man. Let them run to the Enlightener, let them run, believe, receive the clay made of the saliva. The Word is as it were the saliva; the flesh is the earth. Let them wash the face in the pool of Siloam. Now it was the Evangelist's place to explain to us what Siloam means, and he said, "which is translated, Sent" (Jn. 9:7). Who is this Who is Sent, but He Who in this very lesson said, "I must work the works of Him Who sent Me" (Jn. 9:4). Behold, Siloam! Wash your face, be baptized, that you may be enlightened, and that you who did not see before, may now see.

#### 2.

Behold, first open your eyes to that which is said, "I have come," says He, "to work the works of Him Who sent Me." Now here at once stands forth the Arian, and says, "Here you see that Christ did not His Own works, but the Father's Who sent Him." Would he say this, if he saw, that is, if he had washed his face in Him Who was sent, as it were in Siloam? What then do you say? "Behold," he says, "Himself said it." What did He say? "I have come to work the works of Him Who sent Me." Are they not then His Own? No. What then is that which the Siloam Himself says, the Sent Himself, the Son Himself, the Only Son Himself, Whom you complain of as degenerate? What is that He says, "All things that the Father has are Mine." You say that He did the works of another, in that

---

[3] St. Augustine, *Sermon 85*, NPNF s. 1, v. 6, pp. 1107, 1108.

He said, "I must work the works of Him Who sent Me." I say that the Father had the things of another: I am speaking according to your principles. Why would you object to me that Christ said, "I have come to do His works" as if, "not My own but 'His Who sent Me?'"

### 3.

I ask You, O Lord Christ, resolve the difficulty, put an end to the contention. "All things," He says, "that the Father has are Mine" (Jn. 16:15). Are they then not the Father's, if they are Yours? For He does not say, "All things that the Father has He has given unto Me"; although, if He had said even this, He would have shown His equality. But the difficulty is that He said, "All things that the Father has are Mine." If you understand it correctly, all things that the Father has are the Son's; all things that the Son has are the Father's. Hear Him in another place, "All Mine are Yours, and Yours are Mine" (Jn. 17:10). The question is finished, as to the things which the Father and the Son have. They have them with one consent, do not introduce any dissension. What He calls the works of the Father, are His Own works; for, "Yours are Mine," for He speaks of the works of that Father, to Whom He said, "All Mine are Yours, and Yours are Mine." So then, My works are Yours, and Your works are Mine. "For whatever [the Father] does," He Himself has said, the Lord has said, the Only-Begotten has said, the Son has said, the Truth has said. What has He said? "Whatever He does, the Son also does in like manner" (Jn. 5:19). Signal expression! Signal truth! Signal equality! "All things that the Father does, these does the Son also." Was it enough to say, "All things that the Father does, these does the Son also?" It is not enough; I add "in like manner." Why do I add "in like manner?" Because those who do not understand, and who walk with eyes not yet open want to say, "The Father does them by way of command, the Son of obedience, therefore not in like manner." But if in like manner, as the One, so the Other; so what things the One, the same the Other.

### 4.

"But," says he, "the Father commands, that the Son may execute." Carnal indeed is your conceit, but without prejudice to the truth, I grant it to you. Behold, the Father commands, the Son obeys. Therefore, is the

Son not of the same nature because the One commands and the Other obeys? Give me two men, father and son; they are two men. He who commands is a man; he who obeys is a man. He who commands and he who obeys have the same nature. Does not he who commands beget a son of his own nature? Does he who obeys, by obeying, lose his nature?

Now take for the present, as you thus take two men, the Father commanding, the Son obeying, yet God and God. But the first two together are two men, the Latter together is but One God. This is a divine miracle.

Meanwhile if you would that with you I acknowledge the obedience, do you first with me acknowledge the nature. The Father begot that which Himself is. If the Father begot one other than what Himself is, He did not beget a true Son. The Father says to the Son, "From the womb before the morning star, I have begotten You" (Ps. 109:3). What does "before the morning star" mean? By the morning star times are signified. So then before times, before all that is called "before." Before all that is not, or before all that is. For the gospel does not say, "In the beginning God made the Word," but, "In the beginning God made the heaven and the earth" (Gen. 1:1). Neither, "In the beginning the Word was born," nor, "In the beginning God begot the Word." But what does it say? "He was, He was, He was." You hear, "He was," believe! "In the beginning *was* the Word, and the Word *was* with God, and the Word *was* God" (Jn. 1:1). So often do you hear, was seek not for time, for that He always was. He then Who always was, and was always with the Son (for God is able to beget without you) He said to the Son, "From the womb before the morning star, I have begotten You."

What does "from the womb" mean? Does God have a womb? Shall we imagine that God was fashioned with bodily members? God forbid! But He said, "from the womb," so it might be understood that He begot Him from His Own essence? So then from the womb came forth that which Himself was Who begot. For if He Who begot was one thing, and another came forth out of the womb; it would be a monster, not a Son.

5.

Therefore let the Son work the works of Him Who sent Him, and the Father also does the works of the Son. "At all events," you say, "the Father wills, the Son executes." Behold, I show, that the Son wills, and the Father executes. Are you asking, "how can you prove this?" I will show it at once. "Father, I desire" (Jn. 17:24). Now here if I had a mind to object, behold, the Son commands, and the Father executes. What do You will? That they "may be with Me where I am." We have escaped, there shall we be, where He is; there shall we be, we have escaped. Who can undo the "I desire" of the Almighty?

You hear the will of His power, hear now the power of His will. "For as the Father," He says, "raises the dead and gives life to them, even so the Son gives life to whom He will" (Jn. 5:21). He does not say, "The Son raises them, whom the Father commands Him to raise, but "He raises...whom He will." So then whom the Father will, and whom Himself will: because where there is One Power, there is One Will. Let us then in a heart blind no more hold fast that the nature of the Father and the Son is One and the Same; because the Father is very Father, the Son is very Son. What He is, that did He beget: because the Begotten was not degenerate.

6.

There is something in the words of that man who was blind which may cause perplexity and might make many who misunderstand them despair. For among the rest of his words, the same man whose eyes were opened said, "We know that God does not hear sinners" (Jn. 9:1). What shall we do, if God does not hear sinners? Dare we pray to God if He does not hear sinners?

Give me one who may pray; behold, here is One to hear. Give me one who may pray. Sift thoroughly the human race from the imperfect to the perfect. Mount up from the spring to the summer; for this we have just chanted, "You have formed summer and spring" (Ps. 73:17), that is, "Those who are already spiritual, and those who are still carnal You have made." For so the Son Himself says, "Your eyes saw Me when I was unformed" (Ps. 138:16). That which is imperfect in my body, Your eyes have seen. So, then, should those who are imperfect have hope? Undoubtedly they have.

Hear what follows, "and all men shall be written in Your Book" (Ps. 138:16). But perhaps, brethren, the spiritual pray and are heard because they are not sinners? What then must the carnal do? What must they do? Shall they perish? Shall they not pray to God? God forbid!

Give me that Publican in the gospel. Come, you Publican, stand forth, show your hope, that the weak may not lose hope. For behold the publican went up with the Pharisee to pray, and with face cast down upon the ground, standing afar off, beating his breast, he said, "God, be merciful to me a sinner!" and "went down to his house justified rather than the [Pharisee]" (Lk. 18:13, 14). Was the one who said, "Be merciful to me a sinner!" right or wrong? If he spoke truly, he was a sinner; yet was he heard and justified.

Why then did you, whose eyes the Lord opened, say, "We know that God does not hear sinners?" Behold, God does hear sinners. But wash your inferior face, let that be done in your heart, which has been done in your face; and you will see that God does hear sinners. The imagination of your heart has deceived you. There is still something for Him to do to you. We see that this man was cast out of the synagogue; Jesus heard of it, came to him, and said to him, "Do you believe in the Son of God?" (Jn. 9:35) And He said, "Who is He, Lord, that I may believe in Him?" (Jn. 9:36). He saw, and did not see; he saw with the eyes, but he did not yet see with the heart. The Lord said to him,

"You have both seen Him," that is, with the eyes, "and it is He Who is talking with you." Then he washed the face of his heart.

### 7.

You sinners, apply yourselves then earnestly to prayer! Confess your sins, pray that they may be blotted out, pray that they may be diminished, pray that as you increase, they may decrease. But, do not despair, sinners though you are, and pray. For who has not sinned? Begin with the priests. To the priests it is said, "First offer sacrifices for your own sins, and then for the people's" (cf. Lev. 16; Heb. 7:27). The sacrifices convicted the priests that if any one should call himself righteous and without sin, it might be answered him, "I look not at what you say, but at what you offer. Your own victim convicts you. Why do you offer for your own sins, if you have no sins? Do you in your sacrifice lie to God?" But perhaps the priests of the ancient people were sinners; of the new people are not sinners.

Truly, brethren, for that God has so willed, I am His priest. I am a sinner; with you do I beat the breast, with you I ask for pardon, with you I hope that God will be merciful. But perhaps the apostles, those first and highest leaders of the flock, shepherds, members of the Shepherd, these perhaps had no sin. Yes, indeed, even they had. They had indeed. They are not angry at this, for they confess it. I should not dare. First hear the Lord Himself saying to the apostles, "In this manner...pray" (Mt. 6:9). As those other priests were convicted by the sacrifices, so these by prayer. And among the other things which He commanded them to pray for, He appointed this also, "Forgive us our trespasses, as we forgive those who trespass against us." What do the apostles say? Every day they pray for their debts to be forgiven them. They come in debtors, they depart absolved, and return debtors to prayer. This life is not without sin, that as often as prayer is made, so often should sins be forgiven.

### 8.

But what shall I say? Perhaps when they learned the prayer, they were still weak. Someone, perhaps, will say this. When the Lord Jesus taught them that prayer, they were yet babes, weak, carnal; they were not yet spiritual, who have no sin. What then, brethren? When they became spiritual, did they cease to pray? Then Christ should have said, "Pray in such manner now" and to have given them, when spiritual, another prayer. It is the same. He Who gave it is One and the Same; use it then in prayer in the Church. But we will take away all controversy, when you say the holy apostles were spiritual, up to the time of the Lord's Passion they were carnal; this you must say. And indeed, the truth is, as He was hanging, they were in alarm, and the apostles then despaired when the robber believed.

Peter dared to follow when the Lord was led to suffering. He dared to follow; he came to the house, was wearied in the palace, stood at the fire, and was cold. He stood at the fire; he was frozen with a chilling fear. Being questioned by the maidservant, he denied Christ once; being questioned a second time, he denied Him; being questioned a third time, he denied Him. Thanks be to God that the questioning ceased. If the questioning had not ceased, the denial would have been repeated. But after He rose again, then He confirmed them, and then they became spiritual. But did they have no sin then?

You say, "The spiritual apostles wrote spiritual epistles and they sent them to the churches. So, they had no sin." But, I do not believe you. Let us ask them. Tell us, O holy apostles, after the Lord rose again, and confirmed you with the Holy Spirit sent from heaven, did you cease to have sin? Tell us, I beseech you. Let us hear, that sinners may not despair, that they may not leave off to pray to God, because they are not without sin. Tell us, one of them says. And who? He whom the Lord loved the most, and who was leaning on the Lord's bosom (cf. Jn. 13:23), and drank in the mysteries of the Kingdom of Heaven which he was to pour forth again. Him I ask: "Do you have sin or not?" He answers and says, "If we say that we have no sin, we deceive ourselves, and the truth is not in us" (1 Jn. 1:8). Now it is the same John who said, "In the beginning was the Word, and the Word was with God, and the Word was God" (Jn. 1:1). See what heights he had passed, that he could reach to the Word! Such a great person—who like an eagle soared above the clouds, who in the serene clearness of his mind saw, "In the beginning was the Word"—has said, "If we say that we have no sin, we deceive ourselves, and the truth is not in us. If we confess our sins, He is faithful and just to forgive us our sins and to cleanse us from all unrighteousness" (1 Jn. 1:8, 9). Therefore pray!

## "THE TRUE LIGHT AND HIS DISCIPLES"
### *The Scholar Origen*[4]

He said, then, that He was the Light of the world; and we have to examine, along with this title, those which are parallel to it; and, indeed, are thought by some to be not merely parallel, but identical with it. He is the True Light, and the Light of the Gentiles. In the opening of the Gospel now before us He is the Light of men: "That which was made," it says, "was life in Him, and the life was the Light of men; and the light

---

[4] Origen, *Epistle to Gregory*, ANF v. 10, 524-528.

shines in darkness, and the darkness did not comprehend it" (Jn. 1:4,5) A little further on, in the same passage, He is called the True Light: "The True Light, Which gives light to every man coming into the world" (Jn. 1:9). In Isaiah, He is the Light of the Gentiles, as we said before. "Behold, I have set You for a Light of the Gentiles, that You should be for salvation to the end of the earth" (Is. 49:6).

Now the sensible light of the world is the sun, and after it comes very worthily the moon, and the same title may be applied to the stars. But those lights of the world are said in Moses to have come into existence on the fourth day, and as they shed light on the things on the earth, they are not the True Light. But the Savior shines on creatures which have intellect and sovereign reason, that their minds may behold their proper objects of vision, and so He is the Light of the intellectual world, that is to say, of the reasonable souls which are in the sensible world, and if there be any beings beyond these in the world from which He declares Himself to be our Savior.

He is, indeed, the most determining and distinguished part of that world, and, as we may say, the Sun Who makes the great day of the Lord. In view of this day He says to those who partake of His light, "Work while it is day; the night is coming when no man can work. As long as I am in the world, I am the Light of the world" (Jn. 9:4, 5). Then He says to His disciples, "You are the light of the world," and "Let your light so shine before men" (Mt. 5:14, 16).

Thus we see the Church, the Bride, to present an analogy to the moon and stars, and the disciples have a light, which is their own or borrowed from the true Sun, so that they are able to illuminate those who have no command of any spring of light in themselves. We may say that Paul and Peter are the light of the world, and that those of their disciples who are enlightened themselves, but are not able to enlighten others, are the world of which the apostles were the light.

But the Savior, being the light of the world, illuminates not bodies, but by His incorporeal power the incorporeal intellect, to the end that each of us, enlightened as by the sun, may be able to discern the rest of the things of the mind. And as when the sun is shining the moon and the stars lose their power of giving light, so those who are irradiated by Christ and receive His beams have no need of the ministering apostles and prophets—

we must have courage to declare this truth. I will add that neither do the angels have need even of the greater powers when they are disciples of that first-born light. To those who do not receive the solar beams of Christ, the ministering saints do afford an illumination much less than the former; this illumination is as much as those persons can receive, and it completely fills them.

Christ, again, the Light of the world, is the True Light as distinguished from the light of sense; nothing that is sensible is true. Yet though the sensible is other than the true, it does not follow that the sensible is false, for the sensible may have an analogy with the intellectual, and not everything that is not true can correctly be called false. Now I ask whether the Light of the World is the same thing with the Light of men, and I conceive that a higher power of light is intended by the former phrase than by the latter, for the world in one sense is not only men. Paul shows that the world is something more than men when he writes to the Corinthians in his first Epistle: "for we have been made a spectacle to the world, both to angels and to men" (1 Cor. 4:9). In one sense, too, it may be considered, the world is the creation which is being delivered from the bondage of corruption into the liberty of the glory of the children of God, whose earnest expectation is waiting for the manifestation of the sons of God.

We also draw attention to the comparison which may be drawn between the statement, "I am the Light of the world" (Jn. 9:5), and the words addressed to the disciples, "You are the light of the world" (Mt. 5:14). Some suppose that the genuine disciples of Jesus are greater than other creatures, some seeking the reason of this ill the natural growth of these disciples, others inferring it from their harder struggle. For those beings which are in flesh and blood have greater labors and a life more full of dangers than those which are in an ethereal body, and the lights of heaven might not, if they had put on bodies of earth, have accomplished this life of ours free from danger and from error. Those who incline to this argument may appeal to those texts of Scripture which say the most exalted things about men, and to the fact that the Gospel is addressed directly to men; not so much is said about the creation, or, as we understand it, about the world.

We read, "As I and You are One, that they also may be one in Us" (Jn. 17:21), and "Where I am, there will be also My servant" (Jn. 12:26). These sayings, plainly, are about men. However, concerning the creation it is said that it is delivered from the bondage of corruption into the liberty of the glory of the children of God. It might be added that not even when it is delivered will it take part in the glory of the sons of God. Nor will those who hold this view forget that the First-born over all creation (Col. 1:15), honoring man above all else, became man. For it was not any of the constellations existing in the sky, but one of another order, appointed for this purpose and in the service of the knowledge of Jesus, that was made to be the Star of the East (Mt. 2:2), whether it was like the other stars or perhaps better than they, to be the sign of Him Who is the most excellent of all. And if the boasting of the saints is in their tribulations, since "tribulation produces perseverance; and perseverance, character; and character, hope. Now hope does not disappoint" (Rom. 5:3-5). Then the afflicted creation cannot have the like patience with man, nor the like probation, nor the like hope, but another degree of these, since "the creation was subjected to futility, not willingly, but because of Him Who subjected it in hope" (Rom. 8:20).

Now he who shrinks from conferring such great attributes on man will turn to another direction and say that the creature being subjected to vanity groans and suffers greater affliction than those who groan in this tabernacle, for has she not suffered for the utmost extent of time in her service of vanity —no, many times as long as man? For why does she do this not willingly, but that it is against her nature to be subject to vanity, and not to have the best arrangement of her life, that which she shall receive when she is set free, when the world is destroyed and released even from the vanity of bodies.

Here, however, we may appear to be stretching too far, and aiming at more than the question now before us requires. We may return, therefore, to the point from which we set out, and ask for what reason the Savior is called the Light of the world, the True Light, and the Light of men. Now we saw that He is called the True Light concerning the sensible light of the world and that the Light of the world is the same thing as the Light of men, or that we may at least enquire whether they are the same. This discussion is not superfluous. Some students do not take anything at all out of the statement that the Savior is the Word, and it is important for us to assure ourselves that we are not chargeable with caprice in fixing our attention on that notion. If it admits of being taken in a metaphorical sense we should not take it literally. When we apply the mystical and allegorical method to the expression "light of the world" and the many analogous terms mentioned above, we should surely do so with this expression also.

## "The Light of the World"

### *St. John Chrysostom*[5]

"When He had said these things, He spat on the ground and made clay with the saliva; and He anointed the eyes of the blind man with the clay. And He said to him, 'Go, wash in the pool of Siloam…'"

### 1.

Those who intend to gain any advantage from what they read, must not pass by even any small portion of the words; and on this account we are bidden to search the Scriptures, because most of the words, although at first sight easy, appear to have in their depth much hidden meaning. For observe of what sort is the present case. "When He had said these things," it says, "He spat on the ground." What things? That "the works of God should be revealed," and that, "I must work the works of Him Who sent Me." For not without a cause has the Evangelist mentioned to us His words, and added that, He spat, but to show that He confirmed His words by deeds. And why didn't He use water instead of saliva for the clay? He was about to send the man to Siloam: in order that nothing might be ascribed to the fountain, but He spat on the ground so you might learn that the power proceeding from His mouth[6] is the same

---

[5] St. John Chrysostom, *Homily 57 on John*, NPNF s. 1, v. 14.
[6] St. Cyril of Alexandria makes a similar point concerning the power of the flesh of Christ: "When the life-giving Word of God dwelt in human flesh, He changed it into that good thing which is distinctively His, namely, life; and by being wholly united to the flesh in a way beyond our comprehension, He gave It the life-giving power which He has by His very nature. Therefore, the Body of Christ gives life to those who receive It. Its presence in mortal men expels death and drives away corruption because It contains within Itself in His

one which both formed and opened the man's eyes. This, at least, the Evangelist signified when he said, "And made clay with the saliva." Then, that the successful issue might not seem to be of the earth, He asked him to wash.

But why did He not this at once, instead of sending him to Siloam? That you may learn the faith of the blind man, and that the obstinacy of the Jews might be silenced. For it was probable that they would all see him as he departed, having the clay spread upon his eyes, since by the strangeness of the thing he would attract to himself all, both those who did and those who did not know him, and they would observe him exactly. Since it is not easy to recognize a blind man who has recovered sight, He first makes by the length of way many to be witnesses, and by the strangeness of the spectacle exact observers, that being more attentive they may no longer be able to say, "It is Him. It is not Him."

Moreover, by sending him to Siloam, He desires to prove that He is not estranged from the Law and the Old (Covenant), nor could it afterwards be feared that Siloam would receive the glory, since many who had often washed their eyes there gained no such benefit; for there also it was the power of Christ that wrought all. For this reason, the Evangelist adds for us the interpretation of the name. Having said, in Siloam, he adds, "Which is, Sent," that you may learn that there also it was Christ Who healed him. As Paul says, "They drank of that spiritual Rock that followed them, and that Rock was Christ" (1 Cor. 10:4). As then Christ was the spiritual Rock, so also was He the spiritual Siloam. To me also the sudden coming in of the water seems to hint an ineffable mystery. What is that? The unlooked for (nature) of His appearance, beyond all expectation

---

entirety the Word Who totally abolishes corruption." *Commentary on the Gospel of John*. PG 73:563-6.

Elsewhere, St. Cyril comments on how the Lord touched the coffin of the widow of Nain's son as He raised him from the dead. He asks, "How was not a word enough for raising him who was lying there? What is so difficult to it or past accomplishment? What is more powerful than the Word of God? Why then did He not work the miracle by only a word but also touched the coffin? It was, my beloved, that you might learn that the Holy Body of Christ is productive for the salvation of man " Homily 36, *Commentary on the Gospel of St. Luke* (n.p.: Studion Publishers, 1983), 155. Thus, the Lord in many instances demonstrates the power of His flesh to teach us that His Body, of which we partake in the Mystery of the Eucharist, is necessary for our salvation.

But observe the mind of the blind man, obedient in everything. He did not say, "If it is really the clay or the saliva which gives me eyes, why do I need Siloam?" Or, "If I need Siloam, why do I need of the clay? Why did He anoint me? Why did He bid me to wash?" But he entertained no such thoughts. He held himself prepared for one thing only: to obey in all things Him Who gave the command, and nothing that was done offended him. If anyone asked, "How then did he recover his sight, when he had removed the clay?" he will hear no other answer from us than that we know not the manner. And what wonder if we know it not, since not even the Evangelist knew, nor the very man that was healed? What had been done he knew, but the manner of doing it he could not comprehend. So when he was asked he said, "He put clay on my eyes, and I washed, and I see." But how this took place he cannot tell them, though they ask ten thousand times.

**"Therefore the neighbors and those who previously had seen that he was blind said, 'Is not this he who sat and begged?' Some said, 'This is he...'"**

The strangeness of what had been brought to pass led them even to unbelief, though so much had been contrived that they might not disbelieve. They said, Is not this he that sat and begged? O the lovingkindness of God! Where did He descend to, when with great kindness He healed even beggars, and so silenced the Jews, because He deemed not the illustrious, nor the distinguished, nor the rulers, but men of no mark to be fit objects of the same providence. For He came for the salvation of all.

And what happened in the case of the paralytic happened also with this man, for neither one knew Who it was that healed him. And this was caused by the retirement of Christ. For Jesus when He healed always retired, that all suspicion might be removed from the miracles. Since how could they who knew not Who He was flatter Him, or join in contriving what had been done? Neither was this man one of those who went about, but of those who sat at the doors of the Temple. Now when all were doubting concerning him, what does he say?

"I am he."

He was neither ashamed of his former blindness, nor did he fear the wrath of the people, nor did he decline showing himself that he might proclaim his Benefactor.

2.

"Therefore they said to him, 'How were your eyes opened?' He answered and said, 'A Man called Jesus made clay and anointed my eyes...'"

Observe how truthful he is. He does not say from where He made [the clay], for he speaks not of what he does not know. He did not see that He spat on the ground, but that He spread it on he knew from sense and touch.

"...and said to me, 'Go to the pool of Siloam and wash...'"

This too his hearing witnessed to him. But how did he recognize His voice? From His conversation with the disciples. And saying all this, and having received the witness by the works, the manner (of the cure) he cannot tell. Now if faith is needed in matters which are felt and handled, much more in the case of things invisible.

"Then they said unto him, 'Where is He?' He said, 'I do not know...'"

They said "Where is He?" having already murderous intentions against Him. But observe the modesty of Christ, how He continued not with those who were healed because He neither desired to reap glory, nor to draw a multitude, nor to make a show of Himself. Observe too how truthfully the blind man makes all his answers. The Jews desired to find Christ to bring Him to the priests, but when they did not find Him, they brought the blind man to the Pharisees, as to those who would question him more severely. For which reason the Evangelist remarks, that it was the Sabbath (Jn. 9:14), in order to point out their wicked thoughts, and the cause for which they sought Him. As though they had found a handle, and could belittle the miracle by means of what appeared to be a transgression of the Law. And this is clear from their saying immediately on seeing him nothing but, "How did He open your eyes?" Observe also the manner of their speech. They do not say, "How did you receive your sight?" but "How did He open your eyes?" thus affording him an excuse for slandering Jesus, because of His having worked [on the Sabbath]. But he speaks to them shortly, as to men who had already heard. For without mentioning His Name, or that He said to me, "Go, wash," he immediately says,

"He put clay upon my eyes, and I washed, and I see.'

Because the slander was now become great, and the Jews had said, "Behold what work Jesus does on the Sabbath day; He anoints with clay!" But observe, I pray you, how the blind man is not disturbed. When being questioned he spoke in the presence of those others without danger. It was no such great thing to tell the truth, but the wonder is, that now when he is placed in a situation of greater fear, he neither denies nor contradicts what he had said before. What then did the Pharisees, or rather what did the others also do? They had brought him (to the Pharisees), as being about to deny. But, on the contrary, that befell them which they desired not, and they learned more exactly. And this they everywhere have to endure, in the case of miracles. But this point we will more clearly demonstrate in what follows. What did the Pharisees say?

"Therefore some of the Pharisees said," not all, but the more forward, "'This Man is not from God, because He does not keep the Sabbath.' Others said, 'How can a man who is a sinner do such signs?'"

Do you see that they were led up by the miracles? For hear what they say now, who before this had sent to bring Him. And if all did not so, (for being rulers through vainglory they fell into unbelief), yet still the greater number even of the rulers believed on Him, but confessed Him not. Now the multitude was easily overlooked, as being of no great account in their synagogue, but the rulers being more conspicuous had the greater difficulty in speaking boldly, or some the love of rule restrained, others cowardice, and the fear of the many. Therefore He also said, "How can you believe who receive honor from one another?" (Jn. 5:44). And these who were seeking to kill Him unjustly said that they were of God, but that He Who healed the blind could not be of God, because He does not keep the Sabbath. To this, the others objected since a sinner could not do such miracles.

Those first maliciously keeping silence about what had taken place, brought forward the seeming transgression. For they did not say, "He heals on the Sabbath day," but "He does not keep the Sabbath." These, on the other hand, replied weakly, for when they should have shown that the Sabbath was not broken, they rely only upon the miracles; and with reason, for they still thought that He was a man. If this had not been the case, they might besides have urged in His defense, that He was Lord of the Sabbath which Himself had made. But as yet they had not this opinion. Anyhow, none of them dared to say what he wished openly, or in the way of an assertion, but only in the way of doubt, some from not having boldness of speech, others through love of rule.

There was therefore a division among them. This division first began among the people, then later among the rulers also, and, "Some said, 'He is good'; others said, 'No, on the contrary, He deceives the people'" (Jn. 7:12). Do you see that the rulers were more void of understanding than the many, since they were divided later than they? And after they were divided, they did not exhibit any noble feeling, when they saw the Pharisees pressing upon them. Since had they been entirely separated from them, they would soon have known the truth. For it is possible to do well in separating. Therefore He also has said, "I have come not to bring peace upon the earth but a sword" (Mt. 10:34). For there is an evil concord, and there is a good disagreement.

Thus, those who built the tower (Gen. 11:4) agreed together to their own hurt. These also were divided, though unwillingly, yet for their good. Also Koran and his company agreed together for evil, therefore they were separated for good. And Judas agreed with the Jews for evil. So division may be good, and agreement may be evil. Therefore, it says, "If your eye causes you to sin, pluck it out; if your foot, cut it off" (cf. Mt. 5:29, 18:8). Now if we must separate ourselves from an ill-joined limb, must we not much more from friends united to us for evil? So that agreement is not in all cases a good, just as division is not in all cases an evil.

### 3.

These things I say, that we may shun wicked men, and follow the good; for if in the case of our limbs we cut off that which is rotten and incurable, fearing lest the rest of the body should catch the same disease, and if we do this not as having no care for that part, but rather as desiring to preserve the remainder, how much more must we do this in the case of those who consent with us for evil? If we can set them right without receiving injury ourselves, we should use every means to do so. But if they remain unrepentant and may injure us, it is necessary to cut them off and cast them away. For so they will often be gainers rather (than losers). Therefore, Paul also exhorted, saying, "And you shall put away from among yourselves that wicked person" (1 Cor. 5:13). And, that he that has done this deed may be put away from among you. A dreadful thing, dreadful indeed, is the society of wicked men; not so quickly does the pestilence seize or the itch infect those that come in contact with such as are under the disease, as does the wickedness of evil men. "Evil company corrupts good habits" (1 Cor. 15:33). And again, the prophet says, "Come out from among her, and separate yourselves" (Is. 52:11).

Let no one then have a wicked man for his friend. For if when we have bad sons we publicly disclaim them, without regarding nature or its laws, or the constraint which it lays upon us, much more ought we to fly from our companions and acquaintances when they are wicked. Because even if we receive no injury from them, we shall anyhow not be able to escape ill report, for strangers search not into our lives, but judge us from our companions. This advice I address to young men and maidens. "Having regard," it says, "for good things," not only in the sight of the Lord, but also "in the sight of all men" (Rom. 12:17).

Let us then use every means that our neighbor be not offended. For a life, though it be very upright, if it offend others has lost everything. But how is it possible for the life that is upright to offend? When the society of those that are not upright invests it with an evil reputation. For when, trusting in ourselves, we consort with bad men, even though we are not harmed, we offend others. These things I say to men and women and maidens, leaving it to their conscience to see exactly how many evils are produced from this source. Neither I, perhaps, nor any of the more perfect, suspect any ill; but the simpler brother is harmed by occasion of your perfection; and you should be careful also for his infirmity. Even if he receives no injury, yet the Greek is harmed. Now Paul bids us to be without offense, "either to Jews or to the Greeks, or to the Church of God" (1 Cor. 10:32).

I think no evil of the virgin, for I love virginity, and love "thinks no evil" (1 Cor. 13:5). But I am a great admirer of that state of life, and I cannot have so much as an unseemly thought about it.

How shall we persuade those that are outside? For we must take forethought for them also. Let us then so order what relates to ourselves, that none of the unbelievers may be able even to find a just handle of accusation against us. For as those who show forth a right life glorify God, so those who do the contrary cause Him to be blasphemed. May no such persons be among us! But may our works so shine, that our Father Who is in Heaven may be glorified (cf. Mt. 5:16), and that we may enjoy the honor which is from Him. To which may we all attain, through the grace and loving-kindness of our Lord Jesus Christ, by Whom and with Whom, to the Father and the Holy Spirit, be glory forever and ever. Amen.

## "THE BLIND WORLD"

### *St. Augustine of Hippo*[7]

#### 1.

We have heard the lesson of the Holy Gospel which we are in the habit of hearing, but it is a good thing to be reminded: good to refresh the memory from the lethargy of forgetfulness. And in fact, this very old lesson has given us as much pleasure as if it were new. Christ gave sight to one blind from his birth; why do we marvel? Christ is the Savior; by an act of mercy He made up that which He had not given in the womb. Now when He gave that man no eyes, it was no mistake of His surely; but a delay with a view to a miracle.

You might be asking, "How do you know this?" I have heard it from Him. He just now said it; we heard it all together. For when His disciples asked Him saying, "Rabbi, who sinned, this man or his parents, that he was born blind?" (Jn. 9:2), both you and I heard the answer He gave: "Neither this man nor his parents sinned, but that the works of God should be revealed in him" (Jn. 9:3). Behold, then it was that He delayed

---

[7] St. Augustine, *Selected Sermons on the New Testament,* Sermon 86, NPNF, s. 2, v. 6.

when He gave him no eyes. He did not give what He could give, He did not give what He knew He should give, when the need existed.

Yet do not suppose, brethren, that this man's parents had no sin, or that he himself had no sin when he was born and contracted ancestral sin. For it is of this sin that infants are baptized unto remission of sins. That blindness was neither because of his parents' sin, nor because of his own sin; but so that the works of God should be made manifest in him. For we all when we were born contracted ancestral sin, and yet we were not born blind. However, inquire carefully, for we were born blind. For who was not born blind? Blind in heart, that is. But the Lord Jesus had created both, and He cured both.

2.

With the eyes of faith you have seen this man blind, you have seen him too of blind seeing; but you have heard him erring. Where this blind man erred, I will tell you. First, in that, he thought Christ was a prophet, and he did not know that He was the Son of God. Thus, we have heard an answer of his entirely false; for he said, "We know that God does not hear sinners" (Jn. 9:31). If God does not hear sinners, what hope do we have? If God does not hear sinners, why do we pray, and publish the record of our sin by the beating of the breast?

Where again is that Publican, who went up with the Pharisee into the temple and while the Pharisee was boasting, parading his own merits, he standing afar off, and with his eyes fastened on the ground, and beating his breast, was confessing his sins? And this man, who confessed his sins, went down from the temple justified rather than the other Pharisee (Lk. 18:14). Assuredly then God does hear sinners. But he who spoke these words had not yet washed the face of the heart in Siloam. The sacrament had gone before on his eyes, but the blessing of the grace had not been yet effected in the heart.

When did this blind man wash the face of his heart? When the Lord admitted him into Himself after he had been cast out by the Jews. For He found him, and said to him as we have heard, "Do you believe in the Son of God? And he said, "Who is He, Lord, that I may believe in Him?" (Jn. 9:35, 36). With the eyes, it is true, he saw already; but did he see already in the heart? No, not yet. Wait, he will see presently. Jesus answered him, "I Who speak to you am He."[8] Did he doubt? No, he immediately washed his face, for he was speaking with that Siloam, which is by interpretation, "Sent." Who is the Sent, but Christ, Who often bore witness, saying, "I do the will of My Father Who sent Me"? He then was Himself the Siloam. The man approached blind in heart, he heard, believed, adored; washed the face, saw.

### 3.

But they who cast him out continued blind, forasmuch as they mocked the Lord, that it was the Sabbath when He made clay of the saliva, and anointed the eyes of the blind man. For when the Lord cured with a word, the Jews openly mocked. For He did no work on the Sabbath day, when He spoke, and it was done. It was a manifest mockery. They mocked Him merely commanding. They mocked at Him speaking, as if they did not themselves speak all the Sabbath day. I might say that they do not speak not only on the Sabbath, but on no day, forasmuch as they have kept back from the praises of the True God. Nevertheless, as I have said, brethren, it was a manifest mockery. The Lord said to a certain man, "Stretch out your hand" (Mt. 12:13, Mk. 3:5, Lk. 6:10) he was made whole, and they mocked because He healed on the Sabbath day.

What did He do? What work did He do? What burden did He bear? But in this instance, the spitting on the ground, the making clay, and anointing the man's eyes, is doing some work. Let no one doubt it, it was doing a work. The Lord did break the Sabbath; but was not therefore guilty. What is that I have said He broke the Sabbath? He, the Light, had come, He was removing the shadows.

For the Sabbath was enjoined by the Lord God, enjoined by Christ Himself, Who was with the Father, when that Law was given. It was enjoined by Him, but in shadow of what was to come. "So let no one judge you in food or in drink, or regarding a festival or a new moon or sabbaths, which are a shadow of things to come" (Col. 2:16, 17).

---

[8] Our Lord's actual response is "You have both seen Him and it is He who is talking with you" (Jn. 9:37). St. Augustine here is citing Christ's response to the Samaritan Woman (Jn. 4:26).

He had now come whose coming these things announced. Why do the shadows delight us? Open your eyes, you Jews; the Sun is present. "We know." What do you know, you blind in heart? What do you know? That this Man is not of God because He breaks the Sabbath day. The Sabbath, unhappy men, this very Sabbath that Christ ordained, Who you say is not of God. You observe the Sabbath in a carnal manner, you have not the spittle of Christ. In this earth of the Sabbath look also for the spittle of Christ, and you will understand that by the Sabbath Christ was prophesied. But you, because you have not the spittle of Christ in the earth upon your eyes, you have not come to Siloam, and have not washed the face, and have continued blind, blind to the good of this blind man, who is now no longer blind either in body or heart. He received clay with the saliva, his eyes were anointed, he came to Siloam, he washed his face, he believed on Christ, he saw, he continued not in that exceedingly fearful judgment. "For judgment I have come into this world, that those who do not see may see, and that those who see may be made blind" (Jn. 9:39).

4.

Exceeding alarm! That those who see not may see: good! It is a Savior's office, a profession of healing power, that they which see not may see. But what, Lord, is that You have added, that they which see may be made blind? If we understand, it is most true, most righteous. Yet what is, they which see? They are the Jews. Do they then see? According to their own words, they see; according to the truth, they do not see.

What then is, they see? They think they see, they believe they see. For they believed they did see, when they maintained the Law against Christ. We know; therefore, they see. What is we know, but we see? What is "This Man is not from God, because He does not keep the Sabbath" (Jn. 9:16)? They see; they read what the Law said. For it was enjoined that whoever breaks the Sabbath day should be stoned. Therefore, they said that He was not of God; but though seeing, they were blind to this, that for judgment He came into the world who is to be the Judge of living and dead.

Why did He come? That those who see not may see; that those who confess that they do not see, may be enlightened. And that those who see may be made blind—that is, that those who confess not their own blindness, may be the more hardened. In fact, "that those who see may be made blind," has been fulfilled. The defenders of the Law, the doctors of the Law, the teachers of the Law, the understanders of the Law, crucified the Author of the Law.

O blindness, this is that which in part has happened to Israel! That Christ might be crucified, and the fullness of the Gentiles might come in, "blindness in part has happened to Israel" (Rom. 11:25). What does "that those who do not see may see" mean? That the fullness of the Gentiles might come in, "blindness in part has happened to Israel." The whole world lay in blindness; but He came "that those who do not see may see, and that those who see may be made blind." He was disowned by the Jews, He was crucified by the Jews; of His Blood He made saliva for the blind. Those who boasted that they saw the light, being more hardened, being made blind, crucified the Light. What great blindness? They killed the Light, but the Light Crucified enlightened the blind!

5.

Hear one seeing, who once was blind. Behold, against what a cross they have miserably stumbled, who would not confess their blindness to the Physician! The Law had continued with them. What serves the Law without grace? Unhappy men, what can the Law do without grace? What does the earth without the spittle of Christ? What does the Law without grace, but make them more guilty? Why? Because hearers of the Law and not doers, and hereby sinners and transgressors. The son of the hostess of the man of God was dead, and his staff was sent by his servant, and laid upon his face, but he did not revive (2 Kgs. 4:31). What does the Law do without grace? What says the Apostle, now seeing, now of blind, enlightened? "For if there had been a Law given which could have given life, truly righteousness would have been by the Law" (Gal. 3:21). Take heed. Let us answer and say, what is this that he has said? "If there had been a Law given which could have given life, truly righteousness would have been by the Law." If it could not give life, why was it given?

He went on and added, "But the Scripture has confined all under sin, that the promise by faith in Jesus Christ might be given to those who believe" (Gal. 3:22). That the promise of illumination, the promise of love by the faith of Jesus Christ might be given to those who believe, that

Scripture, that is the Law, has concluded all under sin. What is, has concluded all under sin? I had not known lust, except the Law had said, "You shall not lust" (cf. Ex. 20:17).

What does "confined all under sin" mean? [The Law] has made the sinner a transgressor also. For it could not heal the sinner. It has concluded all under sin; but with what hope? The hope of grace, the hope of mercy. You have received the Law. You wished to keep it. You were not able. You have fallen from pride. You have seen your weakness; run to the Physician; wash your face; long for Christ; confess Christ; believe in Christ! The Spirit is added to the letter, and you will be saved. For if you take away the Spirit from the letter, the letter kills (2 Cor. 3:6). But if it kills, where is hope? But the Spirit gives life.

Let then Gehazi, Elisha's servant, receive the staff (2 Kgs. 4:29-31), as Moses the servant of God received the Law. Let him receive the staff, receive it, run, go before, anticipate him, lay the staff upon the face of the dead child. And so it was. He did receive it, he ran, he laid the staff on the face of the dead child. But to what purpose? What serves the staff? If there had been a Law given which could give life, the boy might have been raised to life by the staff. But seeing that the Scripture has concluded all under sin, he still lies dead. Why has it confined all under sin? That the promise by the faith of Jesus Christ might be given to those who believe.

Then let Elisha come, who sent the staff by the servant to prove that he was dead. Let him come himself, come in his own person, himself enter into the woman's house, go up to the child, find him dead, conform himself to the members of the dead child, himself not dead, but living. For this he did; he laid his face upon his face, his eyes upon his eyes, his hands upon his hands, his feet upon his feet. He straitened, he contracted himself, being great, he made himself little. He contracted himself, so to say, he lessened himself. For "being in the Form of God, He emptied Himself, taking the form of a servant" (Phil. 2:6, 7).

What is He conformed Himself, alive to the dead? Do you ask, what this is? Hear the Apostle, "God...sent His Son" (1 Jn. 4:9, 10). What is, He conformed Himself to the dead? Do you ask this? Let him tell this, let him go on and declare it again, "in the likeness of sinful flesh" (Rom. 8:3). This is to conform Himself alive to the dead—to come to us in the likeness of sinful flesh, not in the flesh of sin. Man lay dead in a flesh of sin, the likeness of flesh of sin conformed Himself to him. For He died Who had no reason to die. He died, alone free among the dead; since as the whole flesh of men was indeed a flesh of sin. And how should it rise again, had not He Who had no sin, conforming Himself to the dead, come in the likeness of sinful flesh?

O Lord Jesus, Who has suffered for us, not for Yourself, Who had no guilt, and endured its punishment, that You might dissolve at once the guilt and punishment!

## "Commentary on the Sunday of the Man Born Blind"
### St. Cyril of Alexandria[9]

**"Now as Jesus passed by, He saw a man who was blind from birth."**

While the Jews were raging against Him and now attempting to wound Him with stones, immediately He goes forth from the temple that is among them, and takes Him away from the unholiness of His pursuers. And in passing by, immediately He sees one blind from his birth, and sets him as a token and that most clear that He will remove from the abominable behavior of the Jews, and will leave the multitude of the God-opposers, and will rather visit the Gentiles, and to them transfer the abundance of His Compassion. And He likens them to the man "blind from his birth" by reason of their having been made in error and that they are from their first age as it were bereft of the true knowledge of God, and that they have not the light from God, i.e. the illumination through the Spirit.

It is proper to observe again what Christ's visiting the blind man as He "passed by" signifies. And it comes to me to think that Christ strictly speaking came not for the Gentiles but for Israel's sake alone—as Himself too somewhere says, "I was not sent except to the lost sheep of the house of Israel" (Mt. 15:24). Yet, the recovery of sight was given to the Gentiles, Christ transferring His Mercy to them as passing by the way, because of

---

[9] St. Cyril of Alexandria, *Commentary on St. John*, v. 1, bk. 6, ch. 1-2, 683, 684.

the disobedience of Israel. This again was sung previously through Moses, "I will provoke them to jealousy with them that are no nation, I will anger them with a nation void of understanding" (Deut. 32:21). For a foolish nation was it which serves the creature more than Creator (Rom. 1:25) and like irrational beasts feeds on just all unlearning, and gives heed only to things of the earth.

But since Israel, which was wise by reason of the Law and prudent from having Prophets, angered [God], it in its turn was angered by God, they who previously were not prudent being taken into the place belonging to these, for to them through faith was Christ made wisdom, sanctification, and redemption, as it is written, i.e., both light and recovery of sight.[10]

**"And His disciples asked Him, saying, 'Rabbi, who sinned, this man or his parents, that he was born blind?' Jesus answered, 'Neither this man nor his parents sinned, but that the works of God should be revealed in him.'"**

Being desirous (and not without good reason) that the mystery should be explained, or rather being divinely guided, the most wise disciples were urged to ask instruction on the subject. And they are inquisitive with profit, by this means furnishing an advantage not so much for themselves as for us. For we are benefited greatly both by hearing the true explanation of these things from the Omniscient,[11] and in addition also by being warned off from the abomination of infertile doctrines.

These errors not only used to exist among the Jews, but are also advocated now by some who are unbearably conceited in their knowledge of inspired Scripture and seem to pass for Christians. Such persons of a truth also delight much in their own sophistries, indulging their private fancies, and not fearing to mingle Greek error with the doctrines of the Church. For the Jews, when they were in misery, greatly murmured, as if merely suffering the penalty of their forefathers' impiety, or as if God were

---

[10] Here ends St. Cyril's commentary on v. 1, bk. 6, ch. 9 and starts v. 2, bk. 6, ch. 1, entitled, "That not from sins of the soul prior to birth do bodily sufferings befall any, nor yet does God bring the sins of their fathers upon any, punishing those who have nothing sinned, but brings righteous doom upon all."

[11] i.e., the "All-Knowing" or "All-Wise."

most unreasonably laying upon them the sins of their fathers, and scoffed at it as a most unjust punishment. They even said in a proverb, "The fathers ate sour grapes, and the children's teeth were set on edge" (Jer. 31:29). Being afflicted with a like and kindred ignorance to those just mentioned by us, they earnestly maintain that the souls of men existed before the creation of their bodies, and turned willingly to sin even before the existence of their bodies. Then souls and bodies became united when, in the order of rebuke, the souls received birth in the flesh.

But in one brief statement the follies of both these parties are exposed by Christ, Who confidently affirms that neither had the blind man sinned nor his parents. He refutes the doctrine of the Jews by saying that the man had not been born blind because of any sin either of himself or of his ancestors— no, not even of his father or mother. And He also overthrows the silly nonsense of the others, who say that souls sin before their existence in the body.

For someone will say to them and very reasonably: "How, tell me, does Christ say that neither had the blind man sinned nor his parents, and yet we could not grant that they were altogether free from sin?" For, inasmuch as they were human, it is (I suppose) in every way likely or rather it of necessity follows that they fell into errors. Pray then, what time does Christ mean to define as that concerning which His word shall appears to us true, that neither did the man himself sin, nor indeed his parents? Surely He speaks of that which is previous to birth, when having no existence whatever, they did not sin.

Again, concerning such matters, how truly frivolous and beside the mark it is to think that souls sinned before the existence of their bodies, and on that account were embodied and sent into this world. We have argued at length at the beginning of the present gospel, in interpreting and commenting on the words, "That was the True Light Which gives light to every man coming into the world" (Jn. 1:9). So, it would be superfluous for us to discuss the subject again. But it is necessary to say when it occurred to the Jews to fall into this opinion and supposition; and to show clearly that from inability to understand the Divine Word, they mistook its proper meaning.

Israel once dwelt in tents in the wilderness, and God called His divinely inspired Moses on Mount Sinai. But when Moses extended his stay there with God to the number of forty days, he seemed to be a loiterer to those who had influence with the people, who both rose up against Aaron then being alone, and falling back in contempt upon the idolatries of Egypt, cried saying: "Make us gods who shall go before us; for as for this man, Moses, who brought us out of Egypt, we do not know what is become of him" (Ex. 32:23). Then what followed thereupon I think it necessary to speak of briefly.

They made a calf, as it is written, and at this God was justly provoked to anger. Then, indeed, He threatened to destroy the whole congregation at once. Moses fell down before Him and sought for pardon with much entreaty. The Creator of the universe granted forgiveness, and promised to punish the people no further than that He would not continue to go up with them to the Land of Promise, but would send with them instead His special angel as it were in the position of leader. At this Moses was sorely grieved, and as God was not willing to go up with the people, he inferred with some likelihood indeed that the divine anger was not yet thoroughly satisfied.

So he prayed again earnestly that God would accompany them, knowing that the mere guidance of an angel would not suffice some of the Israelites, and perhaps also fearing the weakness of the people and therefore deploring the holy angels' hatred of evil. And he entreated the Good One, the Lover of mankind, the Supreme King and Lord over all, to be willing rather to be present with those so prone to transgress. For he knew that God would pardon them not once only but many times, and that He would grant mercy to those who would offend Him. And God also consented to this.

Then Moses sought a sign from Him, even that he might see Him, as a full assurance and testimony that He had forgiven them completely. For he said, "If then I have found grace in Your sight, reveal Yourself to me, that I may evidently see You; that I may find grace in Your sight, and that I may know that this great nation is Your people" (Ex 33:13). This also God granted, as far as it was possible, assuring in every way His own servant both that He had forgiven the people their sin and that He would go up with them to the Land of Promise.

Then, giving as it were a sort of finishing touch to the promises, which seemed wanting, He commands Moses to carve out two other tablets for

Him, the former ones as we know having been broken in pieces, so that He might write down the Law yet again for the people; even in this affording no small evidence of His kindness towards them. And when Moses was ready also for this, "The Lord descended in a cloud," as it is written, "and stood with him there, and proclaimed the Name of the Lord. And the Lord passed by before his face and proclaimed, 'The Lord God is beneficent and merciful, long-suffering and very compassionate, and true, and keeping justice, and showing mercy unto thousands, taking away iniquities and unrighteousness and sins; and He will not clear the guilty; visiting the sins of fathers upon children and upon children's children unto the third and fourth generation" (Ex. 34:5-7).

But now attend carefully, for I am about to take up again the question proposed at first. God declares Himself to show His kindness and His incomparable love for mankind in a manner suitable to deity. For we maintain that these were the words of God, not of any other speaker; not (as some think) the words of the all-wise Moses, offering up laudatory prayers on behalf of the people.

For that it is the Lord of all Himself speaking these things of Himself, no other than the blessed Moses himself will bear witness to us, teaching in the Book of Numbers, when the Israelites had again taken offense from unseasonable cowardice, because some, who by Moses at God's command had been sent to spy it out, spoke evil of the Land of Promise. For when they returned from the land of the strangers and had come again to their own people, they spat out bitter words concerning it.

Affirming the land to be so wild and rugged that it was capable of eating up its inhabitants, they excited so much hatred of it in the minds of their hearers, that bursting into tears they now desired again to be in Egypt with all its hardships. And they said, "Let us make a ruler and let us return to Egypt" (Num. 14:4). And when God threatened to destroy them, Moses again prayed, and all but reminding Him also of the promise He had given, went on to cry: "And now, O Lord, let Your strength be exalted, as You have spoken, saying, 'The Lord is long-suffering and of great mercy, and true, forgiving transgressions and iniquities and sins; and He will by no means clear the guilty, visiting the sins of the fathers upon the children to the third and fourth generation. Forgive this people their sin according to Your great mercy, as You have been favorable to them from Egypt even until now'" (Num. 14:17-19).

It appears therefore that He Who is God over all attributes to Himself love of men and the greatest forbearance towards evil. It will be fitting in the next place to set forth the cause on account of which the Jews, being deceived, could suppose our good God to be mindful of injury and exceeding wrathful.

For my part, I do not think them able to lay hold of the divine oracles in any way, or to mock at them as if they have not expressed what is most excellent or have strayed far from the law of fairness. On the other hand, I think that they only indulge their own ignorance in this matter, to suppose the sins of fathers to be really brought upon children, and the divine anger to be stretched so far that it may even reach to the third and fourth generation, exacting unjustly from innocent persons the penalties of others' crimes.

Would it not at all events be more attractive to them, if they were wise, to hold the opinion that the Source of righteousness and of our moral laws would do nothing so shameful? For even men inflict punishments according to the laws upon habitual transgressors, but by no means visit them on their children, unless perhaps they are detected as partners and associates in the misdeeds. And as to Him Who prescribed to us the laws of all justice, how can He be detected in inflicting penalties such as among ourselves are greatly condemned? Then this also in addition is to be considered.

By the mouth of Moses He published laws innumerable, and in many cases those living in bad habits were ordered to be punished. But nowhere is a command from Him to be found that children should share the penalties incurred by their sinning fathers. For penalty is for those who are detected in crime, and it was ordained that it was fitting to punish those only who offended the Law. To think as the Jews do is therefore surely impious, but it is certainly the part of a wise man to investigate the divine mind and by every means to observe what things are agreeable to nature, the queen of all things.

Rightly, therefore, let us hold that the God of the universe, setting as it were before Him His inherent compassion, willing to be admired for His pure love of men and to this end proclaiming: "The Lord is long-suffering and of great mercy and true, forgiving transgressions and sins," would not wish to be known as so mindful of evil that He extends His anger even to the fourth generation inclusive. For how can He still be long-suffering and of great mercy, or how does He forgive transgressions and sins, Who cannot endure to limit the infliction of penalty to the person of the sinner, but extends it beyond the third generation, and like a sort of thunderbolt assaults even the innocent? Surely then it is quite incredible and of almost utter folly, to suppose that God attributes to Himself, together with love of men and gentleness, anger so lasting and so unreasonable.

To these things another may be added by those who support the Jewish opinion, and do not allow that God knows a suitable time for every kind of action. For if He promises long-suffering and is found to yield very easily in laying aside His anger, why is He seen to have added, "Visiting the sins of fathers upon children unto the third and fourth generation" (Num. 14:18)? Of course this was done for no other reason than a wish to frighten those who expect remission of sins from Him, as showing that the object of their hopes should never be realized, since He Who with reason is grieved with them is so mindful of evil and tenacious in anger.

Furthermore, tell me what the divinely inspired Moses himself indicates to us. Would he not seem to do a thing most opposite to all reason, if, when Israel had given offense and was about to suffer punishment, he proceeded to pray for them, and, while asking for oblivion of the offense and an exhibition of God's love for men, he should unseasonably say to God, "You are of such a nature that You avenge the sins of fathers upon children's children?" For this would be rather the way of one instigating to anger than of one calling for mercy, and of one asking mindfulness of injury rather than long-suffering.

In my opinion, by these words he seemed to beseech God and to recall to His memory almost the very words which He Himself uttered, when He publicly proclaimed His inherent goodness. For in what way He is long-suffering and of great mercy, and how He is by nature One Who takes away sins and transgressions, will be most excellently discerned, in the very dealings wherein He seems to be somewhat bitter.

In the next place then, I think, it is fitting to set forth in what way we may rightly understand the words which were spoken by God. "The Lord,"

He says, "is long-suffering and of great mercy, taking away transgressions and sins." Then we will read that which immediately follows as if with a note of interrogation: "And will He not surely purge the guilty?" So that you may understand something like this: "Will not," He says, "the long-suffering and of greatly merciful God, Who takes away transgressions and sins surely clear the guilty?" Of course, it is not to be doubted. Certainly He will thoroughly purge him. For how is He "long-suffering and of great mercy" and how does He at all take away sins, unless He purges the guilty?

At these words He goes off to a demonstration of His inherent long-suffering and forbearance, even that He will visit the sins of the fathers upon children unto the third and fourth generation: not chastising the son for the father. Do not think this. No, not even does He lay upon a descendant the faults of his ancestors like a burden. But this means something of this sort.

There was (we will suppose) a certain man, a transgressor of laws, having his mind full of all wickedness, and who, being taken in this manner of living, deserved to be punished without any relief. Yet, God in forbearance dealt with him patiently, not bringing upon him the wrath he had merited. Then to him was born a son, a rival of his father in impious deeds and outdoing his parent in villainy. God also showed long-suffering towards this man. But from him is born a third, and from the third a fourth, in no way inferior to their ancestors in wickedness, but practicing equal impiety with them. Then God pours out wrath upon them, already even from the beginning deserved by the whole race, after He has tolerated as much as, and even more than, expected of Him. A postponement of vengeance even unto the fourth generation, how is it not truly a commendation of divine gentleness?

For that He is accustomed to chastise neither son for father, nor father for son, it is not hard to learn from those words which by the voice of the prophet Ezekiel He clearly spoke to the Jews themselves, when over this same thing they murmured and said: "The fathers have eaten sour grapes and the children's teeth are set on edge? 'As I live,' says the Lord, 'this proverb shall be said no more in Israel. For all souls are Mine; as the soul of the father, so also the soul of the son; they are Mine. The soul that sins, it shall die...The son shall not bear the iniquity of the father, neither shall the father bear the iniquity of his son, each in his own iniquity in which he has sinned, in that shall he die" (Ezek. 18:2-4, 20).

But I suppose no one is so foolish as to think that God did not at the beginning legislate in the most excellent way, but somehow changed His plans and altered His ideas for the better, and like one of ourselves was with difficulty and after subsequent deliberation able to improve His legislation to what was most fitting. In such a case, if we praise the earlier laws we shall clearly be blaming the later, and if we express an opinion that the later laws are superior we shall condemn the earlier by our lower estimation of them.

God also will legislate in opposition to Himself, and will have fallen short, as we may have done, of a perfect standard, by ordaining one thing at one time and a different thing at another time. But I suppose every one will say that the divine nature cannot be in any way subject to such inconsistencies as this, and could not even have ever fallen short of absolute perfection.

It is then as a demonstration of His incomparable generosity that He alleges the words quoted above, i.e., "visiting the sins of fathers upon children unto the third and fourth generation" (Num. 14:18). For, the merciful God is accustomed to punish sinners not immediately. Rather, you will understand from His own words that He does so reluctantly and puts off punishments for long seasons: "And I was full of My anger and restrained it, and did not utterly destroy them" (cf. Is. 48:9, Jer. 32:31). Again, in another place, He says, "For the iniquity of the Amorites is not yet fulfilled" (Gen. 15:16).

You see that He was indeed full of anger, for some were perpetrating deeds deserving fullness of anger, but as God He forbore patiently and delayed to make a full end of those who offended Him. In order that we may exhibit to you as in a picture the proof of what we have said and from actual events demonstrate the praise of God's love for men to be contained in this text, I will bring forward something recorded in the Sacred Books, and will endeavor from the Divine Scripture itself to show the sins of fathers visited on children even to the third and fourth generation; not unjustly, but justly, and in a manner merited by the sufferers themselves. The story shall be summarized, because of the length of the narrative.

Well, then, in the First Book of Kings we read that after other kings, Ahab reigned over Israel, and burning with a most unrighteous desire for another man's vineyard, he slew the lord of it, even Naboth. For although he did not himself command that deed, yet he expressed no anger at the wickedness of his wife. At this God was of course enraged, and spoke to Ahab by Elijah the prophet: "Thus said the Lord, 'Forasmuch as you have killed and also taken possession,' therefore thus says the Lord, 'In the place where the swine and the dogs licked the blood of Naboth, there shall the dogs lick your blood; and the harlots shall wash themselves in your blood'" (1 Kgs. 20:19).

And again immediately, thus says the Lord: "Behold I bring evil upon you, and will kindle a fire behind you, and will utterly destroy from Ahab every male and him that is shut up and left in Israel. And I will make your house like the house of Jeroboam the son of Nebat, and like the house of Baasha the son of Ahab, for the provocations with which you have provoked Me to anger, and made Israel to sin" (1 Kgs. 20:21, 22). And of Jezebel He spoke, saying, "The dogs shall eat her within the outer-wall of Jezreel. And him who dies of Ahab in the city the dogs shall devour, and him who dies in the field the birds of the air shall devour" (1 Kgs. 16:4).

When the Lord of all unmistakably threatened to do all these things and to inflict them, Ahab rent his garment and entered into his house. As it is written, "He was pricked to the heart, and burst bitterly into tears, and girded his loins with sackcloth" (cf. 1 Kgs. 20:16).[12] In which state God pities him, and begins to allay His anger, and putting as it were a bridle to His sudden fury says to the Prophet, "Have you seen how Ahab was pricked to the heart before Me? I will not bring these things in his days, but in his son's days I will bring the evil" (1 Kgs. 20:29).

Will it not therefore be right to inquire upon whom these things were fulfilled? Well, the son of Ahab was Ahaziah, who, Scripture says, "did evil in the sight of the Lord and walked in the way of his father Ahab" (2 Kgs. 8:27) and in the way of Jezebel his mother. Then the son of Ahaziah was, Scripture says, Joram, of whom again it is written that he walked in the sins of the house of Jeroboam (cf. 2 Kgs. 8:27). Next to Joram reigned a

---

[12] cf. New King James Version, 1 Kgs. 21:27.

third Ahaziah, of whom again the language of the narrative says that he "did evil in the sight of the Lord, as did the house of Ahab" (2 Kgs. 8:27). But when the time had now come for punishing the house of Ahab, which had not ceased from impiety towards God even to the fourth generation, there was anointed to be the next king over Israel Jehoshaphat son of Nimshi, who slew Ahaziah, and beside him Jezebel; he slew also seventy other sons of Ahab (cf. 2 Kgs. 10:6, 7), carrying out as it were the divine wrath to the uttermost, so that he obtained both honor and favor on account of it.

For what did God say to him? "Because of all your deeds which you have acted well in doing that which was right in My eyes, according to all things which you have done to the house of Ahab as they were in My heart, your sons to the fourth generation shall sit upon the throne of Israel" (2 Kgs. 10:30). You see, therefore, that He reluctantly punished in the fourth generation the wicked descendants of wicked men, whereas to him from whom He received honor He extends His mercy even to the fourth generation.

Therefore, cease, O Jew, to accuse the righteousness of God. As a form of encomium certainly we will accept that saying, "Visiting the sins of fathers upon children unto the third and fourth generation" (Num. 14:18).

**"...but that the works of God should be revealed in him..."**

That which lies before us is hard to explain and capable of causing much perplexity, so that it would be perhaps not unlearned to pass it over in silence, and because of its excessive difficulty to leave it. But when the Jewish doctrines have been refuted, lest another thing akin to them, "lest any root of bitterness springing up cause trouble" (Heb. 12:15), as Paul says (for perhaps some will hence suspect that the bodies of men are affected with sufferings, in order that the works of God may be made manifest in them).

I, for my part, think it seasonable to subjoin a few words with reference to this, that thereby we may both keep off any injuries arising from this source, and leave no loophole for deceptive arguments. That God does not bring the sins of parents upon children unless they are partakers of their wickedness, and further, that embodiment is not on account of sins previously committed by the soul, we have shown. For by speaking in opposition to these two errors, Christ in a wonderful manner overturned them, since He unquestionably knows all things, as God. Or rather, since He Himself is the ruler over our affairs, and the ordainer of those things which befit and are deserved by every man.

For in that He says the blind man had not sinned, nor was suffering blindness on that account, He shows that it is foolish to suppose the soul of man to be guilty of sins previous to its birth in the body. Moreover, when He openly says that neither had his parents sinned that their son should be born blind, He refutes the silly suspicion of the Jews. Therefore, after He had taught His disciples as much as was necessary for them to know in order to refute the doctrines which we have above stated, and imparted to them as much as it was fitting to exhibit to the understanding of man, He is silent as to the rest, and sets forth no further with clearness the reason why he was born blind who was guilty of no sin previous to birth, attributing to the divine nature alone the knowledge of all such things and a management of affairs which is past finding out. But again He very skillfully transfers the language of His answer to something else and says, "But that the works of God should be revealed in him."

"Does, then," someone will say, "the Lord declare to us these words here as a certain doctrine, as if for this single reason ailments attack the bodies of men, that the works of God should be revealed in them?" It does not seem so at all to me, but rather it is evidently absurd so to imagine or suppose. He certainly is not dogmatizing at all (as some might think) when He says this. For that it happens to some to be punished on account of their sins, we have often learned from the Holy Scriptures.

Paul indeed plainly writes to those who with feet as it were unwashed dared to approach the holy altar, and with profane and unholy hand to touch the Mystical Eucharist,[13] "For this reason many are weak and sick among you, and many sleep. For if we would judge ourselves, we would not be judged. But when we are judged, we are chastened by the Lord, that we may not be condemned with the world" (1 Cor. 11:30-32).

---

[13] Commenting on Ex. 30:17-21, St. Cyril makes a similar connection in his *De Adoratione, 9*. See also his commentary on Malachi, *In Mal.* 594.7-2, 580.13-15.

Accordingly, it is sometimes by divine wrath that the suffering has been brought upon the sick and dead. But, our Lord Jesus Christ Himself, after He had loosed the paralytic from a long disease, and had miraculously cured him, says, "See, you have been made well. Sin no more, lest a worse thing come upon you" (Jn. 5:14). Surely He says this as though it might happen that unless the man took heed he would suffer something worse for his sin, although he had once escaped and by the Lord's favor been restored to health.

But perhaps some may say, "We will grant that these things are rightly said. But as to those who suffer something terrible from the cradle and their earliest years, or even from the very womb are afflicted with diseases, it is not easy to understand what kind of explanation any one can satisfactorily give."

For we do not believe that the soul previously existed. Nor indeed can we think that it sinned before the body, for how can that sin, which has not yet been called to birth? But if there has been no sin nor fault preceding the suffering, what then shall we allege as the cause of the suffering? Truly, by our minds we cannot comprehend those things which are far above us, and I should advise the prudent, and myself above all, to abstain from wishing to thoroughly scrutinize them. For we should recall to mind what we have been commanded, and not curiously examine things which are too deep, nor pry into those which are too hard, nor rashly attempt to discover those which are hidden in the divine and ineffable counsel alone.

Rather concerning such matters we should piously acknowledge that God alone knows some things, peculiar to Himself and excellent. At the same time we should maintain and believe that since He is the fountain of all righteousness, He will neither do nor determine anything whatever in human affairs, or in those of the rest of creation, which is unbecoming to Himself, or differs at all from the true principle of justice.

Therefore, since it becomes us to be affected in this way, I say, that the Lord does not speak dogmatically when He says that "the works of God should be revealed in him." Rather, He says it to draw off the answer of the questioner in another direction, and to lead us from things too deep for us to more suitable ones. For that is a thing He was somehow inclined to do.

And that this assertion is true, hear again how when the holy disciples were earnestly inquiring about the end of the world, and very curiously putting questions concerning His Second Coming, and going far beyond the limits proper for man, He very evidently draws them away from such interrogations. "It is not for you," He says, "to know times or seasons which the Father has put in His own authority. But you shall receive power when the Holy Spirit has come upon you; and you shall be witnesses to Me in Jerusalem, and in all Judea" (Acts 1:7, 8). Do you hear that He does not permit us at all to seek into those things which no way are fit for us, but rather directs us to come back to what is necessary?

So also in this place, having spoken plainly what was proper for us to learn, He reserves the rest in silence, knowing that it was proper for Himself alone to understand this. Lest by being altogether silent He should as it were invite them again to ask Him about the same things, in the manner of alleging a reason, and as though politely fashioning some such answer as the questions seemed to deserve, He says, "But that the works of God should be revealed in him" (Jn. 9:3). This is just as if He had said, in different and simpler language: "The man was neither born blind on account of his own sins nor the sins of his parents. But since it has happened that he was so affected, it is possible that in him God may be glorified." For when, by power from above, he shall be found free from the affliction which lies upon him and troubles him, who will not admire the Physician? Who will not recognize the power of the Healer shown forth in Him?

I think this sense is hidden in the words before us. But let those who are clever think out the more perfect meaning. And if any think it proper to be contentious and say that the man was born blind for the very end that Christ might be glorified in him, we will say to them in reply: "Do you suppose, O good people, that this was the only man in Judea who was blind from birth in the time of the coming of our Savior, and that there was no other whatever?"

Surely, even though unwilling, they will confess, I think, that in all likelihood very many such were found in all the land. How was it then that Christ only exhibited His kindness and power to one of them, or at all events to but a small number? Concerning these things, however, I deem it superfluous to hold an argument. Therefore, the other opinion being rejected as foolish, we will hold it true, that after Christ had revealed to us as much about the questions asked as was meet for us to learn, He passed on to another subject, skillfully turning aside His own disciple from searching into such things.

"I[14] must work the works of Him Who sent Me while it is day; the night is coming when no one can work."

Behold, here again in these words, plainly and reasonably, He rebukes in a similar manner the disciples, as if they had done something they should not have, and having left the high road, well-trodden and firm, had ventured on another which seemed not at all fit for them. "For, why do you ask," He says, "things which it should remain in silence? Or why, leaving that which suits the time, do you hasten to learn things beyond the capacity of man? It is not a time for such curiosity," He says, "but for work and intense zeal. For I consider it more proper, passing by such questions, to execute God's commands zealously, and since He has appointed us apostles, to fulfill the works of the apostleship."

When the Lord numbers Himself with those who are sent, and enrolls Himself among those who should work, in no way does He make Himself really one of us, or say that He Himself is subject (as we are) by a certain servile necessity to the will of a commander. But He uses a common habit of speech, even to ourselves trite and familiar. For, especially when the bare substance of an argument is not calculated to impress our hearers, we are inclined to join ourselves to them, and to consider ourselves with them.

For which reason doubtless the most wise Paul addressed the Corinthians as if concerning himself and Apollos, and at last added, "Now these things, brethren, I have figuratively transferred to myself and Apollos for your sakes, that you may learn in us not to think beyond what is written" (1 Cor. 4:6). Therefore, He says, "Let us work the works of Him Who sent us; for the night is coming, when no one can work" (Jn. 9:4). In these words He calls the time of bodily life, "day," and the time we are in death, He calls "night." For since the day was given for works, but the night for rest and sleep, therefore the time of life in which we should work

---

[14] New King James Version uses "I" while NU and Pusey's translation of Cyril reads "We."

what is good, people call day; and the time of sleeping, in which nothing whatever can be done, they call night. "For he who has died has been freed[15] from sin" (Rom. 6:7), according to the saying of Paul, being found unable to do anything, and therefore unable to sin.

Thus Holy Scripture really does recognize a theory of a metaphorical day, and in no less degree a corresponding theory of night. And if taken into consideration at the right moment each of these metaphorical interpretations exhibits the aspect of the questions under investigation in a manner free from error. Concerning unsuitable subjects, and when it should not be done, to attempt violently to drag round to a spiritual interpretation that which should be taken historically, is nothing else than unlearnedly to confuse what is profitable if understood simply, and to spoil its usefulness through excess of ignorance.

**"As long as I am in the world, I am the Light of the world."**

Shall we then think that Christ is now not at all in the world, or do we believe that He, having ascended to heaven after His restoration to life from the dead, no longer dwells among those in this present life? Yet, being very God, He fills and tends not only the heavens and what is beyond the firmament, but also the world which we inhabit. While He associated in the flesh with men, He was not absent from heaven. So if we think rightly we shall hold the opinion that even though He is out of the world regarding the flesh, His divine and ineffable nature is yet no less present among those who dwell in the world. Yes, it overrules the universe, being absent from nothing that exists, neither having abandoned anything, but present everywhere in all things; and is fully contained by itself alone, filling the entire visible universe and whatever may be conceived of as beyond it.

Therefore, the next thing is to understand is what the Lord says in these words. Having cast aside as a stale thing the suspicion of the Jews, and shown that they were foolishly entangled in unsound doctrines; having given counsel to His own disciples that it was more becoming for them to strive to love the things that please God, and to leave off pursuing a search

---

[15] Alternatively, "justified."

into what was altogether beyond them; and having in a manner warned them that the time for work will slip away from those who do nothing, unless they devote all their zeal to the wish to do well, while they are in the flesh in the world—He holds up Himself as an Example in the matter. "For behold," He says, "I also work at My own proper work, and since I have come to give light to those things that were in want of light, it befits Me to cause light to dwell even in the eyes of the body, if they are diseased with the terrible lack of light, whenever any of the sufferers come before Me."

We will accordingly understand what was said as spoken with reference to the occasion, and in a simple sense. For we do not doubt that the Only-Begotten is indeed a real Light, with the knowledge and power to illumine not only the things that are in this world, but also every other celestial creature. And if we accommodate the sense of the words to the matter in hand, I do not think we shall be found guilty of setting forth anything unworthy of credit.

**"When He had said these things, He spat on the ground and made clay with the saliva; and He anointed the eyes of the blind man with the clay. And He said to him, 'Go, wash in the pool of Siloam' (which is translated, Sent). So he went and washed, and came back seeing."**

Accepting the cure wrought upon this blind man as a type of the calling of the Gentiles, we will again tell the meaning of the mystery, summing it up in few words. First then because it was merely in passing, and after leaving the Jewish temple, that He saw the blind man. Again from this circumstance also, that without plea and anyone's petition, but rather of His own accord and from a spontaneous inclination, the Savior came to a determination to heal the man. Hence we shall profitably look upon the miracle as symbolical. It shows that as no entreaty has been made by the multitude of the Gentiles, for they were all in error. God, being indeed in His nature good, of His own will has come forward to show mercy on them. For how at all or in what way could the vast number of Greeks and of Gentiles beseech God for mercy, having their mind darkened by gross ignorance, to be in no wise able to see the Illuminator?

Therefore, as certainly the man who has been healed, being blind, does not know Jesus, and by an act of mercy and philanthropy receives an unhoped-for benefit; so also has it happened to the Gentiles through Christ. On the Sabbath too was the work of healing accomplished, the Sabbath being capable thereby completely to exhibit to us a type of the last age of the present world, in which the Savior has made light to shine on the Gentiles. For the Sabbath is the end of the week, and the Only-Begotten took up His abode and was manifested to us all in the last time, and in the concluding ages of the world. But at the manner of the healing it is really fit that we should be astonished and say, "O Lord, how great are Your works; in wisdom have You performed them all" (Ps. 104:24).

Someone may say, "Why does He mix up clay from the spittle, and anoint the eyes of the sufferer and seem to prescribe a sort of operation, although He is able to set all things right easily by a word." For He says, "Go, wash in the pool of Siloam?" Surely I deem that some deep meaning is buried beneath these words, for the Savior accomplishes nothing without a purpose. For by anointing with the clay He makes good that which is (so to speak) lacking or impaired in the nature of the eye, and thus shows that He is the One Who formed us in the beginning, the Creator and Fashioner of the universe. And the power of the action possesses a sort of mystical significance; for that which we said just now concerning this, and what we consider may be understood by it, we will mention again. There was no other way possible for the Gentiles to thrust off the blindness which affected them, and to behold the divine and holy light, that is, to receive the knowledge of the Holy and Consubstantial Trinity, except by being made partakers of His Holy Body, and washing away their gloom-producing sin, and renouncing the authority of the devil, namely in holy baptism.

And when the Savior stamped on the blind man the typical mark which was anticipative of the mystery, He meanwhile fully exhibited the power of such participation by the anointing with His spittle. And as an image of holy baptism He commands the man to run and wash in Siloam, a name whose interpretation, the Evangelist, being very wise and divinely inspired, felt it necessary to give.

For we conclude that the "One Sent" is no other than the Only-Begotten God, visiting us and sent from above, even from the Father, to destroy sin and the envy of the devil. And recognizing Him as floating invisibly on the waters of the sacred pool, we by faith are washed, not for the putting away of the filth of the flesh, as it is written, but as it were washing away a sort of defilement and uncleanness of the eyes of the understanding, in order that for the future, being purified, we may be able in pureness to behold the divine beauty. Therefore, since we believe the Body of Christ to be life-giving, since it is the temple and abode of the Word of the Living God, possessing all His energy, so we declare it to be also a patron of light. For it is the Body of Him Who is by nature the True Light. And as, when He raised from death the only son of the widow, He was not satisfied with merely commanding and saying, "Young man, I say unto you, arise" (Lk. 7:14), although accustomed to accomplish all things, whatever He wished, by a word. But He also touched the coffin with His hand, showing that even His Body possesses a life-giving power. So in this case He anoints with His spittle, teaching that His Body is also a cause of light, even by so slight a touch. For it is the Body of the True Light, as we said above.

The blind man accordingly departs with what haste he can, and washes, and without delay performs all that was bidden him, showing as it were in his own person the ready obedience of the Gentiles, concerning whom it is written, "He inclined His ear to the preparation of their hearts" (Ps. 10:17). The wretched Jews then were hard of heart, but they of the Gentiles were altogether submissive in obedience and bear witness of it in experience. The man having immediately, removed his blindness, washing it away together with the clay, now returns, seeing. For it was Christ's pleasure that this should come to pass.

Excellent therefore is faith, which makes God-given grace to be strong in us; and harmful is hesitation. For the "double-minded man [is] unstable in all his ways" as it is written (Jas. 1:8), and shall receive nothing at all from the Lord (cf. Jas. 1:7).

**"Therefore the neighbors and those who previously had seen that he was blind said, 'Is not this he who sat and begged?' Some said, 'This is he.' Others said, 'He is like him.' He said, 'I am he.'"**

Hard indeed to be believed are such surpassing wonders, and that which exceeds man's experience, from whatever source it comes, finds the intellect to be intolerant of it, and is scarcely treated with honor when convincingly forced upon people's minds. For the attempt to investigate what is beyond the grasp of reason indicates a state of mind akin to insanity. Hence, I think, the unbelief of some who had previously known the blind man haunting the crossroads, and who were astonished afterwards when they beheld him unexpectedly able to discern objects with clear vision. And they are divided, from uncertainty regarding the event, and some who consider more carefully the greatness of the deed say that it is not the same man, but one remarkably like him whom they had known. Indeed, it really is not strange that this opinion should be expressed by some, who by rejecting the truth were compelled through the greatness of the miracle to adopt an involuntary falsehood. Others again keep their minds free from obvious objections, and in reverence and fear they recognize the wonder, and say that it is the same man. But he who was healed quickly settled the question, by making his own statement, most worthy of credit as concerning himself. For no man can be ignorant of his own identity, even though very ill in delirium. Thus in every way the marvelous deed, discredited on account of the unusual degree of power it displayed, testifies that the Wonderworker is to be reckoned among the great.

**"Therefore they said to him, 'How were your eyes opened?'"**

With difficulty they consent to believe that he was the same man whom they had known previously, and abandoning their hesitation on this point, they ask how he had got rid of his blindness, and what was the manner of such an unhoped-for event. For it seems usual for those who are astonished to make careful inquiries and to investigate the manner of what has been done; and these persons resolved to do the same, not without the guidance of God, in our opinion, but so that even unwillingly they might learn the power of our Savior from the narration and clear announcement which the blind man made to them. You may accept this as a beautiful type of the converts from among the Gentiles becoming teachers to the people of Israel, after escaping from their former blindness and receiving the illumination which comes from our Savior Christ through the Spirit. And that what we have said is true, the events themselves will loudly proclaim.

"He answered and said, 'A Man called Jesus made clay and anointed my eyes and said to me, "Go to the pool of Siloam and wash." So I went and washed, and I received sight.'"

He appears still to be ignorant that the Savior is God by nature, for otherwise he would not have spoken about Him so unworthily. He probably thought of Him and esteemed Him as a holy man, forming this opinion perhaps from the somewhat faint rumor concerning Him that went about all Jerusalem, and was repeated everywhere in the common talk. Moreover, we may observe that those physically afflicted and struggling with extreme poverty never feel excessive zeal in occupying themselves about making acquaintance, because their absolute poverty exhausts their mental faculties. Therefore, he speaks of Him merely as a man, and describes the manner of the healing. He must surely have been compelled by the magnitude of the miracle to attribute a glory beyond the nature of man to the Wonderworker, but from giving credit to the belief that holy men were enabled by God to work miracles, he was probably drawn to look upon Jesus as one of them.

"Then they said to him, 'Where is He?' He said, 'I do not know.'"

Not from devout feelings do they inquire for Jesus, nor are they moved to inquire where and with whom He was uttering discourses, so that they might go and seek some profit from His doings. But being blinded in the eyes of their understanding, even much worse than he had formerly been in those of his body, they are inflamed with a most unjust anger, and a rage like untamable beasts, thinking that our Savior had broken a commandment of the Law, that one namely which forbids any work at all to be done on the Sabbath. And they raved immoderately, because He had actually dared to touch clay, rubbing the dirt around with His finger, and in addition to this had also directed the man to wash it off on the Sabbath.

Why did they, in anger and desperation, spit out the words, "Where is He?" without making any excuse for speaking so rudely? For in their pettiness they bestow abuse upon Him Who rightly deserved the highest honor. If they had been sincere and had known how to honor God's power with befitting praises, they surely would have admired Him.

Thrusting aside in their extravagant maliciousness, which I think they in fairness should have thought and done, they devote themselves to untimely zeal. And falsely supposing that they were performing a duty in supporting the Law which had somehow been wronged, they inquire for Jesus as One Who had worked on the Sabbath and thus wronged the excellent commandment by healing the man. Certainly they may have supposed that God was (so to speak) cruel and not compassionate on the Sabbath, and was very angry when He saw a man healed, who was made according to His own image and likeness, and on whose account the Sabbath was instituted. But "the Son of Man is Lord of the Sabbath," according to the saying of the Savior (Mk. 2:28; Lk. 6:5).

**"They brought him who formerly was blind to the Pharisees. Now it was a Sabbath when Jesus made the clay and opened his eyes."**

They bring the man to the rulers—not that they might learn what had been done to him, and admire it. For it was not likely that men travailing with extreme envy against our Savior Christ could ever be pleased by any such thing—but that they might publicly convict Jesus, as they thought, of a transgression of the Law, and accuse Him of being a wrongdoer in having made clay on the Sabbath. For rejecting the idea of the miracle because of its incredibility, they lay hold of the deed as a transgression. And for a proof of what had been done they exhibit the man upon whom He had dared to perform the miracle.

At the same time they think to succeed in gaining a reputation for piety according to Jewish customs, and continue to strain the legal commandment to the utmost. For in Deuteronomy He, Who by nature is Very God, speaks, enjoining the minds of the pious neither to be drawn aside to another, nor to think there were any gods besides Him. But He bids them to serve Him only in truth, and to hate bitterly those who should dare to counsel them differently: "If your brother by your father or mother, or your son, or your daughter, or your wife in your bosom, or friend who is equal to your own soul entreats you secretly, saying, 'Let us go and serve other gods,'...you shall not consent to him, neither shall you listen to him, nor shall your eye pity him, you shall feel no regret for him, neither shall you at all protect him; but you shall surely report concerning him" (Deut. 13:6-9).

And so the Jews, looking only at the errors of others, and foolishly treating everything by the regulation laid down concerning one thing, brought before the magistrates those who were detected in, any action contrary to the Law, thinking that thereby they were honoring the Lawgiver. For this reason I think they sought for Jesus, saying, "Where is He?" But being unable to find Him anywhere, they take as it were in the second place him upon whom the wonder had been wrought, that he might seal with his own voice the testimony to the breach of the law which had been committed by the actions of the One Who healed him on the Sabbath.

When the blessed Evangelist clarifies to us that they were immoderately vexed at the making of clay on the Sabbath, he fitly hints at the absurdity of the thing, by adding, "Now it was the Sabbath when Jesus made the clay."

**"Then the Pharisees also asked him again how he had received his sight."**

They busy themselves about the manner of the healing, stirring up as it were the fire of malice which was in them to a greater heat, and ask unnecessary questions, not failing, as it seems to me, to recognize the miracle. For is it not altogether absurd to suppose that they, who had come bringing to them the man who previously was blind, had not expressed at all the reason for which they had brought him? But as if they were not sufficient to accuse Christ, the magistrates compel him to confess with his own mouth what had been done, believing that by this means the malicious accusation would have greater force. For observe that they do not ask simply and barely if he had been healed, but they seek rather to hear how he received his sight. This was what they were particularly anxious to hear, "He made clay, and anointed my eyes." For it was in this that they foolishly conceived all the transgression of the law to lie, and imagining that laws from above were violated, they thought they were righteously vexed, and that punishment should be inflicted on Him Who vexed them.

**"He said to them, 'He put clay on my eyes, and I washed, and I see.'"**

They receive eagerly, as if it were a sort of food for their envy, his confession of the marvel, and gladly seize upon the excuse for their rage against Jesus. For the man who had been blind relates everything on this occasion very simply, and speaks very abruptly, in brief expressions praising, as it were, his Physician: for he is somewhat astounded at the nature of the deed. Probably he may have thought in his mind that Jesus had miraculously enabled him to see by anointing him with clay, an unusual treatment.

And it seems to me that it was very significantly and with sharp meaning that he said, "He made clay, and anointed my eyes."[16] For it was as though one might suppose him to say, "I know that I am speaking to a malicious audience, but nevertheless I will not on that account conceal the truth. I will repay my Benefactor with my thanks. I will be above unseasonable silence. I will honor by my confession the Physician, Who did not trouble me by an elaborate process of healing, or perform the operation by the knife and surgery, or effect what was necessary by compound mixtures of drugs, or adopt any ordinary method, but rather exhibited His power by strange devices. He made clay, and anointed my eyes, and I washed, and I see."

It is perhaps worthy of notice that the man very rightly added, as the climax to his description of these events, the words, "And I see." For it is almost as though he said, "I will prove to you that the power of the Healer was not exerted in vain. I will not deny the favor I received, for I now possess what I formerly longed for. "I," he says, "who was blind from birth and afflicted from the womb, having been anointed with clay, am healed, and I see. That is, I do not merely show you my eye opened, concealing the darkness in its depth, but I really see. From now on, I am able to look at the things which formerly I could only hear about. Behold, the bright light of the sun is shining around me! Behold, the beauty of strange sights surrounds my eye! A short time ago I scarcely knew what Jerusalem was like. Now I see glittering in her the temple of God, and I behold in its midst the truly venerable altar. And if I stood outside the gate, I could look around on the country of Judea, and could recognize one thing as a hill and another as a tree. And when the time changes to evening, my eye will no

---

[16] It is noteworthy that St. Cyril (or at least the biblical text he quotes) conflates John 9:15 with 9:6. The text of John 9:15 in the New King James version reads, "When He had said these things, He spat on the ground and made clay with the saliva; and He anointed the eyes of the blind man with the clay," while in John 9:15 the text reads, "He put clay on my eyes, and I washed, and I see."

longer fail to notice the beauty of the wondrous objects on high, the brilliant company of the stars, and the golden light of the moon. Shortly after, I shall be amazed at the skill of Him Who made them; from the beauty of the creatures I, as well as others, shall acknowledge the Great Creator."

So that however little breadth of imagination or elegance of argument he uttered, his language is pregnant with all this power when he adds, "and I see," after saying, "He made clay and anointed my eyes." For the preacher's style of argument, which we employ, does not exclude all that is graceful in imagination, or reject it as useless. He therefore who had received mercy from Christ, when questioned before the priests, speaks as we have said, declaring in a truly innocent manner, and to the best of his ability, the power of the One Who had healed him.

**"Therefore some of the Pharisees said, 'This Man is not from God, because He does not keep the Sabbath.'"**

In their folly they say He is not from God, Who has the power to work the works of God. And although they see the Son crowned with an equal measure of glory with the Almighty Father, they are not ashamed unreasonably to cast upon him the blame of impiety. Disregarding the report of the miracle, they attack the Wonderworker with their peculiar envy, and carelessly accuse as an evildoer Him Who knew no sin.

They foolishly believe the whole Law to have been broken by His daring to move one finger on the Sabbath, although they would themselves loose their ox from the stall and lead it away to water. Moreover, if a sheep "falls into a pit," as it is written (Mt. 12:11), with much eagerness they would lift it out. So they strain out the gnat, according to the Savior's word (Mt. 23:24), for this was their ordinary custom. With much folly and very desperately they do not give credit to Christ for the marvelous deed, nor from the work of healing do they henceforth acknowledge Him to be what He is.

But they object pettily about the Sabbath, and, as if in their opinion all virtue was observed by merely remaining unemployed on the Sabbath, they totally deny His relationship to God, saying that He was not from God. Although they should rather have understood that the One before them had authority over His own laws, and that it was pleasing and acceptable to God to do good even on the Sabbath, and not to leave without hope one who needed mercy.

For whenever will any of you refuse to praise the doer of good deeds, or what set time can exercise a tyranny against virtue? Yet while they admire the ancient hero Joshua, who captured Jericho on the Sabbath, and commanded their forefathers to do such things as are customary for conquerors, and himself by no means observed the proper Sabbath rest. They persistently attack Christ, and as their personal ill-feeling prompted them, not only strive to take away from Him the glory due to God, but also to rob Him of the honor due to holy men. And being stirred up by their mere malice to speak very inconsiderately, they pour forth a charge of impiety against Him Who justifies the world, and for that very purpose came from the Father to us.

**"Others said, 'How can a man who is a sinner do such signs?' And there was a division among them."**

Even these still think too contemptibly, speaking and considering as of a mere man. Only, being convinced by the marvelous deed, they give the palm to Christ rather than to the Law; and, putting the proof afforded by the divine sign in opposition to the Sabbath rest on this occasion, they appear in a better light as just judges. Yet, was it not acting greatly in opposition to the precepts laid down respecting the Sabbath, to withdraw altogether the charge of transgression, and to acquit Him of sin, Who had not hesitated, when He thought fit, to do something even on the Sabbath?

But, coming to this conclusion by reasoning which seems unanswerable and has much common sense in it, they argue thus. For it is manifest and acknowledged beyond question, that to those who neglect the divine law, and set at nought precepts ratified from on high, God would never give the power to achieve anything wonderful.

To Christ, however, in the opinion of the Jews, He gave such power, although He slighted the law respecting the Sabbath. Certainly the doing something on the Sabbath, does not necessarily involve sin, but neither can anyone doubt that the doing of good works is far better than remaining unemployed on that day. At all events, as the Savior Himself somewhere else says, it is permitted for Levites to minister on the Sabbath, and they exercise their functions on that day without blame, or rather their remaining unemployed would be blamable. For would any one find fault if they were detected sacrificing oxen on the Sabbath, or even attending to other kinds of offerings?

He would on the other hand more probably accuse them if they were not doing their duty and fulfilling the regulations of divine service. When therefore things dedicated according to the law for the good of certain persons are brought to the divine altar even on the Sabbath without prohibition, is it not more fitting still that a kind action should be performed unto a man, for whose sake the marvelous deed might be acceptable even on the Sabbath?

Therefore, just by reasoning, some of the Jews are inclined to an excellent judgment, and putting off by an effort from the eyes of their understanding the mist of ignorance that characterizes their nation, they admire the glory of the Savior, (although as yet not very ardently, for they speak of Him less worthily than they should) and they separate themselves from those who are actually condemning Him. For the one part unholily allowed themselves to be swayed by envy more than by just reasoning, and treat as a transgression that which in its nature could not in any wise be blamed; whereas the others, rightly considering the nature of the action, condemn such a foolish accusation.

It is of course possible that it was with reference to some other matter that they chose to say, "How can a man who is a sinner do such signs?" ( Jn. 9:16). Perhaps, to put it briefly, they are eager to defend the general practice of holy men. For, they say, if we allow that it is quite possible for habitual transgressors to make themselves glorious by extraordinary actions and to be seen working marvelous deeds, what is there any longer to hinder those fond of making accusations from bringing charges against most of the prophets, or indeed incidentally attacking the blessed Moses himself, and lightly esteeming one so venerable, even though he was borne witness to by the most mighty actions of all? These men therefore may be contending for the reputation of the fathers as at stake in Christ, treating the circumstances respecting Him as a sort of pretext for showing their love towards them.

**"They said to the blind man again, 'What do you say about Him because He opened your eyes?'"**

They imagine those who are disposed to judge fairly to be wandering in their wits, and they seem to me to have forgotten altogether Him Who says: Judge righteous judgment; and having been taken captive as it were in the bonds of envy, they cannot endure to listen at all to any word that honors Christ. Turning away from any one wishing to speak of His miracles as from someone most hostile to themselves, and mistrusting their own powers of explanation, they haughtily address their words to the man that had been healed.

Again they ask what had been many times told them, having already proclaimed their belief that He Who had performed an action contrary to the Sabbath was both worthless and wicked. They think that in this way the blind man will join them in condemning Him, and take his cue from their words; that he will suppress all outward signs of gratitude, out of fear and trembling before their anger, and readily charge Jesus with contempt of the Law because it was the Sabbath. Evil therefore was the design of the Pharisees, and it cannot be doubted that it was foolish also.

For how could the voice of one thankless man weaken the force of the miracle? Would not Christ's divine glory appear, if it so happened that the blind man, overcome by fear, should deny the kindness he had received, in order to avoid suffering anything from those inclined to inflict pain? But envy is powerful to persuade those who are bursting with it to eagerly do any thing in their passion, even though it involves conduct very fairly open to ridicule.

The mind which is free from such thoughts, however, is not entangled by foolish arguments. But, ever preserving its natural excellence untarnished, is borne directly towards a right conclusion, and does not go beyond the limits of truth. Therefore, the Pharisees are malicious and insolent, thinking that those who choose to think and speak rightly are wandering in their wits, and endeavoring to compel the man to speak evil words concerning Him Who had miraculously bestowed on him an unhoped-for blessing. But he was disposed to express gratitude and had been brought near to a clear knowledge by means of the miracle.

"He said, 'He is a prophet.'"

They receive a sharp arrow into their hearts, who do not admit fair and just reasoning, and are eager to seek that only which gratifies their malice. For, as it is written, "The crafty man shall not meet with prey."[17] For their zealous design is upset, contrary to their expectation; and they are greatly disappointed of their hope when to their surprise they receive the reply, "He is a prophet." For the man who had been healed, judging very rightly, agrees with the opinion of the other party.

For they, not unwisely considering the nature of the action, maintain that a man who was a sinner could not perform such a deed. And he upon whom the marvel has been wrought, all but pursuing the same track of argument, declares Jesus to be a prophet, not yet having accurately learned Who He is in truth, but adopting a notion current among the Jews. For it was customary with them to call the prophets "wonder-workers," deeming that God had testified to their holiness by this.

Accordingly, just as they wisely determine not to dishonor the majesty of the divine sign oat of reverence for the Sabbath, but argue from it that He Who wrought it was altogether guiltless of sin; so also I suppose this man, thrusting aside the petty objection respecting the Sabbath, with worthier thoughts gives glory to Him Who had freely given him sight, and, having allotted Him a place among holy men, calls Him a prophet.

Moreover, he seems to me not to have thought to highly of the regulations of the Law. For [otherwise] he would not have admired Jesus so much, or raised his Physician to the rank of a prophet in spite of His apparent transgression of the sabbatical law. Having certainly derived benefit from the marvelous deed, and having arrived at a better state of mind than that of the

Jews, he is therefore obliged to admit a superiority to legal observances in the Wonderworker, Who, in doing good works, deemed an infringement of the Law altogether blameless.

---

[17] St. Cyril seems to be here citing some version of Prov. 14:17.

"But the Jews did not believe concerning him, that he had been blind and received his sight, until they called the parents of him who had received his sight. And they asked them, saying, 'Is this your son, who you say was born blind? How then does he now see?'"

The envy against the Healer which is hot within them does not allow them to believe what is acknowledged by all. Swayed by the frenzy of madness, they of course care little for the discovery of truth, and speak falsely against Christ. First they applied pressure to the man himself, and now they are seen to be no less rashly distressing his parents, but with the very opposite result to that which they intended.

They propose a most superfluous question to the man's parents, and they seem to me, in their unrestrained folly, to dishonor the very Law which they so venerated and so extravagantly upheld. For the neighbors, as it is written, brought him that previously was blind, and setting him face to face with those who were asking these questions, they reported most clearly that he had been born blind, and bore witness that now he had received sight. Thus, whereas the Law distinctly says that every matter is established by the mouth of two or three witnesses (cf. Deut. 19:15), they set aside the testimony not merely of two or three but probably of many more, and go for further evidence to the parents of him who was healed, thus acting contrary to the law as well as to good manners.

But the law is nothing to them when they are eager to accomplish something agreeable to their private pleasures. For when the testimony borne to the miracle, by the voices both of the neighbors and of the man who was healed, put them out of countenance sorely against their will; they expected to be able to persuade those now being questioned, to make light of truth, and rather to speak as they wished them to speak. For see in how overbearing a manner they put their question, saying, "Is this your son, who you say was born blind?" (Jn. 9:19).

For they all but avow their certain intention to treat them very dreadfully, and they frighten them with unbounded fear, calling as it were by compulsion and violence for that which they wished to hear, namely the answer, "He was not born blind." For they had but one object and that an impious one, namely, to loosen the hold which Christ had on the multitudes, and to turn away the simple faith of such as were now overcome with admiration.

And just as men who strive to take some well-fortified city surround it on every side and besiege it in all manner of ways. At one time they are eager to undermine the foundations, at another they strike blows with battering-rams against the towers. So the shameless Pharisees lay siege to the miracle with all their evil devices and leave no method of impiety untried. But it was not possible to disparage as unworthy of credit what was well known to all, or to distort that at which many had marveled into a less certain conviction.

**"His parents answered them and said, 'We know that this is our son, and that he was born blind; but by what means he now sees we do not know, or who opened his eyes we do not know. He is of age; ask him. He will speak for himself.'"**

They acknowledge as true that which was in no wise doubtful and for which it was hardly likely they would suffer anything disagreeable. For they say that they recognize their own offspring, and do not deny what really was the case at his birth, but distinctly affirm that he was born with the affliction. Nevertheless they shrink from relating the miracle, leaving the nature of the deed to speak for itself, and maintaining that it would be much more suitable to put the question as to how he had been healed to their son himself.

Fear of danger is certainly a powerful motive to turn men aside from what it befits them to do. Being greatly alarmed by the harshness of the Pharisees, they do not observe that which is somewhere well said, "Strive for the truth unto death" (Sir. 4:28). It is likely that they did suffer something of another sort. For the poor man is always timid, and, losing through, his poverty the power to offer bold resistance, often takes refuge in an unwilling silence, and a forced acquiescence. As if already completely crushed in spirit by the vexation of poverty, he seems insensible to being burdened with other misfortunes. We suspect that the parents of the blind man suffered something of this sort, even though their answer on the whole is composed with great plausibility.

For every one would agree that the recognition of the man as their son was a matter as to which it was far more reasonable to interrogate them than the man himself, whereas the question as to the Physician was one not so much, for the parents to answer as for him who had experienced the benefit of the wonderful operation. Thus they distinctly acknowledge what they know, inasmuch as they are fairly called upon for this. But they call upon him to give information about what he could tell more truly, since he had the more accurate knowledge. And this is not without divine guidance.

I think, that they added to their speech the words, "He is of age." For this also seems to indicate the impiety of the Pharisees. Because, if he who received sight was qualified by his time of life to form a sound opinion, when he relates the miracle and how he was treated, he will not speak with the mind of a boy, but with an understanding now well matured, and probably able to support by argument those speakers with whom he agrees. This then will of necessity tend to show the utterly shameless unbelief of the Pharisees. Behold, they will believe neither the neighbors nor the blind man himself, although it is not with an immature intellect that he gives evidence, nor on account of a boyish understanding does he easily glide into falsehood. But "he is of age," is a fact which prevents his being ignorant of the nature of affairs.

**"His parents said these things because they feared the Jews, for the Jews had agreed already that if anyone confessed that He was Christ, he would be put out of the synagogue."**

Well and fitly does our Lord Jesus the Christ utter this woe at the heads of the Pharisees: "Woe to you lawyers! For you have taken away the key of knowledge. You did not enter in yourselves, and those who were entering in you hindered" (Lk. 11:52). For again let the devout person consider if the beauty of truth will not correspond to these words. For Christ could never be deceived.

Behold, besides the unwillingness of any one of them to teach the doctrine of the presence of the Christ among them, they both terrify with cruel fear those who could perceive Him by the brilliance of His actions, and, by imposing a severe compulsion in their savageness, hinder any member of their company who seemed disposed to do so from acknowledging His miracles. For by putting out of the synagogue him who was right-minded and therefore disposed to believe, the wretches do not blush of their own authority to alienate in a manner from God him who cleaves to God; and to persuade him that the Lord of all is a partaker of the madness against all which they themselves possess.

However, the admirable Evangelist defends such, and says that the persons questioned were overcome by fear and therefore unwilling to say that the Christ had healed their son. So that by exposing the magnitude of the fury of the Jews, he might make it evident to those that come after. For what could be more inhuman than the conduct of these men, who deem right-minded persons worthy of punishment, and bring under the necessity of being punished, such as at all understand Him Who was proclaimed by the Law and the Prophets? And we shall find from the Sacred Scriptures that the unholy design of the Jews was known to the holy Prophets.

For "He Who searches the hearts and reins" (Rom. 8:27), "piercing even to the division of soul and spirit, and of joints and marrow, and is a discerner of the thoughts and intents of the heart" (Heb. 4:12). To Whom all things are naked and laid open, Isaiah said: "'Woe to the rebellious children,' says the Lord, "who take counsel, but not by Me; and covenants, but not by My Spirit; to add sins to sins" (Is. 30:1).

For he who says that Jesus is Lord most certainly will "speak by the Holy Spirit" (1 Cor. 12:3), according to the words of Paul. But anyone who professes the contrary will not speak in the Holy Spirit, (how could it be possible?) but rather in Beelzebub. Surely then the covenants of the Jews were not made by the Holy Spirit, for they added sins to sins. They, first of all, draw down the doom of disobedience upon their own heads. Then, they communicate it to others by forbidding them to confess the Christ.

Surely the design is full of the grossest impiety, albeit the Psalmist laughs at those who to their disappointment engage in a fruitless undertaking, saying: "You O Lord shall confound them in Your wrath, and the fire shall devour them; You shall destroy their fruit from the earth, and their seed from among the sons of men. For they intended evil against You; they imagined a device which they shall by no means be not able to perform" (Ps. 20:10-12). For they were quite unable to carry out a design which fought against God, although often and in ten thousand ways they attempted to obscure the glory of Christ. Therefore they were turned back, that is, were driven from the face and presence of the Lord of all, justly being addressed with the words, "Walk in the light of your fire, and in the flame which you have kindled" (Is. 50:11).

> "So they again called the man who was blind, and said to him, 'Give God the glory! We know that this Man is a sinner.'"

Being unable to stop the man from speaking well of Christ, they attempt to attain a similar end by another method, and proceed to entice him in a sort of coaxing way to fulfill their private aim. Trying by many arguments to make him forget Christ altogether, and not even mention Him as a Physician, they say most craftily that he should ascribe glory to God on account of the marvelous deed, thus pretending piety.

Nevertheless they offer him to agree with and believe themselves, even when they maintain the highest impiety possible by saying that "He is a sinner," He Who came to destroy sin. They bring forward no proof whatsoever of this slanderous assertion. But being boasters and thinking something great and extraordinary of themselves, merely because they were leaders of the people, they command implicit confidence to be put in their discernment of character, and lay it down as a matter of duty. For the words, "We know" will be found pregnant with surpassing arrogance by those who closely examine what they imply.

But you may in no small degree wonder at the foolish mind of the Jews from this also, that whereas they decree that glory should be ascribed to God on account of the miracle, since He alone is the doer of such deeds, they condemn the One Who works the works of God by His own might; and not only do the miserable people act thus themselves, but they compel others to agree with them. Yet when they claim that by their own unaided knowledge they are sure that Christ is a sinner, they are ignorant that they assert something most harmful to themselves. For, being inclined to boast greatly of their learning in the Law, and exhibiting intolerable conceit about the Sacred Scriptures, they will suffer a greater penalty; because, it being in their power to know the Mystery of Christ, which by the Law and the Prophets in many ways is typified and proclaimed, they with much heedlessness cling to their self-imposed ignorance.

Or, if they possess accurate knowledge, are always most persistently unwilling to do what they should. For they should rather to instruct the mind of the common people to comprehend the Mysteries of Christ, and to try to lead others to the knowledge of what it was suitable them to know. But they, profuse in arguments and mighty in boasts, and crying out with far too high an opinion of themselves, "We know," set aside the words of the Law, account the voice of Moses as nothing, and think the declarations of prophets to be as vain as those of the thoughtless mob. They quite fail to take notice of what the voice of the Prophet foretells will happen at the time of our Savior Christ's coming. For he says: "Then the eyes of the blind shall be opened, and the ears of the deaf shall hear; then shall the lame man leap as a deer, and the tongue of the dumb shall speak plainly" (Is. 35:5, 6).

The Paralytic was healed at the pool of Bethesda (Jn. 5:2), and after passing through thirty and eight years in his infirmity, as it is written, by one word of the Savior he took up his bed and leaped away like a deer. Yet when they should have admired Jesus for that, they lamented the breach of the Sabbath, and, holding that the law had been transgressed, disparaged the excellence of the miracle.

At another time, when an evil spirit had been cast out of him, the dumb man spoke, but they fell into such terrible folly as not to gain even a little profit from it. The blind man received sight, the prophetic announcement was fulfilled, the word of the Spirit was brought to pass to the uttermost, and what? Again at this they go mad, they condemn the Wonderworker, they attribute sin to Him Who is able to shine forth with divine brightness, and Who displays as actually now present that which had been expected ages ago.

**"He answered and said, 'Whether He is a sinner or not I do not know. One thing I know: that though I was blind, now I see...'"**

The benefit which the man formerly blind had received from Christ appears to have been twofold: his understanding was in some way enlightened at the same time as his bodily eyes, and as he possesses the, light of the physical sun in his fleshly eyes, so the intellectual beam, I mean the illumination by the Spirit, takes up its abode within him, and he receives it into his heart. For hear how he resists the abominable conduct of the magistrates out of his great love towards Christ, and how cleverly he reproaches them as being well-nigh intoxicated and beside themselves.

But he frames his speech with proper respectfulness, and giving them their due honor as the ruling order, courteously says, "Whether He is a sinner, I do not know." We do not argue from this that the man was unaware that Jesus was not a sinner, but shall rather suppose that he so addressed those men with the following design. For he may be imagined to speak thusly: though compelled against my will to acquiesce in what is wrong, I will not endure to slander my Benefactor. I will not join myself to those who wish to dishonor Him Who deserves all honor. I will not say that such a Wonderworker is a sinner. I will not give an unjust vote against One Who is mighty to work the works of God. The miracle wrought in me does not permit me to consent to your words. I was blind and I see. It is not another man's account of His doings that I have believed. I am not carried away by the reports of mere strangers. It is not cures effected upon others that I am led to admire. I myself, he says, am a proof of His power. I stand here seeing, having been formerly blind, as a sort of monument, exhibiting the excellence of His love for men, and flashing forth the greatness of His divine power.

Something like this I conceive to be the real significance of the words used by him who had received his sight. For to say, "Whether He is a sinner, I do not know," and immediately to add: "One thing I know: that though I was blind, now I see," is not in the style of a simple statement, but shows a deeper meaning of very wise reasoning.

**"Then they said to him again, 'What did He do to you? How did He open your eyes?'"**

They again resort to questioning, and inquire about the manner of the divine sign—not doing this out of good feeling or a laudable curiosity, but placing and reckoning the speaking well of Christ by any living being as lower than any villainy and worse than any wickedness. They stir up all these matters afresh, thinking perhaps that the man would no longer repeat the same words, but would vary his account of the event, and say something inconsistent with his former answers, so that they might lay hold of the contradiction and denounce him as an impostor and a liar. For, arrogant in their excessive cleverness, they imagined the force of the miracle to depend on the mere words of the man, as though it were not evident from the fact of what had been done.

Moreover, I think that they may have experienced something of this sort. Those who hate others without cause, when they examine the things done by others and believe these things were not done correctly ask witnesses, not once, but many times, about these things, whether they were rightly done, thereby making more acute their feeble anger. Such as are not backward in hating others unjustly, when they are making inquiries about anything done by them which does not seem to have been rightly done, wish to hear it from the witnesses not once only but over and over again, whetting as it were into keener action the anger which seems too feeble. For, conscience, always testing our motives, makes us uncomfortable, and does not ceases to accuse us of injustice, even though from passionate prejudice we may feel a certain pleasure in the unjust action. The man who had been healed is accordingly provoked and urged against his will to go over the story again and to answer the same questions, while they almost make signs to one another to observe closely whether something illegal might not have been done in the working of this divine sign on the Sabbath. For conscience checks the savage design that rages within them, and (so to speak) puts a bridle on them, though they are unwilling to admit its interference.

**"He answered them, 'I told you already, and you did not listen. Why do you want to hear it again?'"**

"It seems redundant now," he says, "to tell the story over again to a skeptical audience. It is useless for you to inquire so often concerning these things, when you do not gain anything whatsoever, although you learn and have conclusive evidence. But you bid me now again reiterate the same words for no good purpose, as experience proclaims." In such a way, the man who had been healed thoroughly convicts the Pharisees of irrationality, of "turning away their ears from the truth" as it is written (2 Tim. 4:4), not being laudably angry at the law being broken, but by these questions bidding him who wished to speak well of the Wonderworker to appear in the character of an accuser, rather than accepting him as an admirer. For this was in truth their aim, since the transgression of the law was altogether a matter of indifference to them, and passed over as quite unimportant. On this account they set aside just judgment and were only bent on gratifying their prejudice; forgetting God Who says," For the priest's lips should keep knowledge, and they should seek the law at his mouth" (Mal. 2:7).

### "Do you also want to become His disciples?"

He has now confessed distinctly, and without any evasion, that he has been made a disciple, if not by argument yet in consequence of the marvelous deed; and has become a believer, accepting his miraculous sight in the place of instruction. For when he said to them, "Do you also want to become His disciples?" he, as it were, revealed his own condition of mind. For he was not only willing to become, but actually had already become, a disciple. And in some degree even before he had fullness of faith, acting upon the precept, "Freely you have received, freely give" (Mt. 10:8), he was prepared at once and very unselfishly to communicate his advantages to them. He affirms, unhesitatingly and often, his account of the marvelous deed, had they only considered his narrative really as instruction. He certainly therefore observed in an excellent way that in the Book of Proverbs, He speaks in the ears of those who hear (cf. Prov. 5:1, 20:12)

It seems probable that some deep and hidden meaning is obscurely intimated in these words of his, and I will briefly state what it is. There were some of the magistrates who recognized that the Wonderworker was in truth Christ, but keeping their knowledge of Him buried (so to speak) within their hearts, they as yet were unsuspected by the majority of their companions. And our witness will be the wise Evangelist himself, where he says that the rulers knew that He was the Christ, but because of the Pharisees they did not confess it.

The proofs of this will be strengthened also to some extent by Nicodemus, boldly exclaiming and saying to our Lord Jesus Christ, "Rabbi, we know that You are a teacher come from God; for no one can do these signs that You do unless God is with Him" (Jn. 3:2). Therefore some of the rulers certainly knew, and the report of this was spread abroad throughout all Jerusalem. The majority of the Jews suspected that the rulers knew, but were determined not to confess it through malice and envy; and that this also is true, we will show from the evangelical writings themselves.

For the blessed John himself somewhere says that Jesus stood teaching in the very temple and explaining things which, at least to the understanding of His hearers, seemed to be breaking the law (cf. Jn. 8:20). And when the magistrates of the Jews did not proceed at all against Him—no, they did not dare so much as to say: "O fellow, cease teaching what does not harmonize with our ancient laws"—they brought suspicion on themselves among the multitudes as we have just observed.

Thus, for instance, it is written, "Now some of them from Jerusalem said, "Is this not He Whom they seek to kill? But look! He speaks boldly, and they say nothing to Him. Do the rulers know indeed that this is truly the Christ?" (Jn. 7:25, 26). Surely he all but says, "Those whose lot it is to be leaders know that He is indeed the Christ. See, although they are generally considered to be desirous of killing Him, He is speaking with very great boldness and they do not rebuke Him even so much as by words."

Accordingly, this suspicion being spread abroad through all Jerusalem, the blind man had at some time heard it, and had this report about these men ringing in his ears. Gracefully reproving them, as we may suppose, he says: "Surely it is to no purpose that you bid me again utter the same words and again speak the praise of the marvelous deed. Or do you indeed consider the narrative a pleasure, thirsting even now for instruction from Him, although, overcome by fear of others, you allow ungrateful cowardice to stand in the way of such excellent knowledge?"

**"Then they reviled him and said, 'You are His disciple, but we are Moses' disciples.'"**

We almost see the Evangelist smile as he says this. For he beholds those whose lot it was to hold sacred offices degraded in mental stupor so far as to make an object of reviling that which was so excellent, namely discipleship under Christ. Smitten with a worthy love of which, some of the saints say, "How sweet are Your words unto my taste, sweeter than honey and honeycomb to my mouth!" (Ps. 118:103). And again, another, as if speaking to our Lord Jesus the Christ, says concerning those that disobey Him, "Consume them and Your word shall be to me joy and gladness, yes the joy of my heart" (Jer. 12:15, 16).

But they attach no value to His sacred words, and think that one who is being instructed by Him is worthy of blame even on that account alone. Holding so far true opinions even against themselves, they speak of the Christ as the blind man's teacher, and Moses as their own. For in very truth the Gentiles were illuminated by Christ through the evangelical teaching and Israel died in the types given by Moses and was buried in the shadow of the letter. Therefore, Paul also says somewhere about them, "But even to this day, when Moses is read, a veil lies on their heart" (2 Cor. 3:15). And there is no doubt that it was as a type of the Gentiles that we were as in a picture delineating the history of the blind man, fashioning, as in a type, the incidents connected with him to express the truth concerning them.

Yet this also is signified, that to suffer reproach for Christ's sake is a thing delightful and most honorable; for the very means by which those who do not shrink from becoming persecutors think to vex those who love Him, become (though the persecutors know it not) sources of joy to them. Yes, those who persecute Christians cause their excellence to shine more conspicuously and do not so easily succeed in causing them injury. The abandoned Pharisees, then, disparaging as seems probable themselves more than Christ, say of the blind man, "You are His disciple." And being elated and puffed up with pride, foolishly they say of themselves, "But we are Moses' disciples."

**"We know that God spoke to Moses; as for this fellow, we do not know where He is from."**

Boldly do they speak again, armed with that folly which is so familiar and dear to them, and in undiminished shamelessness they once more boastfully exclaim, "We know." When they add, "that God spoke to Moses," thereby recognizing that He deserved great honor, they in another way again insult Him, seeing that they take no account of His precepts. For they ignorantly condemn One Whom as yet they know not, or rather they dishonor Him in spite of what they have learned concerning Him, although the Law forbids them to act unjustly and argumentatively towards anyone, or to judge at all in this way.

Now, they say again something like this: "Confessedly, God has spoken to Moses. There is no sufficient reason for any to be in doubt on this point. He enacted laws by him, and laid down regulations how every thing is to be done. Therefore," he says, "whoever has contrary opinions to those expressed by Moses is certainly a transgressor of the sacred Scriptures. And manifestly the Law concerning the Sabbath has been broken, for you were healed on the Sabbath. It is righteous not to acknowledge one who is detected in this matter and therefore condemned. Now we have good reason to say that He has not observed the divine law." Then, when they say of Christ, "We do not know where He is from," they surely do not say so as being ignorant Who or from where He was, for they are elsewhere found publicly confessing that they know all about Him.

"Is not this the carpenter's Son, Whose father and mother we know?" (Mt. 13:15; Jn. 6:42). How then does He say, "I have come down from heaven" (Jn. 6:41)? Certainly therefore we cannot accept this statement. We know not from where He is, as indicative of ignorance, but we shall look upon it as the expression of the arrogance which was in them. For, throwing contempt on their own previous judgment, and setting it altogether at naught, they make this statement concerning Him. Perhaps, indeed, their words indicate that they argued as follows; for it is only fair to their arguments that we should scrutinize them more carefully. "We know," say they, "that God spoke to Moses. Therefore we must believe without hesitation what was spoken by him, and observe the commandments given to him from God. But this Man we do not know, for God has not spoken to Him, nor have we recognized any such thing with regard to Him."

But the Pharisees, wished to be wise in their own conceit, and boasting much of their knowledge of the divine Word, should have considered that God the Father thus speaks, when by the all-wise Moses He proclaims the future advent of Jesus, "I will raise them up a Prophet from among their brethren like you, and will put My words in His mouth, and He shall speak to them as I shall command Him. And whoever shall not listen to whatever that Prophet shall speak in My Name, I will take vengeance on him" (Deut. 18:18, 19).

Surely anyone might have rebuked the Jews with good reason, and said, "O you who only know how to disbelieve, if you are so readily persuaded by the words of Moses, because God has spoken to him, shouldn't you believe Christ in the same way, when you hear Him publicly declaring, 'The words that I say unto you are not Mine, but the Father's Who sent Me' (cf. Jn. 14:10); and again, 'I have not spoken on My own authority; but the Father Who sent Me gave Me a command, what I should say and what I should speak' (Jn. 17:8)"? Therefore, the words of the Pharisees are certainly a mere excuse, a fiction of vain reasoning. For if they say they should rather follow Moses, on this account, that God spoke to him, why do they not think similarly with regard to Christ, when He distinctly says what we have just mentioned? But while in part they honor the law, and pretend to hold God's will in high esteem, in another way they violate it and dishonor it greatly by refusing to accept its proclamation concerning their time, that namely which was announced by it concerning Christ, that by His Incarnation He should appear in the character of a prophet.

**"The man answered and said to them, 'Why, this is a marvelous thing, that you do not know where He is from; yet He has opened my eyes!'"**

"I am astonished," he says, and very justly, "that you say you do not know One Who is borne witness to by such holiness and by the divine power shown in His actions. Yet you are thought to incessantly give attention to God's teaching; you administer the law; you make the verbal study of the sacred words your great delight; you possess the chief power among the people and especially may be expected to know who are good teachers. For who should rightly know those who by God's power work wonders, if they do not who are appointed to minister in holy things and who have been put in charge of the venerable mysteries?"

And by saying that he is astonished that they are altogether ignorant respecting the divine sign, so wonderful and strange, which had been wrought upon him, the man covertly and by implication rebukes them, hinting that they were so far removed from sanctification and fitness for piety, that they shamelessly confessed themselves utterly ignorant of Him Who is truly holy, that is, Christ.

For let us reveal what we believe to have been the concealed thought. If that is true which is somewhere well said: "Every beast loves his like, and a man loves his neighbor" (Sir. 13:15, 16) how then if they were holy and good did they turn away and refuse to cleave to Him Who was holy and good? Therefore that which was spoken was certainly pregnant with a rebuke of the accursed policy and behavior of the Pharisees. And I think another thing also will help to make this manifest. For I think that the diligent student who devotes his attention to such expressions will perceive more distinctly that which seems to be hidden in each. What then is this?

Many rumors went about through all Judaea concerning our Savior Christ (Lk. 7:17), but they spoke of Him only as a prophet. For thus the Law prophesied that He would come, saying: "The Lord our God will raise up a Prophet from among your brethren" (Deut. 18:16); yet they hoped that when He was revealed in His proper time He would instruct them in things above the Law, and by unfolding the truer intent of the Lawgiver would educate them in worthier manner.

And you need not wonder that there was among the Jews such a hope and opinion, when even among the other nations the same opinion was spread abroad. For instance even that Samaritan woman said: "We[18] know that Messiah is coming (Who is called Christ). When He comes, He will tell us all things" (Jn. 4:25). Most clearly therefore the Jews knew that Christ would come, (for this is what Messiah means), and would interpret to them the higher counsel of God. Moreover that He would also open the eyes of the blind was declared by Isaiah, who says distinctly, "Then shall the eyes of the blind shall be opened" (Is. 35:5).

But there was also another opinion prevalent in Jerusalem, forasmuch as the prophet Isaiah speaks of the Ineffable Son of God the Father as quite unrecognized, saying, "Who shall declare His generation?" (Is. 53:8). The Jews, here also distorting the force of the words in accordance with their own notions, imagined that the Christ would be altogether unrecognized, no one whatever knowing whence He was. However, the Divine Scriptures establish for us very evidently His birth in the flesh, and therefore exclaims, "Behold, the Virgin shall conceive in the womb, and shall bring forth a Son" (Is. 7:14). And that the mind of the Jews in this again was uneducated as regards the comprehension of essential truths, when they supposed that the Christ would be unrecognized, it is easy to see, from what the blessed Evangelist John declared to be evident concerning Him, when speaking to them of Jerusalem. For some of them of Jerusalem said, "Is this not He Whom they seek to kill? But look! He speaks boldly, and they say nothing to Him. Do the rulers know indeed that this is truly the Christ? However, we know where this Man is from;

---

[18] The New King James Version, along with most New Testament translations, follows the Received Greek text (Textus Receptus 1894), which reads, "I know" *(oida)*.

but when the Christ comes, no one knows where He is from" (Jn. 7:25-27).

While the Jews therefore are thus absurdly laying down these opinions concerning Christ, the man who had been blind already forms correct ideas about Him, quickly drawing inferences from the marvelous deed. He all but seizes on the words of the Pharisees in confirmation of his own reasoning. For he says, "Why, this is a marvelous thing, that you do not know where He is from; yet He has opened my eyes!" (Jn. 9:30). "I have two very clear signs," he says, "that He is the Christ. For you do not know where He is from; yet He has opened my eyes." Therefore this is evidently He Who was foretold by the Law, and certainly borne witness to by the voice of Prophets.

**"Now we know that God does not hear sinners; but if anyone is a worshiper of God and does His will, He hears him."**

Having already in some measure shown his delight in the proclamations made by the Prophets and the Law as now fulfilled, both in its being unknown whence Christ was, and in the eyes of the blind being opened, he collects for himself aids to faith from every quarter, and thus discovers something else also. Starting from necessary and acknowledged principles, he makes a show of going on to the inquiry as to what is profitable and fitting, and constructs what may be termed a piece of reasoning well-pleasing to God. For he maintains, and surely there are good grounds for so thinking, that the God Who loves justice and virtue never hears those who love sin.

And laying this down as indisputable and universally acknowledged, he introduces as a contrast the opposite statement as true. So, as contradicted in no quarter, I mean of course that everywhere and always the Lord of all listens to those who are habitually pious.

Although the conclusion to be drawn was designed to refer to the Christ alone, it was so constructed as if it had reference to a general and universal principle. For as I have already pointed out by anticipation, the man who had been blind has an unworthy conception of Christ and has not yet learned accurately that He is by nature God. So that he thinks and speaks of Him as a prophet, to Whom he might without blame ascribe piety. But this does not rightly apply to Christ at all, because He is God by nature, receiving the worship of the pious as it were a spiritual sacrifice.

**"Since the world began it has been unheard of that anyone opened the eyes of one who was born blind."**

Pained as it seems very keenly, and grieving as we may say over their reviling against Christ, so as to be vexed beyond endurance because they contemptuously said, "You are His disciple, but we are Moses' disciples," he is eager to speak on behalf of his Master. Hence, he draws a sort of comparison between the achievements of Moses and the brilliant deeds of our Savior, showing that as the latter is greater in wonder-working, so far He is the better. For indeed, is it not a matter of course that he who accomplishes the greater work should be in every way superior in glory? Surely it is not to be doubted. At the same time he probably signifies something of this sort:

"Whereas a very ancient prophecy foretells and declares thus concerning the coming of Christ, 'Then shall the eyes of the blind be opened' and no one ever before caused astonishment by having done any such deed. Now it has been fulfilled by Him and Him alone, Whom you (I know not why)," he says, "do not hesitate to call a sinner. Moreover, a great company of holy Prophets are spoken of, and a number not easily computed of just men are mentioned throughout the Sacred Scriptures. But 'since the world began it has been unheard of that anyone opened the eyes of one who was born blind.' Is it not therefore certain that this is the Christ, Who accomplishes the declarations of the Prophets, Who thoroughly and completely fulfills the things proclaimed of old? For if no other besides Him opens the eyes of the blind, what from now on shall stand in the way of faith? What shall turn us aside from accepting Him? Or how can we fail, every doubt being cast aside, to attain by the very easiest way the mystery of knowing Him?"

Thus, in these words also the man who was healed speaks on behalf of the Savior Christ. See how cleverly he puts together the argument of his plea? For it would really have been altogether outspoken and frank to say that Christ was better and more illustrious than Moses and the Prophets. But it was not unreasonable to suppose that the Pharisees, frantic at that, would have pretended that they were contending for the saints thus insulted. And with a good excuse they would have attempted to punish the man, that he might not live and be looked upon as a monument of Christ's glory and a sort of representative of the divine power which Christ possessed. Therefore, craftily avoiding the passion that might arise, and depriving their murderous thoughts of this pretext for development, he diverts the application of the argument to what is universal and indefinite, saying, "Since the world began" that which Christ had worked upon him had never been done by any one.

This was nothing else than showing that Christ was certainly greater and more glorious than all, since He manifested by His actions such power and authority to be possessed by Him, as none of the saints had ever possessed. Thus he crowns his Physician with excellent honor in every thing, taking for justification the marvelous deed never before accomplished or attempted, namely, the removal of blindness.

**"If this Man were not from God, He could do nothing."**

He who had just received sight and been miraculously freed from his old blindness, was quicker to perceive truth than those who had been instructed by the law, for see, see how by very many and wise arguments he demonstrates the utter baseness of the Pharisees' opinion. For when they absurdly said of Christ, "as for this fellow, we do not know where He is from" (Jn. 9:28), he in reply severely rebukes them for their unfairness of thought, when they deny all knowledge of One Who worked such wonders. It was evident to all that one who was not from God would be unable to do any of those deeds which are only accomplished by divine energy. For God works such deeds through the saints only, and would never bestow upon a stranger who had not yet entered on the way of godliness the ability to boast of such glories.

Otherwise, let the dumbfounded Pharisee come forward and say what is then the distinction with God between the holy and the profane, the just and the sinner, the impious and the devout. For if He enables each equally to become glorious by the same means, there is no longer any distinction, but at once all things are brought into confusion, and we will say with good reason that which is written: "How shall we fitly serve Him, and what will be the profit if we appear before Him? For if, as one of the Greek poets said, 'The same share is allotted to him who remains at home as to him who fights bravely,"[19] and the evil and the good are held in equal honor, will it not be useless to experience bitter hardships on account of virtue?" But we will not consider that these things are so, and why? Because God says, "I will only honor those who honor Me, and he who sets Me at nought shall be despised" (1 Sam. 2:30).

For my part, I would ask the self-conceited Pharisees, if God indifferently works such deeds even by the hands of sinners, why the magicians of Egypt did not achieve the same things as the great Moses? Why could they not do equally wonderful works and carry off the same glory as he did? But you will say that Moses' rod when it fell on the ground became a serpent, and those of the magicians became so in like manner.

We answer that their rods were not transformed into serpents, but a deceit was practiced, and something which appeared to men like the form of serpents deluded them into error. A certain magical art made their rods look like serpents, while Moses' rod was truly changed into a serpent and suddenly received the nature of that beast. From the distinction which is laid down in the Sacred Scriptures you will see that what I have said is true. For Moses' rod swallowed up their rods. Since the latter were merely in the outward form of serpents; but the former was truly and in nature that which it appeared to be, it was provoked to anger that they should look no longer like rods but like living beings, and devoured them with unheard of power beyond the power of an [ordinary serpent], God rendering such a difficult thing easy to it.

Again, let the Pharisee tell me why these magicians, who caused their own rods to take the outward form of serpents, did not exhibit a leprous hand made clean, but in despair openly confessed, "This is the finger of God?" (Ex. 8:19). And tell me why the priests of Baal did not bring down fire from heaven, and yet Elijah brought it down (2 Kgs. 1:10-14). Are, therefore, God's ways certainly characterized by respect of persons? God forbid! But because He is just and a Lover of just men He works His gracious miracles through the agency of the saints, but by no means through the agency of the sinful. With excellent reason, therefore, the man who had been blind rebukes the impudent chattering of the Pharisees and

---

[19] "Ἴση μοῖρα μένοντι, καί εἰ μάλα τις πολεμίζοι," Homer, *Iliad*, ix. 318.

convicts them of an erroneous opinion, when they say He is not from God Who is proved to have a divine nature by His power of working miracles.

**"They answered and said to him, 'You were completely born in sins, and are you teaching us?' And they cast him out."**

Hard of acceptation to most people are the wounds of refutation, and the consequent correction of error. They are certainly welcome and sweet to the wise, since they convey much profit, and have an improving tendency, although they may carry with them a painful sting. But to those who love sin they are bitter. Why? Because, having fixed their mind on debasing pleasures, they turn away from any warning that draws them from being frustrated, and deem it a loss to be diverted from their pleasures, setting no value on what is truly profitable.

For just as those who fall overboard from a ship—and, being caught by the current of a river, are not strong enough to resist it, and, thinking it dangerous to swim in opposition to the waves, are simply borne on by the current—so I think these men, of whom we were just speaking, overcome by the tyranny of their own pleasures allow those pleasures to rush on unconstrained, and decline to offer any resistance whatsoever. Hence, the wretched Pharisees are displeased, and crying out like wild beasts against him who brought forward excellent arguments, they welcome the beginnings of anger. And spouting forth the extreme rage of madness, they unlawfully revile him. And somehow recurring to the haughtiness so natural to them, they say that the blind man was born in sins, thus maintaining the Jewish errors, and ignorantly supporting a doctrine that will not hold together.

For no living person, either on his own account or on account of his parents, is born blind or with any other bodily infirmity. Moreover, that God does not visit the sins of their fathers upon children, not unskillfully, in my opinion at least, we have shown at some length, when we had to explain the words, "Rabbi, who sinned, this man or his parents, that he was born blind?" (Jn. 9:1). Therefore, since the man who had been born blind knew how to refute the Pharisees, he was on that account not only reviled, but cast out by them. And here again learn that what was done is typical of a true event: for anyone can recognize from what the Pharisees said to that man that the people of Israel were going to utterly loathe the

Gentiles as nurtured in sins from erroneous prejudice. And they expel him, exactly as those who plead the doctrine of Christ are expelled and cast out by the Jews.

**"Jesus heard that they had cast him out..."**

The inspired Evangelist says that our Lord Jesus Christ heard, not implying certainly or of necessity that any one reported the fact to Him, but because, as one of the wise somewhere says, "The Spirit of the Lord fills the world, and the ear of hearing hears all things" (Wis. 1:7). Surely He hears, as the Psalmist says, "He Who planted, the ear, does He not hear? or He Who formed the eye, does He not perceive?" (Ps. 94:9). Therefore, when we suffer insult on His account, or endure any grievous thing from those who like to fight against God, we are bound to believe that most assuredly God is a witness, and listens as it were to the trial that comes upon us. For the very nature of the occurrence, and the sincerity of those who are dishonored on His account, cry aloud in His divine ears.

**"...and when He had found him, He said to him, 'Do you believe in the Son of God?'"**

The man who had been blind has been cast out by the Pharisees, but after no long interval of time Christ seeks him, and finding him, initiates him in Mysteries. Therefore, this also shall be a sign to us that God keeps in mind those who are willing to speak on His behalf and who do not shrink from peril through faith in Him. For you hear how, making Himself manifest as though to give a good recompense, He hastens to implant in him the highest perfection of the doctrines of the faith. And He proposes the question so that He may receive the assent. For this is the way of showing faith.

Why also those who are going to divine baptism are previously as a preparation asked questions concerning their belief, and when they have assented and confessed, then at once we admit them as worthy for the grace.[20] Hence therefore arises the significance of the event to us, and we have learned from our Savior Christ Himself how right it is that this profession of faith should be made. Why also the inspired Paul asserted that [Timothy] confessed the confession of these things with "many witnesses" (1 Tim. 6:12), meaning the holy angels. And if it is an awful thing to falsify what is spoken before angels, how much more so before Christ Himself?

So then He asks the man who had been blind not simply if he was willing to believe, but also mentions on Whom. For the faith [must be] on the Son of God, and not as on a man like ourselves, but as on God Incarnate. Surely this is the fullness of the mystery concerning Christ. And in saying: "Do you believe?" He all but says, "Will you show yourself superior to the madness of those men? Will you bid farewell to their unbelief and accept the Faith?" For the emphatic "you" implies such a contradistinction from other persons in some way.

**"He answered and said, 'Who is He, Lord, that I may believe in Him?'"**

The soul furnished with sound reason, diligently seeking the word of truth with the eyes of the understanding free, without embarrassment makes straight for it like a ship going into port, and obtains its advantages by a chase without fatigue. Again, the man who had been blind will be a proof of what has been said. For when he had already by many arguments and reasonings admired the Mystery concerning Christ—and, moreover, had been struck with astonishment at His unspeakable might, which had been experienced not by any other but by himself, in himself—he is found thus ready to believe and without delay proceeds to do so. For see, see, he earnestly asks upon whom he should fasten that faith which had been already built up within him. For this alone was lacking to him, and he was previously prepared for it, as we have said.

---

[20] St. Cyril here refers to the interrogations which precede baptism in the Coptic rite, an ancient practice which was adopted by many other liturgical traditions in the East and West.

"And Jesus said to him, 'You have both seen Him and it is He Who is talking with you.'"

Being asked upon whom it was proper to believe, Jesus points to Himself, and not simply by saying, "It is I," but by saying that the Person Whom the other was looking at and by Whom he was being addressed, was the Son of God. In every way consulting beforehand our advantage, and in diverse manners constructing aids towards a faith both free from error and unadulterated, lest while thinking ourselves pious we might fall into the meshes of the net of the devil, by foolishly turning aside from the truth of the Mystery.

For even now some of those who think themselves Christians, not accurately understanding the scope of the Incarnation, have dared to separate from God the Word that Temple which was for our sakes taken from woman, and have divided Him Who is truly and indeed One Son into two sons, even because He was made Man. For with great folly they disdain to acknowledge as probable that which the Only-Begotten disdained not even to do for our sakes. For, "He, Who being in the form of God," according to that which is written, "did not consider it robbery to be equal with God, but emptied Himself, taking the form of a bondservant" (Phil. 2:6, 7) that He might become a man like us, of course without sin.

But they in their strange opinions find fault in a sort of way with His divine and philanthropic design, and thrusting away the Temple taken from woman from the true Sonship as far as they can in their thoughts, they do not accept His humiliation. And conceiving an opinion far removed from the truth, they say that the Only-Begotten Son of God the Father, that is, the Word Begotten of His Essence, is One; and that the Son born of woman is yet another.

Still, when the inspired Scripture proclaims the Son and Christ to be One, are they not full of all impiety who sever into two Him Who is truly and indeed One Son?[21] For inasmuch as He is God the Word, He is

---

[21] St. Cyril here refers to heretical teachings concerning our Lord Jesus Christ. The word "heresy" comes from the Greek *haireisthai*, which means "to choose." Thus, the heretics were those who chose their own truth about God, ignoring the Orthodox teaching of the One, Holy, Apostolic Church and its Fathers. Some of the Christological heresies that

thought of as distinct from the flesh. And inasmuch as He is flesh, He is thought of as distinct from the Word. But inasmuch as the Word of God the Father was made flesh, the two will cease to be distinct through their ineffable union and conjunction. For the Son is One and only One, both before His conjunction with flesh, and when He came with flesh. And by flesh we denote man in his integrity, I mean as consisting of soul and body.

Certainly therefore on account of this pretense, with the greatest foresight, the Lord here again when asked, "Who is the Son of God?" did not say, "It is I." For it would then perhaps have been possible for some ignorantly to suppose that the Word alone Who shone forth from God the Father was thereby signified. But He showed Himself forth in the very manner which to some seems so doubtful, by saying, "You have both seen Him," and also indicated that the Word Himself was dwelling in the flesh by speaking again and adding, "and it is He Who is talking with you."

Therefore, you see what a unity the Word possesses. He makes no distinction but says that Himself is both that which presents itself to bodily eyes, and that which is known by speech. Certainly therefore it is altogether ignorant and impious to say as some inconsiderately do say: "O Christ's man." For being God He was made man without being severed from His Divinity, and is the Son also with flesh. And in these things is the most perfect confession and knowledge of faith in Him.

**"Then he said, 'Lord, I believe!' And he worshipped Him."**

Quick to make a confession, I mean as regards his faith, and warm in showing piety, is the man who had been blind. For when he knew that the One present with him and visible to his eyes was truly the Only-Begotten Son, he worshipped Him as God, although beholding Him in the flesh without the glory which is really God-befitting.

But having had his heart illumined by Christ's indwelling power and authority, he advances to wise and good thoughts by fair reasoning, and

---

wrongly teach a separation of Christ into two are Apollinarianism, Docetism, Arianism, and Adoptionism. St. Cyril, however, was prophetically addressing the heresy of Nestorianism, which would plague the Church later and which taught that Christ exists as two persons, the man Jesus and the divine Son of God, or Logos, rather than as One Christ, One Son, and One Lord from two natures.

beholds the beauty of His divine and ineffable nature. For he would not have worshipped Him as God unless he believed Him to be God, having been prepared and led thus to think by what had happened to himself, even the miraculously accomplished marvelous deed. And since we transferred all the circumstances connected with the blind man to the history of the Gentiles, let us now speak again concerning this.

See, I ask you, how he fulfills by the prefiguring of the worship in spirit the type to which the Gentiles were conducted by their faith. For it was the custom for Israel to serve the Lord of all according to the bidding of the Law, with sacrifices of oxen, incense, and with offerings of other animals. But the faithful among the Gentiles do not know this manner of service but were turned to the other, that is, the spiritual, which God says is truly and especially dear and sweet to Him. For He says, "I will not eat the flesh of bulls, neither will I drink the blood of goats" (Ps. 49:13). And in preference He bids us offer the sacrifice of thanksgiving, that is, worship with song, to celebrate which the Psalmist through faith in the Holy Spirit sees that all the Gentiles would go up, and says as if to our Lord and Savior, "All the earth shall worship You, and shall sing unto You; yea they shall sing to Your Name" (Ps. 66:4).

Moreover, our Lord Jesus Christ Himself shows the spiritual to be better than the legal service, when He says to the woman of Samaria: "Woman, believe Me, the hour is coming when you will neither on this mountain, nor in Jerusalem, worship the Father...But the hour is coming, and now is, when the true worshipers will worship the Father in spirit and truth; for the Father is seeking such to worship Him. God is Spirit, and those who worship Him must worship in spirit and truth" (Jn. 4:21, 23, 24).

And if we rightly think, we shall conclude that the holy angels also are distinguished by this kind [of service], presenting unto God such worship as a sort of spiritual offering. For instance when the Spirit gave command to those above to bring God-befitting honor to the Firstborn and Only-Begotten, He says, "Let all the angels of God worship Him" (Heb. 1:6). Moreover the divine Psalmist called us to do this, saying: "O come let us worship and fall down before Him" (Ps. 94:6).

While it would not be difficult to treat of this matter at great length; but putting a convenient limit to our words, we will abstain from bringing forward any more arguments for the present. Except that we will once more repeat that the man who had been blind admirably carries out the type of the service of the Gentiles, making his worship the close companion of his confession of faith.

**"And Jesus said, 'For judgment I have come into this world, that those who do not see may see, and that those who see may be made blind.'"**

Christ, when explaining to us by the voice of Isaiah the cause of His manifestation, I mean in this world, says, "The Spirit of the Lord is upon Me, because He has anointed Me to preach the gospel to the poor; He has sent Me to heal the brokenhearted, to proclaim liberty to the captives and recovery of sight to the blind" (Lk. 4:18). Moreover He said somewhere in another place, "Hear, you deaf; and look up, you blind, that you may see!" (Is. 42:18).

Therefore, when He says that for this cause He was chosen by God the Father, that He might proclaim recovery of sight to the blind, how is it that here He says, "For judgment I have come into this world, that those who do not see may see, and that those who see may be made blind" (Jn. 9:39)?

"Is then," some one will say, "Christ a minister of sin, according to the language of Paul?" God forbid! For He came to accomplish the predetermined intention of His goodness towards us, namely, to illuminate all men by the torch of the Spirit. But the Jews, being obstinate in unbelief did not accept the grace shining upon them, invoking as it were on themselves a self-chosen darkness. For instance, it is written concerning them in the prophetic records, "While they waited for light darkness came upon them" (cf. Job. 30:26); waiting for brightness they walked in obscurity. For inasmuch as He was to come according to the declaration of the Law, the Jews waited for brightness and the Light, that is, Christ. For they accepted the fact that He would come, and expected Him, but they who thought themselves pious in this matter were walking in obscurity, that is, in profound darkness, when there was no other cause why they suffered the gloom that came upon them, except that by their own unbelief they drew the affliction upon themselves.

"I came therefore," He says, "to give sight to the blind through their faith." But the unyielding obstinacy of the stubborn and resistant, which tended greatly to unbelief, caused the coming of the Illuminator to be unto them a coming for judgment. Since they did not believe, they are condemned. The Savior said this more clearly to you in other words also, "Assuredly, I say unto you, he who believes in the Son is not condemned; but he who does not believe in the Son has been condemned already, because he has not believed in the Name of the Only-Begotten Son of God" (Jn. 3:18).

Therefore, with beautiful fitness He mentions this in connection with the event now under our consideration, making the deed miraculously wrought upon the blind man the basis as it were of his discourse. For He declares that man to have received sight not only regarding the body, but also regarding the mind, because he had accepted the faith. However, the Pharisees suffered just the contrary, because they did not behold His glory, although it was shining most clearly, even in that marvelous deed that was so great and so novel.

**"Then some of the Pharisees who were with Him heard these words, and said to Him, Are we blind also?"**

The Pharisees keep close to the Savior Christ and are eager to associate with Him, although they have a sharp arrow shot into their heart, and wither with vexation and envy at His glory. They associate with Him, however, gathering nourishment for their hatred, and devising various slanders against His marvelous deeds, and by these means perverting the guileless mind of such as are more ready to believe. When they heard Christ say these words, they were cut to the heart again, for it was not likely they would fail to know that the aim of the discourse was directed against them.

But when He said at first, vaguely and indefinitely that those who see may become blind (Jn. 9:39) not yet having an occasion to find fault with good reason as being insulted, they maliciously question Him, applying the force of what had been said to their own persons, and demanding as it were that He should say more clearly whether He meant that they were blind also, so that they might now condemn Him again as offending against the commandment of the Law. For being constantly familiar with every part of the writings of Moses, they knew that it was written, "You shalt not speak ill of a ruler of your people" (Ex. 22:28). Therefore, either expecting to be insulted they say such words, so that they might seem with good reason to attack Him, and to be angry, and now without blame to take counsel against Christ; or because they really felt such excess of bitterness in their mind, and were bursting to show the malice which was in them.

For when Christ said, "For judgment came I into this world, that they which see not may see" (cf. Jn. 18:37, 9:39), and indicated by these words the restoration of sight to the blind man, they were unable to endure being reminded of the miracle. Being goaded by envy they again rise up against Him, and endeavor to oppose Him. In His presence they do not shrink from saying what almost amounts to this: "O fellow, You boast strange things, having accomplished none of those deeds which You think Yourself to have done. Do You indeed wish," they say, "to impose even upon us with Your wonderworking? Will You be capable of saying that You have healed us, since we are blind also? Do You wish that we should ascribe to You the glory of a physician and wonderworker, telling lies after the manner of this man, of whom You say that he has received his sight, having been born blind? Will You dare to deal falsely with us by similar statements?"

Certainly, therefore, the language of the Pharisees as they mock at the events relating to the blind man is evil and very bitter, and they deem the whole thing an imposture rather than a truth; for nothing convinces the obstinate.

**"Jesus said to them, 'If you were blind, you would have no sin; but now you say, 'We see.' Therefore your sin remains."**

The Savior again confounds them, tempering His reproof with skill. For He holds distant from all reviling and puts them out of countenance by setting before them the force of the truth. He shows them that they derive no advantage from possessing sight, or rather that they fell into a worse condition than one who could not see at all.

For the blind man, He says, by not beholding any of the deeds miraculously wrought, escaped without sin, and is so far blameless. But those who have been watchers and beholders of the marvelous deed, and through great folly and evilness of disposition have not accepted the faith in consequence of them, make their sin difficult of removal, and it is really hard to escape from the condemnation which such conduct incurs.

Therefore it is not hard to understand the meaning of this regarding bodily blindness and restoration to sight. And when we pass to that which is to be understood by analogy, receiving our impressions from the argument itself, we shall again repeat the same signification. The man who does not understand may claim his pardon with excellent reason from the judge. But he who is keen of intellect and understands his duty, and then, having indulged his debasing inclination in the baser principles of his mind, and given himself to the sway of pleasures and not of duty, shall shamelessly claim compassion—the request for which he should be punished shall in no way be granted. He will very justly perish for having kept in himself a sin without excuse.

For instance, our Lord Jesus Christ signifies exactly the same thing in the gospels, saying that he "who knew his master's will," and did it not "shall be beaten with many stripes" (Lk. 12:47). For the charge against him that knew not is merely that of ignorance; but against him who understood and yet inconsiderately refused to act, the charge is that of overweening presumption.

Observe again how guardedly accurate was the language of the Savior on this occasion also. For He does not say plainly, "You see," but He says, "You say, 'We see.'" For it would of course have been very much beside the mark to ascribe understanding to those who possessed a mind so blind and emptied of light as to dare to say concerning Him, "We know that this Man is a sinner." Self-condemned, therefore, are the Jews, who affirm of themselves that they see, but do not act at all as they should. Yes, most emphatically self-condemned, for they know the will of the Lord, but are so self-conceited that they thus resist even His mightiest miracles.

# Ⲇⲟⲝⲁⲥⲓ ⲟ̀ Ⲑⲉⲟⲥ ⲛ̀ⲙⲱⲛ

*Glory be to God, now and forever, Amen.*

# APPENDIX OF SOURCES AND CHURCH FATHERS

### *St. Ambrose of Milan (340-397AD)*

He was born in Trier, Arles or Lyons, from a Roman Christian family. His father, Ambrosius, was a prefect of Gallia Narbonensis (which included France, Britain and Spain). He was the youngest of three children: his sister, Marcellina became a nun and his brother, Satyrus, became a prefect. With his classical and legal education he was assigned to a government post in Milan around 370. In 373-374 he was baptized and ordained as bishop by popular demand after a child cried out, "Bishop Ambrose," and the crowd responded, apparently against Ambrose's will. St. Ambrose greatly influenced St. Augustine, guided him back to the true faith, and baptized him. His major work on the New Testament was a commentary on the Gospel of Luke. He also wrote treatises such as *To the New Emperor Gratian,* and *On the Holy Spirit* (381), which is taken largely from St. Basil the Great's treatise on the same subject. He mastered the Greek language and literature. Upon his departure Paulinus wrote his biography.

### *St. Athanasius the Apostolic (ca. 295-373 AD)*

This great saint is called "Apostolic" by the Coptic Orthodox Church because he is considered a successor to the Apostles due to his erudite theological and biblical teaching. We know little about his childhood, except for an incident in which he was baptizing children by the sea and was discovered by Pope Alexander, who later began to teach the young Athanasius. He spent three years in the desert under the guidance of St. Antony the Great along with St. Serapion. He spent six years as a reader in Alexandria, was later ordained as a deacon by Pope Alexander, and helped at the Council of Nicaea in 325. According to the Coptic Encomium, he was 33 when he was ordained as pope and patriarch in 328. As the twentieth pope of Alexandria, he fought diligently against Arius and his teachings. He was exiled five times and spent 16 of his 46 years as pope in exile. Among his writings are *On the Incarnation,* the *Orations against the Arians, The Life of Antony, Against Apollinarius,* and various epistles to monks and bishops. We commemorate his departure on 7 Bashans, and the miracle of his return to Alexandria on 30 Tout.

### St. Augustine of Hippo (354-430 AD)

He was a prolific father of the church born in Tagasta, North Africa to Patritius, his pagan father and Roman official, and St. Monica, his faithful Christian mother. At the age of 16, he went to Carthage to study law, literature, and philosophy. He became a teacher of rhetoric in Tagaste, Carthage, and Rome, taught in Rome and Milan, and lived a sinful life. His famous prayer in resisting God, was "Give me chastity and continence, but not yet." Due to the prayers of his mother, the intellect and competence of St. Ambrose of Milan, St. Athanasius' amazing biography of St. Antony, and the impact of Romans 13:13, he was finally baptized at the age of 33 (in 387). In the same year, St. Monica departed. He returned to Italy, established a monastery there, was ordained a priest, and later a bishop of Hippo. He would have attended the Council of Nicaea, but he departed when Barbarians were attacking his diocese in Hippo. His extant writings include the *Confessions, The City of God,* his Commentaries on the Old and New Testaments, *On the Trinity, On Rebuke and Grace, Against the Manicheans, On Christian Doctrine,* and *The Predestination of the Saints,* his last major work. Despite many of his wonderful writings, prayers, and contemplations, he is also attributed with being the source of many problematic teachings such as the *Filioque,* the doctrine of original sin and grace, predestination, purgatory, and other such beliefs. Many claim this was due to his lack of Greek, and thus his lack of knowledge of the Eastern fathers.

### St. Cyril of Alexandria (ca. 380-444AD)

Also known as "The Pillar of Faith" in the Coptic tradition, this father is the twenty-fourth Patriarch of the See of St. Mark. St. Cyril was the son of the sister of Pope Theophilus (23rd patriarch), who trained him in

Theology and Philosophy at the School of Alexandria, then sent him to the monastery of St. Macarius in the wilderness. There he studied the Church books and sayings of the fathers for five years under a righteous monk named Sarabamon. Later he was sent to the honorable bishop Abba Serapion, and he increased in wisdom and knowledge. After St. Cyril returned to Alexandria, Pope Theophilus ordained him a deacon, appointed him a preacher in the cathedral, and made St. Cyril his scribe. When his uncle departed in 412, St. Cyril was enthroned as 24th patriarch of Alexandria on 20 Babeh, 128 AM (October 17, 412). He is famous for his exceptional biblical exegesis and Christological formulas, which he used to defend the faith while presiding over the Council of Ephesus against Nestorius. He remained a pope for 31 years. He is one of the greatest fathers of the ancient Church, whose life and teachings have been decisive in shaping the Orthodox tradition. We commemorate his departure on 3 Abib.

### *St. Cyril of Jerusalem (d. 386 AD)*

Not much is known about his early life, but he was ordained a priest at Jerusalem before 343. Around 348, he was appointed bishop of Jerusalem, despite the attacks from leaders of other sects, and being exiled three separate times. He is most famous for his Catechetical Lectures, which were written for those desiring to join the Christian faith (although a few scholars have attributed this to his successor, John of Jerusalem). His messages focused on the importance of the death and Resurrection of our Lord Jesus Christ. He was exiled by Acacius after selling church vessels to support the needy during a famine in Palestine, but returned to his see in 356 AD. We commemorate his departure on 22 Baramhat.

### *St. Ephrem the Syrian (ca. 306-379AD)*

One of the early fathers of the church from Syria. He was baptized by St. James bishop of Nissibis. He was among those who attended the Council of Nicaea. He is famous for his poetical hymns, especially those relating to the Annunciation, Nativity, and Holy Theotokos. He wrote a famous commentary on Tatian's Diatessaron, the Book of Daniel, and the Pauline Epistles. Often he quoted the Peshitta translation, which is among the earliest manuscripts of the Old Testament today. His writings well represent the Syrian patristic tradition. He is also known for his famous visit to St. Pishoy in Egypt, in what is now El- Surian (The Syrian) Monastery. He also witnessed the departure of St. Basil the Great. We commemorate his departure on 15 Abib.

### St. Gregory of Nazianzus, "the Theologian" (ca. 330-389AD)

This father was born at the country estate belonging to his father called Arianzus, near Nazianzus—a place quite unknown to early writers. His parents were rich Christian landowners and his father was bishop of Nazianzus. Gregory studied in the major centers of learning before being baptized in 358. His father forced him to accept ordination as a priest in 361. In 371, his friend Basil unsuccessfully attempted to persuade him to accept being ordained as a bishop. However, eight years later, St. Gregory finally agreed to accept the responsibility of being the bishop of Constantinople in 379, where he served for two years before resigning. His poetry and theological writings earned him the title of "the

Theologian." He is included among the Cappadocian Fathers, with St. Basil the Great and St. Gregory of Nyssa. We commemorate his departure on 21 Tubah.

### St. Gregory of Nyssa (ca. 330-ca. 396 AD)

He was born in Cappadocia, in the year 330 AD and was ordained bishop by his brother, St. Basil the Great, in the year 372 AD He was exiled during the reign of Emperor Valens, then returned in the year 378 AD, by the order of Emperor Theodosius the Great. He wrote many church books and departed in peace around the year 396 AD.

### St. Ignatius of Antioch (d. 107 AD)

One of the most famous disciples of St. John the Beloved, St. Ignatius was consecrated bishop over the city of Antioch. He is famous for his seven pastoral letters—the Ephesians, Magnesians, Romans, Philadelphians, Smyrna, Tralles, and Polycarp—that were written between 100-107 AD. Although he does not quote from the Old testament, he had a strong focus on eschatology as well as church unity. The theology of his writings foreshadows the later definitions of the Ecumenical Councils.

## St. Irenaeus of Lyons (d. 202 AD)

This saint was born at Smyrna in Asia Minor, where he studied under St. Polycarp, the disciple of St. John the Beloved. After living at Rome for a time, he settled in Lyons in 177, where he was consecrated as bishop of a Greek-speaking community. He mastered the Greek and Latin languages, and served in France and Rome against the Gnostic movement. His most famous work, *Against the Heresies*, describes and refutes the teachings of the Gnostics, while explaining about the gospels, the sacraments, apostolic tradition, and the hierarchy of the Church.

## St. Jerome (350-420AD)

He was born as Sophronius Eusebius Hieronymous and soon showed immense potential as a scholar. He lived for a while in Jerusalem, then was summoned by Pope Damasus of Rome in 382 to revise the Latin translation of the Holy Scriptures, called the Vulgate. He completed his revision of the gospels in 383 or 384, but seems to have largely abandoned the work to devote his energies to the Hebrew Old Testament. He died in 419 or 420. Besides his translations (which include patristic works as well as the Vulgate), he left a number of letters and assorted commentaries plus biographies of "Famous Men." Interestingly, the text used by Jerome in his commentaries often differs from that in the Vulgate.

## St. John Chrysostom (ca. 347-407AD)

St. John Chrysostom was born in Antioch between 347 and 349. His father was a soldier in Syria and his mother was a faithful Christian. After his father died when he was very young, he was raised by his mother, Anthusa. He was so gifted that she arranged for him to study Philosophy, Rhetoric, and Greek. He agreed with two of his classmates, Evagrius and Basil (most probably not Basil the Great), to seek the monastic life, but because of the tears of his mother he agreed to continue his education as an advocate (lawyer) instead. At the age of 18, he studied under Patriarch

Meletius, who encouraged him to stay with him. At 21, he was baptized, and three years later, he was ordained a reader and composed

Against the Jews and many pamphlets. After deceiving his friend, Basil, into ordination, John defended himself with the treatise *On the Priesthood*. Upon the death of his mother, he gave all his goods to the poor, chose one of the poorest monasteries, and meditated on the Scriptures and wrote three treatises on the monastic life. He was later ordained as a deacon, and wrote many more treatises. The Patriarch Flavian ordained him as priest. Some called him "the mouth of Christ," others "a second Paul," and others the "golden-mouthed (Chrysostom)." This last name was given to him by a woman during one of his sermons. He was ordained the bishop of Constantinople by force in 398. His sermons led the city through many crises, but his enemies eventually exiled him three times. He spent his last days of his earthly life in exile. We commemorate his departure on 17 Hatour.

### *St. Justin Martyr (b. 100-110; d. 163-167AD)*

He was born into a pagan family in Samaria between 100 and 110 AD. After practicing Stoic, Peripatetic, and Pythagorean philosophies, he finally converted to Christianity most probably in Ephesus. Due to his philosophical background, he is the first Christian thinker to seek to reconcile the claims of faith and reason. Among his many works, he is most famous for his Apology (ca. 155 AD), addressed to Emperor Antoninus Pius and his colleagues; as well as his *Dialogue with Trypho*, a discussion with a Jew named Trypho about the differences in the two faiths. These, among his other works, make him one of the most important of the apologists of the second century and one of the noblest personalities of early Christian literature. Clothed in the palladium, a cloak worn by Greek philosophers, he traveled about as an itinerant teacher. He arrived in Rome during the reign of Antoninus Pius (138-161 A.D) and founded a school there. One of his pupils was Tatian, destined later to become an apologist. St. Justin suffered martyrdom in Rome between 163 and 167 AD.

## The Scholar Origen (185-254AD)

He was born into a Christian family: his father Leonides was a righteous scholar who was martyred during the persecution of Septimius Severus in 202 AD. At an early age, Origen dedicated his life to reading and scholarly endeavors. St. Jerome praised his love of reading and said that Origen read while eating, walking, resting, etc. When Pope Demetrius, the twelfth Patriarch of Alexandria, heard of his fame, he appointed him dean of the School of Alexandria. He increased its fame and thinking and became a teacher of many bishops and priests, as well as many men, women, young and old. He was famous for his allegorical interpretation, such as his famous interpretation of the Song of Songs. He was imprisoned and tortured for his Christian faith. He was courageous, ascetic and a man of fasting and prayer. He exaggerated in his asceticism by castrating himself (defending his action by saying that he was protecting his chastity). He was such a prolific writer that some of his admirers said, "There is no human mind that can absorb all what he wrote." St. Epiphanius (315-403 AD) stated that Origen had 6,000 manuscripts, including his famous *Hexapla,* 28-year study comparing six manuscripts of the Old Testament and their translations. Pope Demetrius excommunicated Origen for theological mistakes, as well as being ordained in Palestine, outside of his diocese. He spent the rest of his time there, where he established a famous theological school. He is one of the most controversial as well as influential ancient writers.

## Socrates Scholasticus (b. 380 AD)

He was also called Socrates of Constantinople writes and quotes from the historian Eusebius, while completing much of his work with additional information of the Church history from the conversion of Constantine to about 439 AD. He begins by narrating "The particulars which he has left out" through various documents and other sources. His writings are found in NPNF 2:2.

### The Scholar Tertullian (c.160-225AD)

He was a scholar born to a pagan family in Carthage, North Africa. His father was a Roman centurion. He received a good education in Literature and Rhetoric, practiced law in Rome, and visited Athens and Rome in his youth. He was converted to Christianity before 197 AD and returned to his native city as a Christian shortly before the turn of the third century. He wrote extensively against the various enemies of the church. But, like many converts, the fixed life of the official church was not sufficient for him. He wanted a return to prophecy. After some years of trying and failing to restore the spiritual nature of the Church in the West, he became a Montanist (ca. 207). St. Jerome reported that this happened in his "middle age." According to St. Jerome, he became a priest, but there are other indications that he remained a layman. Shortly after 220, Tertullian seems to have tried to form an independent congregation before his death. He was the author of a long list of apologetic, theological, and ascetic works. No list of Tertullian's works is extant, but historians have identified at least 43 titles, of which all or part 31 survive. Some of these, however, were written after he left the Church. Among his apologetic writings he addressed a work *To the Heathen (Ad Nations,* two books), in which he protested against the laws condemning Christians without examining their behavior. Nevertheless, St. Cyprian called him "the master," and made it a policy to read from his works every day. Tertullian's text is rather unique, as he wrote in Latin but apparently used primarily Greek texts which he translated himself. One historian says, "He touched almost nothing which he did not exaggerate."

Manufactured by Amazon.ca
Bolton, ON